ADVANCE PRAISE FOR

# The Call from the Stranger
## on a Journey Home

"Hongyu Wang presents an elegant and insightful journey into cross-cultural self-formation. Readers travel with her through an unusual juxtapositioning of life and academic narrative, of prose and poetry, located in a central rendering of the philosophies of Confucius, Foucault, and Kristeva. The text is revolutionary for its multiplicity of writing forms and for its example of a postmodern self continually in the making. As for all of us, partial selves are Wang: there is no resolution of difference or dissonance either personally or theoretically even as one desires (subconsciously?) wholeness or harmony. This I applaud most of all."

*Lynda Stone, Professor of Philosophy of Education,*
*University of North Carolina at Chapel Hill*

"Hongyu Wang's voice is as clear as a bell in this text and yet, at the same time, she helps me experience myself and my own presumptions and successes and blind-spots anew. It is always a sign of hermeneutic success when, through a 'stranger's' eyes and words, one's own culture begins to appear odd and unique and not simply 'the way things are.' I believe that this is precisely the sort of text that is vitally needed right now: new voices, new conversations, new unearthings of our shared and contested lives in education."

*David Jardine, Professor of Education, University of Calgary*

# The Call from the Stranger on a Journey Home

# A Book Series of Curriculum Studies

William F. Pinar
*General Editor*

VOLUME 7

PETER LANG
New York • Washington, D.C./Baltimore • Bern
Frankfurt am Main • Berlin • Brussels • Vienna • Oxford

HONGYU WANG

# The Call from the Stranger on a Journey Home

## CURRICULUM IN A THIRD SPACE

PETER LANG
New York • Washington, D.C./Baltimore • Bern
Frankfurt am Main • Berlin • Brussels • Vienna • Oxford

Library of Congress Cataloging-in-Publication Data

Wang, Hongyu.
The call from the stranger on a journey home:
curriculum in a third space / Hongyu Wang.
p. cm. — (Complicated conversation; v. 7)
Includes bibliographical references and index.
1. Education—Philosophy. 2. Postmodernism and education.
3. Curriculum change. 4. Educational anthropology.
5. Feminism and education. I. Title. II. Series.
LB14.7.W355  370′.1—dc21  2003011694
ISBN 0-8204-6903-3
ISSN 1534-2816


Bibliographic information published by **Die Deutsche Bibliothek**.
**Die Deutsche Bibliothek** lists this publication in the "Deutsche
Nationalbibliografie"; detailed bibliographic data is available
on the Internet at http://dnb.ddb.de/.

Cover design by Lisa Barfield

© 2004 Peter Lang Publishing, Inc., New York
275 Seventh Avenue, 28th Floor, New York, NY 10001
www.peterlangusa.com

Printed in the United States of America

*Dedicated to*
*my parents,*
*Wang Hezeng and Lin Shuduan*

# Table of Contents

# Preface

Hongyu Wang faces a problem all face when one leaves home and country for foreign lands and then tries to "return." Landing in Beijing after studying in the United States—with me at Louisiana State University—she finds herself estranged: from mother, motherland, mother tongue. In a scene reminiscent of Thomas Wolff's *You Can't Go Home Again,* Hongyu, stepping off the plane last, the cry of her mother, "My Goodness, I thought you missed the flight somewhere!" is both haunting and prophetic. Hongyu finds herself not only a stranger to her mother but to her country and herself. Just who is she? Certainly she is not American, but no longer does she feel Chinese. The hybrid Chinese-American fits her no more than the oxymoron American-Chinese. Her identity has become bicultural: not either, not both, more than either, than both. Unlike Wolff, however, she finds the experience of estrangement rich with possibilities, and finds the exploration, though intense—at times, agonizing—rich and creative, providing a unique perspective for curriculum and cultural studies.

Using the question of identity as a starting point, Hongyu takes the reader on a journey through the intricacies of French, post-structural thought —J. Derrida, M. Foucault, J. Kristeva, and M. Serres, specifically—in search of *self.* In Derrida, Hongyu senses that difference can be liberating, freeing, generating. Only through awareness of our responsibility to others, to life, to the other's otherness can "self" begin to emerge. In Foucault, she realizes that "an aesthetics of self is imbued with power relationships" and begins to recognize that her own power needs to be nurtured with love, care, responsibility. In Kristeva, she finds herself wrestling psychoanalytically with the *uncanny,* the stranger within "a space of interlocking alterities." And so Hongyu asks herself, what is woman's role in society? In Serres, she finds a "third space," one that while always bounded, also holds infinite possibilities. Here Hongyu introduces the notion of a dancing curriculum. In such a curriculum, it is not always the man who leads.

This journey, crossing many borders and boundaries, is ever aided by Dwayne Huebner's call from the other, the transcendent lure of "The Call from the Stranger." In this call from and to her past, Hongyu begins to reclaim the lost roots of her culture (wiped out by the Cultural Revolution), especially China's Confucian thought. In reclaiming this thought, she encounters the ghosts of women past, those no-name women who have for centuries, even millennia, silently played a minorant/majorant role in Chinese society. It may well be that as we try to bridge two cultures—East and West, Male and Female—it is these women who will lead the way.

This book is the tale of one woman's intellectual and emotional struggle to find her "self," to come to grips with her Otherness, in a rapidly shifting, transforming, "post" society. Hongyu shows us that as dark and depressing as this struggle may be, it can also be freeing, liberating. In that "third space" between us and Others, indeed between us and ourselves, a new consciousness can be born, a new sense of curriculum can emerge. The call from the stranger can invite us to create new relationships, to realize what we would not have realized had we stayed "home." We must journey across borders—geographical, social, personal, intellectual, linguistic. In this crossing over we see the possibility of that which is yet to be. The stranger beckons.

As a path into curriculum, nested within William Pinar's series on complicated conversations, this journey invites us to bring forth our lives and our learning into this "third space," one where we converse with the otherness of our Other—our texts, our teachers, our students, our peers, our values, our selves.

Drawing on her own poetic being, Hongyu combines story, poetry, musings (on her thoughts) in a way wherein we not only watch her wrestle with "self," but are ourselves so affected. We probe our own depths of self. In this journey through the labyrinthine layers of post-structural and feminist thought, one crosses the bridge between Asian and European cultures. One sees perspectives not visible from either side of the bridge. I hope other readers will be so moved and will search for their own "third space." The stranger beckons.

For me, to have traveled with Hongyu, at least part way, on this journey has been an inspiring and humbling experience. Remembering the trip to China that she recounts throughout the text, calls forth images of our both working with students there. While I spoke, students were respectful, eager and attentive. Even in the packed rooms, the silence and concentration were palpable. However, in her working with the students, Hongyu brought the situation to life—faces relaxed, body postures changed, interactions bubbled to life—inspiring an amazing transformation, exemplifying a teacher who leads by journeying with. It is both joy and a daunting task to introduce this book. Hongyu has journeyed far beyond my field, and yet I feel at home with her strong faith in creativity, conversation, and the complexities of life.

—William E. Doll, Jr.

# Acknowledgments

The birth of this book is a result of all interconnections I have experienced as I continuously moved from one place to another place. If I could thank all those who have been important to me, as I would like to, my acknowledgments would be too long. To make it possible, let me start with my teachers.

First of all, I wish to thank my influential American professors who have guided, supported, and transformed my sense of the self intellectually, emotionally, and spiritually. Dr. William E. Doll, Jr., my major professor, with his wisdom, nurturance, and mentorship, has artfully reached into the depth of my soul, has patiently guided me through struggles of my heart, and has persistently held my hands, not letting me slip away. Dr. Petra Munro with her sharp intelligence and challenging teaching style has always encouraged me to go further, to question more, to understand from yet another angle. Dr. Denise Egéa-Kuehne, with her kindness and detailed critique, has opened up my intellectual landscape by bringing important French thinkers such as Jacques Derrida and Michel Serres into my life. Dr. Wendy Kohli, with her humor and loving support, has guided me through the entrance into Michel Foucault's discourse. Dr. William F. Pinar, with his insightful and inspiring teachings, has brought me closer to the rhythm of language and thus closer to myself. I am especially indebted to his unyielding support of this book project and his final masterly editing of the manuscript with grace and care. All of their scholarship and mentoring, and their openness to me as a person, have been such gifts to sustain my courage in constantly becoming more than what I am.

It is also a book indebted to all my influential teachers in China. Liu Zhen, my language teacher, gently introduced me into the beauty of ancient Chinese poetry, essay, and calligraphy. Professor Wu Yuqi, as a personal exemplar of his own belief, has given me the promise of Chinese traditions in contemporary life. Professor Zhong Qiquan, my advisor, with his faith in my intellectual ability and his open-mindedness, has led me beyond my own world. Professor Du Diankun, with his caring mentorship, unwaveringly supported my own choice and encouraged me, even on his deathbed, to write more. Dr. Yuan Guilin, my undergraduate professor, with his gentleness, generosity, and modesty, befriends me.

I wish to thank American and Chinese professors at the Nanjing–Hopkins Center for Chinese and American Studies for opening a window for me to have a glimpse of another world. My admiration goes to the Chinese co-director Professor Wang Zhigang, who, in his unique manner, inspires my imagination about Chinese and American jointly educated intellectuals. Professor Dana Ward and his family and Professor Mary Rothchild and her family not only intellectually influenced my view of the world but also personally transformed my sense of the self. Once the window is open, the other side beckons.

All my teachers saw my potential before I realized I had any, and have helped me to bring it out one way or another. Their loving words have opened up my own words and I am forever indebted to all of them.

I thank all my colleagues, friends, and students who have read the different drafts of this book and provided both encouragement and critique. First of all, I owe my heartfelt gratitude to Lisa Cary, Michael Gungenhauser, and Yu Tianlong who gracefully read the whole manuscript on very short notice and provided me valuable suggestions. I thank Zhao Guoping for investing time in her early motherhood to read the major chapters of my draft and initiate debates with me so that I have been challenged to further articulate my thoughts. I also wish to thank Kathryn Castle, Claudia Eppert, jan jagodzinski, Clare Penlington, Li Xin, and Donna Trueit for reading various chapters and gently leading me toward another level of thinking and writing. Jacqueline Bach, Diane Knapp (I particularly thank her for bringing my attention to Michel Serres's *Troubadour of Knowledge*), Lo Yi-hsuan, Cody Carr, Sibongile Mtshali-Dlamini, Jared Rothstein, and Bob Wallace read the first four chapters of the manuscript and engaged in a lively conversation about it, making a great contribution to the book's revision. All the reading and critiquing they have provided make the book a better one and inspire me to think further, beyond the book.

I thank Aymen Kassaimih who has patiently and carefully helped me with the bibliography. Frances Griffin and Betty Ann Sisson, my professional editors, have done marvelous jobs in editing and polishing my writings. I am grateful to Peter Lang for providing a home for this work and particularly thank Christopher Myers, Bernadette Shade, Sophie Appel, and Rodney Williams for all their wonderful work in bringing this manuscript into press.

I wish to thank Pam Fry, my senior faculty mentor and department chair, for strongly supporting and gracefully guiding my teaching and writing through difficult times. Nadine Olson, who co-taught a class with me, has remained a friend ever since. She has helped me understand more about American students, particularly in Oklahoma, and brings a stronger sense of interconnection to my journey toward the third space. The friendships from colleagues Pam Brown and Gretchen Schwarz have helped me tune in with my new life in Oklahoma. The love and support from all my friends have made it possible for me to marry my words to my life in the book. An Shu-hua, Nichole Guillory, James Heller, Vikki Hillis, Hua Na (and her son, Samuel), Tayari Kwa Salaam, Li Liuzhen, Liu Xuemei, and Wu Mei are in the long list that I cannot make complete here. I particularly wish to ac-knowledge my Chinese-Australian friend, Chou Bon-Wai who persistently knocked on my door when I only wanted to shut the world out.

I wish to attribute my deepest thanks to my family who has lovingly sus-tained my confidence in living a meaningful life. My mother, with her wis-dom, inner strength, and laughing spirit, has supported—without any reservation—my constant pursuit of something beyond myself. My father, with his fondness for novels, introduced me into the world of literature that has brought joy to my life since my childhood. Xu Xiaoyun, who was my husband for almost a decade, although we have split, persistently supported and took pride in my intellectual aspirations. His contagious passion for life has also taught me the art of living. My three sisters, Wang Hongmei, Wang Hongkun, and Wang Hongyan, who have moved around the world, make all those international telephone calls to connect with one another with humor and laughter. And with great affection, I thank my nephew, Mengmeng (Gu Meizhang) who teaches me about the complexity of childhood.

Finally but not the least, I am grateful to two lakes along which I jogged and walked when I wrote this book on hot summer days. One is the Univer-sity Lake at Louisiana State University in Baton Rouge and the other is Boomer Lake in Stillwater. They have both comforted and inspired me as I struggle with my writings.

The birth of this book made possible by all of you leads to the rebirth of my life that I have shared, am sharing, and will share with you as I continue my journey home, listening to the call from the stranger.

*******************************

The poems used at the beginning and the end of the book are reprinted with the permission of the following publishers:

Excerpt from "Fruit Gathering-Verse VII," reprinted with the permission of Scribner, an imprint of Simon & Schuster Adult Publishing Group, from

# Chapter 1
# Introduction: The Call from the Stranger on a Journey Home

ALAS, I cannot stay in the house, and home has become no home to me, for the eternal Stranger calls, he is going along the road.

The sound of his footfall knocks at my breast; it pains me!

The wind is up, the sea is moaning.

I leave all my cares and doubts to follow the homeless tide, for the Stranger calls me, he is going along the road.

(Rabindranath Tagore, 1937, p. 142)

A prayer. A silent prayer for a more peaceful and loving world. A song. A voiceless song singing the call from the stranger. A swing. A swing back and forth, simultaneously between different landscapes, different ways of life. A story. An unspeakable story of how a common soul struggles to reach out for the light. A dance. A motionless dance across the ocean on a journey home. A journey. A journey of a speechless girl learning to speak, to sing, and to laugh. A journey of a woman leaving home in search of mother's invisible traces. A journey of a Chinese woman in exile longing for an im/possible co-creative union between self and universe. A journey of creating home, in a third space, among the multiple, with singular strokes of handwriting. A conversation. A heartfelt conversation a daughter attempts to initiate between mother and father, with the world. A curriculum. A curriculum by the sea, calling us to journey beyond, to reach yet another shore...

## A Journey Back Home

In a general sense, home is a mode of life. In a deep sense, home is a sense of longing and attachment. Only someone who goes on a long journey has a strong longing for home. Only someone who goes on a long journey has a deep sense of home.

(Yu Qiuyu,[1] 1999, p. 177)

The most basic purpose of going on a journey, then, is the very ordinary one of learning to be at home in a more creative way, in a good way, a healthy way, a way tuned to the deepest truth of things.

(David Geoffrey Smith, 1999b, p. 2)

A hot summer day. The flight from Detroit to Beijing. A journey home. The plane almost reaches Beijing: I start to look for the Great Wall—the symbol of Chinese civilization. Unfortunately no matter how hard I try, I just cannot see it. Somehow I am disappointed. Somehow I am relieved.

Due to the luggage problem, I am the last person to appear at the welcome gate. A friend of my mother's finds me first and calls to my mother, who is at another gate. Mom comes over—her hair turning all white, her face filled with worries. She rushes to me and cries out: "My goodness, I thought you missed the flight somewhere!" At the moment of seeing my mother, with so many people around her greeting each other—the airport waiting room was as crowded as the streets—I am overwhelmed. Wow, I am in a different world! Mother has become a stranger to me somehow. Julia Kristeva (1991) says that foreigners are people who have lost their mother. Have I lost my mother after my stay in the United States?

The first thing we need to do in Beijing is get a visa for my reentrance into the United States. Three times my mother and I ride together on the bus traveling between her friend's house and the American embassy in order to get that official stamp. Mother has usually been with me when I venture into the public and has been my mentor. Now she accompanies me to get permission to leave home again. The classical psychoanalytic picture of a powerful father stepping into the asocial bond between mother and child to bring the child out into the public is absent in my story.

*In Eastern culture, mother plays a very important role in children's lives, even after children grow up, despite her submissive status to her husband. Julia Kristeva (1977a) also observes that the mother occupies a[n] (empty) center in Chinese culture. They make me question myself. To what extent are my own experiences that I used to hold as only personal actually culturally constructed? To what extent are they the results of the dynamics of a particular household not confined within cultural norms? Since psychoanalysis is mainly a Western creation, to what degree can it apply to Chinese or Eastern culture? Actually it is not only a cross-cultural issue. From her own perspective as a working-class Western woman, Carolyn Steedman (1987) attempts to understand how complex human relationships challenge a universal theoretical framework in psychoanalysis. Is not a powerful father a myth?[2]*

After we get my visa, we are on the train to Harbin—my hometown, a northern city in the coldest area in China. According to Yu Qiuyu (1999), Ningan County, which is near my hometown, was the place of exile for intellectuals and rebels during the Qing dynasty (A.D. 1644–1911). What may exile and estrangement bring to one's life?

In Harbin, I take a walk with my mother every night. We talk, argue, and end up in disagreement every time. She must think she is losing me to the United States. One day I half-jokingly say: "You and father fight inside of me." Mother immediately retorts: "Of course not. It is China and the United States that fight inside of you." Actually both are true.

Mother is fond of telling me how as a little girl I held books, newspapers, or anything with Chinese characters on it to read aloud using my own "language." I do not remember. What I do remember is that when I began my struggle to speak as a teenager, I usually could not find my own voice. That is because, some feminists say, the child is delivered to the father's symbolic order. We women alienate ourselves in the word of the father. We do not have our own language to speak.

*In Chinese culture, silence is not something necessarily negative. It could be a symbol of wisdom. It could be a sign of reservation or modesty. A child who is quiet but produces good work is usually praised rather than being encouraged to speak. Writing as a physical, visual, emotional, and intellectual practice is privileged over speech. Moreover, in general, action is much more important than words. Chinese tend to express their feelings in action rather than in words. The situation might be different in Western culture.[3] Silence is something that you must break through in order to reveal what is suppressed by this silence. In feminist discourses, voice is often used to imply the presence of women's differences. However, in poststructural critiques, such a notion of presence is problematic, and the embodiment of voice in an essentialized understanding of the self is challenged. In his deconstructive analysis, Derrida (1991) directly questions the privilege of speech-as-presence over writing-as-absence in Western thought. Approaching silence as something negative in promoting a person's self-cultivation, am I imposing a traditional Westernized discourse upon the Chinese situation? If voice is not that important, why must silence be broken to expose what is inside? On the other hand, if Western logocentrism is in question, why shouldn't the Chinese tradition, in which writing dominates over speech, be deconstructed?*

Is language necessarily masculine? My mother taught me Chinese poetry when I was two. I loved it. Such is not an uncommon practice in Chinese families. I suspect it is the musical rhythm of the Chinese language that is so attractive to young children. As a written language, Chinese is embodied and intersubjective, not necessarily symbolizing the disconnection with mother. Studies (Wu & Liu, 1996; Chen, 1996) of Chinese as a language have shown that Chinese characters are much more context dependent in reading and comprehension and more visually represented than are the letters in alphabetic language systems such as English, and that understanding Chinese occurs more at the sentence level than the alphabetic word level. The graphic aspects of Chinese script, more often than not, indicate a certain "conversational" or interactive mode, as components of one script can convey different meanings but complement one another to form the meaning of one character. For example, the Chinese character 泪 means the lacrimal "tear." The left part means "water" and the right part (目) means "eye." Tracing it back to the pictorial representations of more than two thousand years ago, it communicated water falling down from eyes (Li, 1996, p. 149). Such a correspondence between meanings and graphic structures is not unusual, especially if one studies the evolution of the Chinese characters. All these qualities make it difficult to view the Chinese language as only "paternal" in psychoanalytic terms.

*In* About Chinese Women, *Kristeva (1977a) wonders whether the Chinese language, due to its intonation and its visual and physical written aspects, maintains its pre-Oedipal qualities. That is fascinating to me. But I want to ask: If the Chinese language has pre-Oedipal attributes, if the interaction between* yin *and* yang *questions the dichotomy between man and woman, if the Western ideal of autonomy and independence is absent in Chinese culture, to what degree is the Oedipal struggle (framed in the West but taken as universal) applicable to the Chinese psyche? If Chinese is a more embodied language, to what extent is Kristeva's distinction between the semiotic and the symbolic aspects of language equally applicable to the Chinese self?*

For me, language itself is not necessarily patriarchal, but the power relations embedded in its usage and construction are implicated in social control. Kristeva (1996) also acknowledges that language is a heterogeneous construction from which femininity is not excluded.

In *Bitter Travel in Culture,* Yu (1992) quotes Tagore's poem which I used above. In Chinese, "stranger" is translated as "someone who has left home," implying a strong sense of journeying, but without religious implications. Upon reading the poem, I immediately felt the call from the stranger to go along the winding paths into ever-changing new landscapes of life. Such an opening to the stranger has carried me to see both the world and the self in a different way, but it also has thrown me into an unexpected world of ambiguity, uncertainty, and perplexity. What does it mean for a woman to leave mother/land for a father/foreign land?

*Is a foreign country necessarily a fatherland? How about those who feel at home in a foreign land? While my personal story coincides with the transition from a culture which claims relationships to a culture which claims autonomy, the fluidity of national boundaries in such a globalized contemporary society challenges the fixed notions of mother/father tales.*

My longing for the Great Wall and my wish to be away from it indicate conflicting but coexisting directions. What is simultaneous is the strong desire for belonging somewhere, safe from attack, and the equally strong urge to break through, to wander around, and to be on my own. Can this journey beyond the given be a process of simultaneously leaving and creating home? Is home necessarily stable anyway?

In the West, the notion of journey conveys a strong sense of the self leaving home on the road to explore through the breaching of frontiers, becoming autonomous and independent, or one with God in religious contexts. This abandonment of home for the sake of travel to become (heroic) men "through performances of masculinity" (Smith, 1996, p. 51) can be implicated in the denial of an original connection with mother. However, I would argue, home is not necessarily hospitable to women, although home is always associated with women. Only after I left home for college did I begin to appreciate my mother's strength in her nurturance; only after I left China did I understand more about the traditions and legacies of my homeland. For Kristeva, woman has the peculiar status of the stranger who alienates herself from both home and the public world. The stranger within her whisper words from the shadow.

A journey for a woman is first of all a journey within, in search of lost voices and invisible traces. To some extent, this is a journey home for the return of what is repressed, excluded, and alienated. At the same time, a journey home is made possible only by a journey of leaving home at a symbolic level, not only in the sense of challenging father, but also in the sense of seeking the necessary independence from mother so that a woman can transfigure the familiar and thus bring forth something new. During a journey out, home becomes irreversibly different and is renewed every time she has a new starting point. As Virginia Woolf suggests, "thinking back through our mothers is not aimed at becoming them" (quoted in Grumet, 1988, p. 187). Nancy Chodorow (1978) also emphasizes the necessity of both connection and independence. In journeying beyond the domestic space of home, to places mother may not be able to go, woman expands her femininity.

While a journey may be personal first of all, for the Chinese it is inevitably cultural and historical at the same time. In *Bitter Travel in Culture*, Yu (1992) talks about his travels around China and his cultural reflections during the journey. At those moments of facing a landscape, Yu feels that people, history, and nature are all mingled in telling a unique story. The image of an autonomous and independent self in isolation from others has not really existed in the Chinese psyche. This mingling of the personal, the cultural, and the historical is evident in Yu's comments:

> Now that it is a wandering journey, every stopping cannot negate a new beginning.... I dare not make a wish for our huge culture, but I hope the words flowing out of my pen can bring you some taste after bitterness, understanding smiles after worries, relaxation after deep pondering, and youth after agedness. (p. 5)

While talking about his own travels, he reflects on Chinese culture, a culture with both a glorious and a humiliating history. This heavy sense of historical, social, and cultural responsibility has always been with many Chinese—as the ancient poet Fan Zhongyan says, "to be worried before the world is worried; to be happy after the world is happy." In the Chinese imagination, the self can never be separated from society and culture. The Chinese ideal of the union between the universe and the person stays with me, too, as I travel across the ocean to search for new ways of life. Such an intercultural—and also gendered—journey is the very process of my curriculum, a journey that Dwayne Huebner (1999) terms "transcendent," to convey the "moreness" and "beyondness" of education listening to the call of the stranger.

Home is not something preexistent, but in a process of creation. A Chinese poet, Yang Ming, says: "Were not all hometowns foreign towns at the beginning? The so-called hometown is actually the last place where our ancestors stopped in their wandering journey" (quoted in Yu, 1992, p. 4). For women exiled from themselves, a home embracing both difference and connection has yet to be born. Only when women's difference is no longer denied can meaningful relationships be built and our children be freed from suffering lost maternal connections as they grow up.

In a Derridian sense, the permanent deferral of a central presence in exile constantly deconstructs the possibility of being at home. As an already exiled woman, I long for the possibility of creating new homes along this wandering journey. Home does not have to be a place, a family, or a permanent location; for me, it is more a spiritual locus—not fixed, but unstable and regenerative—from which the passion of the soul can gain both release and rest. Jo Anne Pagano (1990) tells me, "But as exiles, we can form our own communities. We can speak together a common language and make a home for ourselves in this world" (p. 155). Can a common language create a new home? Whose language? Mother's language? I travel back home in order to talk with my mother but we no longer speak the same language. Perhaps we have never really shared a common language. Going back home does not bring me home but has turned my mother into a stranger. I have become a stranger to myself too.

## The Call from the Stranger

The space of freedom for the individual is love—it is the only place, the only moment in life, where the various precautions, defenses, conservatisms break down, and one tries to go to the limit of one's being; so it is fundamental.

(Julia Kristeva, 1996, p. 121)

I am walking in this vast field
Searching, along the footprints of the heart
Whatever is lost
Is upon reflection

(Liang Xiaobin, 1980, p. 8)

Eternity is the moment of eyes meeting.

(Muo Fei, 1997, p. 357)

The gaze of the stranger. Stern. Unreachable. I cannot stay with it. I cannot leave. Struggling, I reach out. Yet the moment I stand up, the stranger is gone. Across the ocean, I journey, following distant calls. The gaze of the stranger. Intimate. Affectionate. Melting into the stranger's eyes, I am at one with the world. Yet into the stranger, I lose the sight of it. I am lost too. The moment I find freeing words and step out, the stranger is gone. The stranger calls. I follow its echoes. There is a winding path ahead, disappearing into the distance.

The stranger also calls inside of me. I listen closely. My twin sister within leaps out and waves to me. I run after her...

A journey out, a journey within. Along the road, between me and the stranger, in a third space, are my unique dancing steps. The encounter between the self and the stranger. The meeting of each other's potential. A journey beyond, a journey inward. A journey home at a simultaneous moment of in and out, the moment of eyes meeting.

Confucius' best disciple, Yan Hui (*The Analects*, 9.11), once commented on how the Way of Confucius was beyond his grasp and how there was always something more that could not be comprehended no matter how hard he tried. The master always led him on to something different. Isn't this relationship between the self and the stranger one central theme of education? The willingness and capacity of the self for relating to the other—be this a person, a text, or a landscape—in such a way that the other's alterity is acknowledged through a loving relationship is necessary for initiating an educative process. In such an expansive process, one risks feeling uncomfortable even among the familiar, but it inaugurates the very possibility of education: learning from something different and other than the self. Huebner (1999) clearly states the educative implications of the stranger in our midst when he says, "Our task is to bring the stranger, and the fruits of her comings and goings, into the presence of the person to be educated—to be led forth" (p. 362).

However, walking toward the stranger can be dangerous.

A beautiful autumn day. Baton Rouge. Sitting in front of my reading desk, I pull out my journal. All I can find is blank page after blank page. I listen attentively. The silence of the pages in their emptiness yells: What is my own space? Where is my home? I have lost myself in the (lost) stranger's eyes. Seduced into the promised adventure into freedom, I become mute. I cannot become the stranger. I cannot be myself, either. In silence, I struggle.

Kristeva's (1991) writings keep whispering to me that the stranger can be within the self. One cannot master it; one has to live with it. Am I releasing my own stranger within in the process of encountering the other? But if I am divided, how can I deal with this conflicting double? The "lure of the transcendent" (Huebner, 1999) hovers over me; the "intellectual exile" discussed by Edward Said (1996) awakens my spirit; the new ontology of the subject formulated by Michel Foucault (1997) firmly assures me that the self can be created anew; and the Way of Confucius promises me new stories. All of these concepts call me to consciously dwell in a cross-cultural/intercultural space (also a gendered space) working through the pains of loss, fragmentation, and alienation. Perhaps what is important is to turn the site of the stranger into a creative space which sustains the transformation of both self and other. No longer subsumed by love, disciplined by a stern gaze, or seduced by freedom, am I emerging? Am I emerging in a new space in which the self and the stranger call each other to reach beyond, yet without losing each other's alterity? Don't we need to redefine love, freedom, and independence? The trap of the conflicting in-between is gradually loosening its grip.

At Christmas. Baton Rouge. Passing by the Indian mound on campus which witnessed my identity crisis, I notice something I have never paid any attention to before. Curiously, I climb a little bit to reach it. To my astonishment, it is the root of an oak tree. Root. Home. There is an old Chinese saying: When a leaf falls down, it returns to the root of the tree. A root in a mound on which Indians performed their religious rituals a thousand years ago. Thousands of miles away from my hometown. Yang Ming has told me that home could be a foreign town. I sit by the root and on the root. Looking ahead, I see a tree, an old oak tree on the other mound, with a twisted trunk standing there quietly. Suddenly, I am caught by a moment of feeling at home. I am at peace. Time stops at that moment and space exists eternally. I am forgetting myself, yet at the same time I am fully aware of my own existence. I am not thinking of anything, yet at the same time everything is in my mind. I feel calm and peaceful, yet passion flows through my whole body. Why do I try so hard to find a home? I ask myself. Home is nowhere in the Derridian sense; home is everywhere, wherever stranger/strangeness, other/otherness, foreigner/foreignness are welcome, regardless of the limitations of time and place. Home itself can be a third space. A space in which the self and the stranger transform each other. A space embracing the conflicting double, yet leading beyond the trap of the in-between. The space is transformed too. A mobile home. We may not have a common language, and actually we do not need a common language—a common language always runs the risk of suppressing differences and the singularity of an individual person. Still a woman can create her own home in which m/other is welcome to speak, to sing, and to laugh. Embracing differences and multiplicity, home becomes a place where people can live together expressing their own uniqueness without doing violence to one another.

A third space. Three is a magical number to me. It refers to the multiple in ancient Chinese and can be a symbol of creativity, as in the Taoist myth that three gives birth to the universe. According to Homi Bhabha (1990), the "third space" comes from two original moments in cultural translation and its hybridity supports the emergence of new positions, structures, and activities. Inspired by Bhabha's thoughts, David Smith's (1996) elaboration of identity and pedagogy also calls for the third space, which is neither East nor West but contests the given intellectual and cultural binary. Michel Serres (1997) also enchants a poetics of "the third place." In my imagination, a third space is not only cultural but can also be gendered, national, or psychic. It is a space situated in the mutual transformation of both parties of the conflicting double without assuming that they must meet each other in full embrace. In such a space, contradictions are not only acknowledged and accepted but also put into movement to enable new layers of the self. Thus it also becomes a space of creating one's own subjectivity among and through the multiple. Conflicts, as a result of these dynamics, are not dissolved but transformed.

My own journey is enabled by "a complicated conversation" (Pinar, Reynolds, Slattery, & Taubman, 1995) that is curriculum among multiple layers of the conflicting double. Trapped between two very different cultures with the shadows of their own gendered stories, I am forever lost until I realize I need to go beyond the "in-between" into a new space. The process of coming to terms with my own strangeness brought forth by the other gradually leads me into a third space which gives birth to new senses of self, a self neither confined by national or cultural identity nor losing its own spiritual roots, a self hosting and transforming ambiguity. As dangerous and difficult as it is, the walk to the stranger is a necessary step for imagining life otherwise. What one needs to be cautious about is not to lose the self into the stranger, not to become the stranger. Being assimilated into the other can happen—out of the need to survive or due to genuine admiration—especially when the stranger holds more power in society or the international world. However, in renouncing one's self, one's renewal potential through mutual encounter is lost. Only in mutual movement does this dance of the self with the stranger form and transform curriculum along the complex lines of "an autobiographics of alterity" (Pinar, 2001, p. 2), through freedom, full of love.

"At seventy I could follow my heart to do whatever I wanted to do without transgressing what was right" (*The Analects*, 2.4). Confucius regarded this as his highest achievement, as it indicates a creative harmony between the self and the (moral) Way. This harmonious sense of freedom is different from the Western notion of "autonomous" freedom. Is it possible to have another version of freedom, based not upon individual autonomy but on relationships? Can freedom be reclaimed by an interactive view of both autonomy and relationships? Can one be really free without being at ease *with* others and *with* the world? On the other hand, can a loving relationship be possible without devouring the beloved if the alterity of each party is not respected? Is not the independence of the (emerging) subject of the beloved the foundation of any loving relationship? The loving respect for a student's own subjectivity—while also acknowledging the teacher's own potential for growth—is essential to any education offering the student freedom to explore, to question, and to create.

Michel Foucault (1986, 1997) believes that the care of the self is the practice of freedom that goes beyond limits. Confucius tells me that personal cultivation is possible only through a loving (*ren*) relationship with others and with the world. Carrying my own tradition, entering into the realm of freedom, I attempt to search for a third space, a space beyond the in-between, a space embodying both love and freedom but also transcending both, for a possible creative transformation of selfhood. This sense of both freedom and love, as implied by Kristeva (1996), is made possible in our willingness and ability to take exile, strangeness, and foreignness as a site of creation. It is a peculiar position for a woman and for a foreigner, but also a position for anyone who wants to form an inventive relationship with the self, a relationship always open to the other, the otherness of the other.

*To imply that my cultural tradition is relational and that Western culture holds the ideal of freedom undoubtedly simplifies the complexity of each cul-*

*ture. The multiplicity within each culture makes such a reductionism impossible. Could such a tension be eased somehow by taking such an angle as only one focus of a kaleidoscope to glance at an ever-changing picture of the self?*

The traditional relationality of the Chinese self is a patriarchal concept in which women are inferior to men. In its affirmation of independence and autonomy, Western selfhood has the potential to counteract suppressive relationships. However, it is also a myth with a veil of patriarchy. Woman does not really have a self. Whether relational or autonomous, woman cannot find her home in either discourse. Beyond traditions in search of a new space, as Kristeva suggests, we need to listen to the call of the stranger who is woman.

What is the self? What can Yu Qiuyu's (1992) search for the self during the heyday of the Cultural Revolution teach me as a Chinese woman?

> I do not know why this courtyard [the lyceum] has touched a certain layer existing deeply in my soul. This layer is not something cultivated in all my born days, but existed much earlier. If there is indeed a previous existence, I must have been here and lived here for a long time. I vaguely feel I have found myself. What is the self? The self is a mysterious courtyard. If you enter it by chance one day but are no longer willing to go out of it, and you feel it is dearer to you than the house you were born in and the current house you are living in, that is your self. (p. 131)

The sense of the self that Yu tries to convey in this message is deeply rooted in the cultural, in the historical, and in the collective unconscious of Chinese intellectuals. Reading the affirmation of his search for a scholarly self grounded in the collective past, however, I cannot help but think about whether or not women can claim themselves in a similar way. Considering the great difficulties of tracing women's recorded traditions, can the call from those no-name women be heard?

## Listening to the Ghost of the No-Name (Chinese) Woman

> To worry or to smile, such is the choice when we are assailed by the strange; our decision depends on how familiar we are with our own ghosts.
> (Julia Kristeva, 1991, p. 191)

> Not as fragrant as flower, as tall as tree
> I am a piece of unnoticed little grass
> Never feel lonely never feel worried
> Look at my companion everywhere
> With spring wind and sunshine, I turn into green
> River and mountains hold me

Earth mother dearly embraces me

(a Chinese song)

A piece of unnoticed little grass is a symbol of the common soul to me. I once read a newspaper article titled "How Far Can a Common Soul Go?" It told the story of a Chinese woman fighting against cancer to finish her Ph.D. dissertation in the United States. It is a touching story. It told me that a common soul can go as far as possible, as long as one follows one's heart to bring life into blossom, even under the threat of death. Ever since I read this article, this thought has stayed with me.

A woman's story. A woman who regards herself as a common girl but shows her brilliance and free spirit. Her name is Yuan He. She has a name. She has a story that can be told in public. There are women's stories that are not allowed to be told, especially those of women who transgress the boundaries and do not follow rules. There are women's stories that are deliberately forgotten. There are women's stories that are not recorded simply because they are women, not men.

In *The Woman Warrior*, Maxine Hong Kingston (1989) tells the story of a no-name Chinese woman. She was Kingston's aunt, who killed herself by jumping into the family's well with her illegitimate newborn baby. To give birth to a baby out of wedlock was unforgivable, not only by the family but also the whole community. The attack from the community and the silence in the family drove her aunt to suicide on the day of her baby's birth. After her death, her name was never mentioned in the family, as if she had never existed. It was a secret that one day Maxine Kingston's mother revealed to her, warning her never to tell others about it. Kingston had ever since been haunted by her aunt. A tearful ghost not able to tell her own story. A courageous ghost protests silently.

The ghost of this no-name woman has haunted me ever since I read the book. Horrified by her fate and by many other women's fates, I am speechless, confronting the pain, tears, silent screams, and madness of women who are suppressed by the tyranny of patriarchy. The ghost is also part of me as a Chinese woman. I am carrying her call in my own struggles, trying hard to find a space to breathe, to love, and to explore. Is it possible for me to find a women's lyceum, wandering around the world one day, just as Yu found his home and self? Do I have to find a lyceum? Perhaps what I need is the flame, that hidden fire shining through generations of women, as Kim Chernin (1994) pictures so well:

> An image comes to me. I see generations of women bearing a flame. It is hidden, buried deep within, yet they are handing it down from one to another, burning. It is a gift of fire, transported from a world far off and far away, but never extinguished....

I must keep it alive, I must manage not to be consumed by it, I must hand it on when the time comes to my daughter. (p. 16)

Like a hidden flame, women's traditions and stories burn with the hope for every generation of daughters to carry on their legacy, exploring new paths for the next generation of daughters. To carry a mother's legacy, though, does not mean to follow the mother's steps. The constant fight between Kim Chernin and her mother and their final spiritual compromise show how a daughter can seek independence from a mother to follow her own calling without abandoning the mother's legacy. Kim's persistence upon her own path is the way she carries the flame her mother has handed on to her. A mother can be reclaimed by a daughter who leaves home to walk into new territories, to journey through unexpected routes, and to dig tunnels to reach alternative grounds. Mary Aswell Doll (1995) depicts her magnificent journey of turning the mother–daughter "relationship of mutual negativity" (p. 19) into sharing the feminine time of myths, dreams, and ghosts so that the connection between mother and daughter in the mother-world of implicit link instead of the father-world of explicit law can be traced and claimed. Here the departure from home symbolizes the move away from the patriarchal house and the entrance into the underground of feminine consciousness.

This burning flame carries the call from those ghosts who try to tell us their stories and invite us to speak for them, and speak for ourselves. As Gerda Lerner (1993) argues, traditional Western criticism against patriarchy tends to regard women not as active subjects but as passive victims of the system. Such a criticism ignores the fact that women not only have participated in but also have resisted this system actively. Dorothy Ko (1994) also argues that the May Fourth Chinese enlightenment movement depicts women in an oversimplified way as the victims of the Chinese family who need to be liberated by modernization and freedom. Not listening to women themselves, not understanding how women acted upon the family system to find their own spaces, and talking about women as if they were merely passive receivers of traditional institutions do not do justice to women's own struggles. We do not have much in written records—recently there have emerged many feminist studies of ordinary women—about the struggles of those common souls who tried to reach out for light in various forms of resistance, but we can follow our hearts to listen to their call. To renew this flame. To hand it on to the next generation, who will continue our struggles.

*His-tory described in official records is mainly about great men. Because women are usually nameless, it becomes especially necessary to rewrite and rethink his(?)tory through common souls.*

> Listening is love. . . . Listening, like engagement with a text, effects a dissolution of
> the boundaries of self. So does love. Simultaneously frightening and exhilarating, it
> allows the "outside" to come "inside," opening up channels of possibility, sharing
> languages, inspiring action. (Edgerton, 1996, p. 83)

In listening to the calling of women ghosts, we allow ourselves to go beyond the usual boundary of the self, to reach inside, getting in touch with our
shadowed twin within. This inner revolution of "inside" coming out disrupts
the given. Such a movement of inside out is simultaneous with outside in.
Listening to stories of womankind, we expand ourselves through connections
by love. The stranger within the self on most occasions whispers to us only
when we are off-guard. She can flash through our minds when we are not
prepared for her visit. Sometimes she can also leap out when we are caught
by a moment of anger, frustration, or ambivalence. These moments can be
easily channeled into our established way of life. If we are not attentive and
receptive, with opened ears and loving eyes, we cannot catch the deeper
meaning of the whisper or the flash that slips away as quickly as it comes.
The necessity of listening in a caring way asks us not to be restrained by the
routine, but through a loving dance of inside and outside, to journey out so
that a journey within can be enriched simultaneously. My own travel across
national borders helps me get in touch with the ghosts of Chinese women.

*In Chinese fairy tales, a ghost is usually a sad, vengeful image. A ghost*
*can be loving, though. There are beautiful love stories between ghosts and*
*humans. Interestingly, the ghost usually appears in a woman's figure. The*
*ghost's wish—whether positive or negative—must be respected. Otherwise,*
*the ghost will keep disturbing man's world on the ground. The call of the*
*ghost must be listened to and answered. Women, as shown in* The Joy Luck
Club, *may take advantage of this fear of the ghost to fulfill their (impossible)*
*wishes. Is this fear related, one way or another, to the fear of feminine*
*power?*

Those ghosts are actually still part of us today. Women are strangers.
Women are the other. The theme of woman as stranger and as other is not
uncommon in feminist literature. As early as Simone de Beauvoir (1952), the
issues of women as other, in contrast to men as ideal, are explicitly discussed. Even earlier, Virginia Woolf (1929) was concerned with the issue of
women as the inessential and the inferior. In searching for and constructing a
women's literary tradition, she honors a different way of writing which challenges the (male) norm. From a psychoanalytic perspective, Kristeva (1991,
1996) approaches the strangeness and foreignness of woman as a creative
site on which the drama of different landscapes of humanity can be staged.
For her, woman's journey is implicated in the process of attending to what

has been repressed, speaking the unspeakable. Getting in touch with the feminine is not intended to overthrow the paternal but, instead, to transform it.

Our curriculum visions can also be informed by ghosts (Doll & Gough, 2002). This attending to the haunting of the ghosts promises an imaginative realm in which curriculum negotiates a public world intimately related to students' personal journeys, borrowing Pinar and Grumet's (1976) notion of *currere*, which focuses on an autobiographical experiencing of life rather than a limited sense of schooling. This intimacy is enabled by "nourishing words" (Atwell-Vasey, 1998a, 1998b), through recovering students' lost connection with the maternal and facilitating students' own negotiations between the maternal and the paternal. Such a creative recovery is achieved by encounters with the stranger that are both intracultural and intercultural (Trueit, Doll, Wang, & Pinar, 2003; Pinar, 2003), initiating the psychic transformation of the personal situated in a third space. Informed (but not trapped) by ghosts, curriculum is envisaged otherwise.

The ability to converse with the ghosts deep inside ourselves brings us new consciousness and invites us to create new relationships. The call from the stranger is not only from others who are foreign to us, but also from the hidden yearning inside of ourselves. The no-name Chinese woman confronts me with my own past, the past that existed before I was born. Her calling from the collective unconscious of Chinese women shocks me into sudden awareness. She will always be with me as I continue my search for mother's invisible traces and pursue my own path, a path embedded in a difficult but necessary negotiation between the maternal and the paternal.

## In Search of a Third Space: The Outline of the Book

Why cannot I tell the true shape of the Mountain Lu?
Only because I am wandering so deeply in the mountain.
    (Su Shi [1037–1101], *Written on the Wall of Xilin Monastery*)

Every time when I walk upon a bridge, I always feel that I cannot go across—
perhaps because where I want to arrive is not what the bridge can reach.
    (Wang Jiaxin, 1993, p. 277)

As a Chinese woman who travels back and forth between Chinese culture and American (Western) culture, I attempt to work at the intersection of culture and gender, searching for a third space in which the movement of the self across cultural and gendered differences becomes creative through dynamic interconnections. Such a search is complicated by both the "identity crisis" in the West and the dramatic transformation in contemporary China, although they follow different directions. The contradictory nature of differences between Chinese and Western cultures constantly challenges me to reconcile these differences into a creative site where new subjectivities can emerge. Embracing both cultures through a third space of mutual transformation enables me to approach the issues of self, relationships, and differences in a new way.

Both Bhabha (1990) and Smith (1996) focus on the cultural aspect of the third space. The third space I am interested in is a space in which both parts of a conflicting double—whether cultural, gendered, national, psychic, or intellectual—interact with and transform each other, especially through the multiplicity of the self, giving rise to new realms of inter/subjectivity. Such a space is particularly enabling for me to live with "aporias" (Derrida, 1993) of identity. It is characterized not by erasing conflicts to reach agreement but by movement among differences to generate a new sense of the familiar self capable of creative activities. It is a space unfolding an inventive, shifting, and winding path between the self and the stranger on a journey beyond the current forms of life. What follows is a brief outline, situated in my search for a third space, of the chapters of this book.

My own journey of claiming myself through cultural and gendered layers of identity while at the same time questioning the very concept of naming has carried me beyond the notion of "bicultural identity" (Young, 1998). Bicultural identity implies the coexistence of two different cultures but is problematic if conflicts and contradictions between the two cultures are not addressed in generative rather than resolvable ways. What we need is a third space embodying both cultures but at the same time, honoring the otherness of each and encouraging passages and interactions between them. Such a third space is a transformative space in which different cultural layers of the self shift, intersect, and constantly reform. This effort to promote interaction across differences refuses the position of "either/or," addresses the tensions produced by "both/and," and utilizes the in-between interstices for cultivating new thoughts. Such passages, such a dialogue, such a cross-cultural inquiry, does not intend to achieve consensus but aims at a deeper and richer understanding of each, providing space for multiplicity and contradiction which can further generate more singularity and more passages.

The deconstruction of the subject in the contemporary West leaves an open space for rethinking the issue of the self. Michel Foucault takes up this space to elaborate a new sense of self-creation through tracing back to the Greco-Roman tradition of self-cultivation (Chapter 2). A stranger such as Foucault, a very Western man who nevertheless powerfully challenges Western traditions, provides an unsettling yet enticing view for me. As I wander around in quest of the self, Foucault's discourse of the subject as creative becoming offers a certain promise for my own journey, yet my engagement with Foucault's discourse both as a woman and as a Chinese cannot really initiate self-transformation without critical reflection. Such an engagement sends me back home to reclaim the Confucian self in its relational and cosmic connections (Chapter 3). This return is not a homecoming in its literal sense; it is a journey, since my understanding of the Confucian self has been transformed by my encounter with the West.

Foucault's genealogical analysis of the evolution of the Greco-Roman notion of "the care of the self" into the Christian confessional notion of "knowing thyself" has a striking parallel with the development of the classical Confucian notion of personal cultivation into the Neo-Confucian notion of the rational self. Both the Greco-Roman tradition and classical Confucianism exhibit a relational view of the self, while the Christian "knowing oneself" and Neo-Confucianism subdue the self within the control of absolute truth or moral reason. On the other hand, the Foucauldian subject and the Confucian self exist in almost utter opposition: They are strangers to each other. Although neither Foucault nor Confucius is concerned with the essence of the self, Foucault emphasizes the transgressive aspect of the subject, its rupture with traditions and institutions, while Confucius emphasizes the relational aspect of the self, in harmony with society and nature. However, contradictions can be generative. In Chinese traditions, contradiction flows in dynamics of *yin* and *yang* beyond mere confrontation. An interactive flow between the Foucauldian subject and the Confucian self can mutually transform both to reach new grounds of inter/subjectivity. I attempt to initiate, in Chapter 3, a cross-cultural dialogue to envisage a third space in which new notions of individuality and relationality can emerge.

If Foucault focuses more on the creative aspect of the subject and Confucius more on the relational aspect of the self, how can one build connections in such a way that the creativity of relational individuality can be encouraged and cultivated? The relation between self and other through *difference* is implicated in one's relation with oneself, as Kristeva suggests (Chapter 4). As a woman, I do not feel fulfilled in either the Foucauldian subject or the Confucian self, as neither can answer the call from the woman. For me, the issue of otherness in general is not dealt with successfully by either of them. This sense of unfulfillment takes me to Julia Kristeva, a French psychoanalyst and linguist, who approaches the subject through the depth of the psyche which holds the stranger within. As an exiled intellectual woman, she reformulates the relationships between femininity and masculinity, and between self and other.

Kristeva calls for the embodiment of the semiotic in forming and developing the individual psyche through its dynamic interaction with the symbolic, since the feminine semiotic is usually suppressed socially and culturally. Such a call is not unique to women because strangeness within the self is universal, but women's unique experiences of the semiotic give them a peculiar position for becoming subjects relationally, in process, and in alterity. Utilizing psychoanalytic theory, Kristeva (1996) argues that the relationship with the stranger is also a relationship with the self, leading to a "paradoxical community" (p. 41) which welcomes foreigners/foreignness. Her efforts to regenerate the semiotic directly challenge the rigid control of the symbolic and endow woman with the distinctive role of creating the subject anew. While questioning, under the contexts of the Chinese language and self, the psychoanalytic notion of a universal foundation of subjectivity upon separation (from the maternal) in Chapter 4, I construct a notion of a loving third space—psychically, socially, pedagogically—inspired by the Kristevian subject. Such a notion takes the psychic double of the semiotic and the symbolic and the gendered double of femininity and masculinity to a third space of creative transformation.

Traveling through the complexity and ambiguity of a third space in which the selves of both West and East, both man and woman—without claiming an essence of each identity—intersect, coexist, and contradict each other, I attempt to draw a multilayered landscape of the human/woman self whose different angles are depicted simultaneously. My journeying to Michel Foucault's self-creation, then back home to Confucius' relationality, and further into Julia Kristeva's stranger-within places me in unsettling positions, in contradictory gestures, and in a situation of aporia. Through dwelling with aporias, in Chapter 5, I discuss how the theory of the self engages the human psyche to generate a fuller, deeper, richer sense of intersubjective individuality contextualized within and across cultures and genders. This third space of the self is both multiple and singular.

Shifting in this contradictory yet generative space, I elaborate a transformative curriculum (Doll, 1993) and a transcendent pedagogy in intimacy in which both teacher and student continuously create both themselves and curriculum. In Chapter 6, based upon renewed understandings of individuality, relationality, and creativity, I suggest a vision of curriculum for the creative transformation of selfhood through autobiographical musings, alternating between my second trip back to China and my experiences as an educator here in the United States. Reflections on curriculum as *currere* have been woven into the whole book explicitly and implicitly, so this final chapter serves as a concluding remark resisting conclusion, inviting readers to start anew.

What is important to point out here is that, in this book, I have no intention of making a comprehensive study of any thinker. I will focus only on specific aspects of Foucault, Confucius, and Kristeva's works which particularly speak to my own journey of searching for and dwelling in a third space of the self. Most of all, I do not try to unify these thinkers' thoughts; they cannot be unified. Without any final synthesis, they nevertheless come together in the lived experience of myself as a cross-cultural being through space and time. Encountering each of these thinkers but refusing to be confined by any of them, I invite readers to travel with me through Foucauldian, Confucian, and Kristevian discourses into your own realm of self-creation and co-creation. In this contemporary age, an age full of multiplicity, contradiction, and fragmentation, but with increasing interconnection, such an attempt at making meanings out of the multiple has both singular and general implications, as conversations about identity, differences, and creativity are already underway in curriculum studies.

Finally, a note on the writing styles of this book. The multiplicity of self, language, and culture that I attempt to bring into a third space leads to different styles of writing within one book. Chapter 1 and Chapter 6 are highly autobiographical, echoing each other. Autobiographical writings are scattered throughout Chapter 2 and Chapter 3. Chapter 4 uses the double voice I already utilized in Chapter 1, albeit in a different way. Chapter 5 weaves the book together in a theoretical style while still allowing a trickle of the poetic which does not always follow the rules of English grammar. Overall, theoretical and narrative voices, which are not separate in life, are mingled in the book, although Chapter 4 separates them for a particular purpose. The multiple styles of writing, to a great degree, are intentional, enabling me to work in a third space which is mobilized by contradictions and ambiguity. Throughout the chapters, especially when I bring narratives into the writing, are several short sentences that do not accord with standard English grammar. By keeping sentences short, I hope to create a literary rhythm and, to some extent, introduce the poetic aspect of the Chinese language which is structured in a different way than English. Such is my experimental effort to mingle theoretical and literary writing so that a space open to differences is created through language. This experiment may not be as satisfactory as I hope, but it is a risk worth taking.

In summary, through cross-cultural philosophical inquiry, gender analysis, psychoanalysis, and autobiography, this book attempts to rethink inter/subjectivity in our so-called postmodern age. As an interdisciplinary effort to renew our understanding of self and curriculum, this inquiry intends to show multiple and different layers of reality simultaneously. This simultaneity in differences may initially cause a sense of uneasiness for readers, but it is necessary for creating a third space. I invite you to bear with me through this difficult journey, struggling toward making sense out of multiple cultural traditions, and thereby envisioning curriculum differently. The transformative and creative third space I am searching for is impossible without a journey both outside and inside, and without listening to the call of the stranger. The call from the stranger on a journey home is a journey into a third space beyond the binaries of self/other, femininity/masculinity, and semiotic/symbolic, so that a transformative vision of the self can be created and re-created. The conflicting doubles of the self—whether at a cultural or a gendered level, or at the intersection of gender and culture—create new layers of the self through movement across differences to reach another sphere of subjectivity which is achieved not by consensus but by "polyphonic dialogue" (Bakhtin, 1984). Curriculum becomes self-generative through such a journey. Both teachers and students are engaged in the process of self-transformation/co-transformation and self-creation/co-creation. So, together "let's go" (Bei, 1991) on a continuous, ever-evolving, and unfinished journeying with the company of the stranger, carving out many third spaces along the way.

## Notes

1. I indeed have taken time to think about how to translate Chinese names. It is customary to translate Chinese names according to the Western naming order in English, which is first name before family name. But names of famous Chinese scholars are translated according to the Chinese naming order, which is family name before first name. In order to avoid confusion, I use the Chinese naming order for Chinese names. The important consideration for such a choice is that I believe different naming orders to some degree reflect different notions of the self. The Chinese naming pattern emphasizes the relational aspect of a person, while the Western naming pattern emphasizes the individuality of a person. Although it may sound far-fetched, I prefer to keep the Chinese naming custom as it is, in its *difference* from Western autonomy.

2. Since the space I am writing in is itself contestable and sometimes contradictory, I hesitate to make any grand generalizations without accompanying questions. What is in italics are my musings, which are often registered on a conflicting subjective site. In this way I intend to show multiple voices—in Mikhail Bakhtin's terms, polyphonic dialogue within the self and with others—without influencing the flow of the main text. The idea of producing a double voice was first suggested by my advisor, Dr. Bill Doll, and I would like to thank him for seeing the potential in my struggles for new ways of writing.

3. Aware of the problematic of using the term *Western culture*, I still use it in a comparative sense—a skewed comparison, since I do not use the term *Eastern culture* because I understand more about the cultural differences of the East. Coming from Chinese culture, my take on Western culture stays more at the level of theorizing about a culture different from mine rather than experiencing different cultures within Western culture. Perhaps as

an outsider, what I can offer are my thoughts as a result of such unbalanced travel between Chinese culture and Western culture(s). Furthermore, my discussions involve Western thinkers who are from different countries, which makes it more difficult to distinguish national/cultural differences within the West.

# Chapter 2

# The Call from the Other Shore: The Care of the Self, Freedom, and Self-Creation

> Is one more faithful to the heritage of a culture by cultivating the difference-to-oneself (*with oneself*) that constitutes identity or by confining oneself to an identity wherein this difference remains *gathered*?
>
> (Jacques Derrida, 1992, p. 11; emphasis in original)

The other shore beats against the ancient wall of an old Chinese capital. Walking on the ancient city wall, looking far into the distance, I can vaguely smell the salty wind of the sea. Through the window of a bilingual education center, Nanjing opens a crack for me to see another world. In a few years, the echoes of the Drum Tower in Nanjing find me across the ocean sitting under the University Tower on campus at Louisiana State University, reading stories of another civilization. The call from "the other heading" (Derrida, 1992) leads me out of myself.

Michel Foucault unfolds the story of Western civilization through a new light. He is a stranger to me, with his piercing gaze, uncompromising posture, and "legendary laugh" (Miller, 1993, p. 328). Yet when I first came across Foucault's writings on the formation of the subject, I was immediately captivated by his call for self-creation as I wandered around the labyrinth of the subject. Is it possible that what is the strangest can be a part of the self? The call of the other shore promises renewed understanding of both self and other. Foucault's unfinished project due to his early death leaves us a challenge and an invitation onto a road less traveled.

As I am drawn to Foucault's new understanding of the subject, a critical distance I attempt to maintain as a Chinese woman keeps whispering, "You cannot afford to get too close! You cannot lose yourself in the stranger!" The road less traveled is not likely a straightforward path leading to an already known destination. Curving around without being afraid to step onto side paths, in this chapter I am going to dwell upon the possibilities that the Foucauldian subject can offer and point out its limitations through a gendered critique. Regarding my cross-cultural analysis of Foucault's theory, I will leave that to the next chapter, when I discuss Confucianism.

## The Problematic of Identity

> As the archaeology of our thought easily shows, man is an invention of recent date.... one can certainly wager that man would be erased, like a face drawn in sand at the edge of the sea.
>
> (Michel Foucault, 1970, p. 387)

The quest for the self is a personal yearning. It is what brings me to the West. Yet my journey here is initiated not by an induction into Western selfhood but, dramatically, by the "deconstruction" of Western traditions, by "the death of the subject." I hear Foucault's announcement about the death of man, Roland Barthes' litany on the death of the author, Jacques Derrida's call for deconstruction of the subject, and Jacques Lacan's embracement of a decentering self. What is at stake in all these unsettling discourses is the very notion of the subject or identity.

As David Geoffrey Smith (1996) points out, contemporary debates in the West, to a great degree, have been centered on the problematic of identity. He locates the crisis of identity in "a profound *desire* for identity" (p. 7) and calls for "a healthy abandonment of the concepts of Self and Other" (p. 9) as Buddhism and Zen teach us. Coming from Chinese culture, I appreciate Eastern wisdom about the co-emergence of self, other, and the universe, but I have doubts about the abandonment of an independent boundary between self and other. I would argue that the attempt to challenge the dualism between subject and object must be coupled with an effort to keep a certain distance between the two, so that the in-depth understanding of both the self and the world is possible. I will discuss this issue further in the next chapter. Here it is sufficient to notice that Western discourses on identity are undergoing a dramatic shift, away from the certainty of the subject in its transcendental essence and toward the ambiguity of the self in its contingency and multiplicity. Postmodern critiques of reason and metaphysics in the modern West unmask the normalizing tendency in a unitary, essential, and universal notion of the subject, with its exclusion of differences and subjugation of margins. Such critiques throw the self into context, fluidity, and plurality, and situate it on the border. Questions remain: If the notion of the subject is already at stake, what can we do with ourselves? If we want to act upon the world, upon what can we rely to be engaged in the project of selfhood?

Foucault approaches the issue of identity first through a negative posture. In his archaeological studies of "subjugated knowledge" and genealogical analysis of madness and psychiatry, crime and punishment, Foucault (1973, 1977a) attempts to show how we constitute ourselves through the exclusion of the other, through the constructions of "madness" and "criminality." He (1977a, 1978) also shows how discursive practices of regulating and producing the subject through disciplining the body reproduce domination. Such a formation of an essential modern subject is practiced at the expense of differences. The very practices of categorizing, essentializing, and labeling the individual, no matter what intentions they carry, identify a stable and fixed self to impose on a concrete person. When the self is seen as a sort of entity with an essence hidden deeply inside, the most we can do is to uncover the predetermined truth. Rejecting this approach, Foucault is interested in opening up critical and creative spaces of subjectivity which cannot be limited by any preestablished essential self. It is not surprising that he remarks, "The relationships we have to have with ourselves are not ones of identity; rather, they must be relationships of differentiation, of creation, of innovation" (1982a, p. 166). Through his suspicion of essentialized identity, he calls for self-creation.

Foucault's discourses on the subject are provocatively situated in an ambiguous zone, claiming for the subject neither complete independence nor passive enslavement. His critique of identity does not prevent him from elaborating the capacity of the subject to grasp its own limitations. He not only shows how identity is constructed socially, historically, and culturally, but he also elaborates the subject's active role in constituting itself. The constructed nature of the subject implies a potential to become different than it is; what is contingent can be changed. For Foucault, the resistance against the social construction of the "normal" individual in its domination and exclusion is much more than a negation; it is creative self-constitution through changing the situation and opening up new modes of individuality not controlled externally by religion, institutions, or media. As early as 1969, when Foucault talked about "author functions," he was already referring to openings in the space left empty by the disappearance of the author (Foucault, 1984c). This opportunity to create a new space is taken up by Foucault in his later works where he articulates a creative notion of the subject. The complicated network of power, knowledge, and subjectivity that he attempts to weave makes it possible to claim "an ontology of ourselves" not based upon a transcendental notion of the self but "at one and the same time [an] historical analysis of the limits imposed on us and an experiment with the possibility of going beyond them" (1984a, p. 319). The ethos of discontinuous becoming is implied by this "limit attitude." This attitude does not provide any essential foundations for human agency but adopts an open-ended mode of emergence and creativity. Without solid ground to rely on, what we are left with is the task of continuously inventing ourselves anew.

As I have already implied, a sense of the self is necessary to renew one's relationship both with oneself and with others. A certain version of the subject under fire does not necessarily lead to the total collapse of the concept. If the self does not have to disappear all together, the issue we need to confront is how to rethink the self. The problematic of identity makes Foucault critical of any truth-claiming project in identity politics—including gay liberation. He does not believe that there is any essential truth about oneself that can guarantee human freedom. Foucault draws a distinction between liberation and freedom. He is suspicious of the notion of liberation because it usually implies a human nature that is "concealed, alienated, or imprisoned in and by mechanisms of repression" (1984b, p. 282), and that by breaking repression and prohibition, one can be liberated; problems can be solved. History has shown that such projects of liberation based upon some essential truth have failed to combat the worst parts of tradition. The practices of freedom, however, are much more concerned with redefining relationships, experimenting with new modes of thought, and crafting one's existence to create a fulfilling life, rather than reaching a predetermined ideal. In other words, human nature is created, not given. Without denying the possibility of liberation under certain historical and cultural conditions, Foucault prefers the concrete exercise of freedom to the abstract appeal of liberation. Such an understanding of freedom does not deny the role of the subject; rather it intensifies the responsibility of the self, which is to not comply with the social norm, despite the constraints imposed on the individual. In his later works, Foucault shifts his attention to a transgressive self which works at the limits of knowledge and history to breathe life into subjectivity. To show the nonnecessity of the modern subject which claims universal truth, he returns to the Greco-Roman tradition of the care of the self for a different construction of subjectivity, working to interrupt the line of historical continuity.

Foucault's critical formulation of a new ontology of the self dissolves the arguments of his critics who, ironically, in conflicting directions, regard his discourse either as too passive to register human agency (Fraser, 1994), or too autonomous, falling back to the philosophy of the transcendental subject (Garrison, 1998). His new relation with the self calls for the simultaneous recognition and transcendence of historical, social, and cultural limitations. According to Foucault, "playing with structure—transforming and transfiguring its limits" instead of "playing inside the structure" (quoted in Miller, 1993, p. 353) is the path one needs to take. This notion of *playing with* indicates Foucault's devotion to a form of self-creation situated at the edge of limits with the potential to go beyond. For Foucault, transformation stays at superficial levels if it merely adjusts the same modes of thought. Deep transformation must break away from the same thought by means of an open and turbulent critique, bringing forth new modes of thought. Creativity is possible only at the limit and cannot remain within any "sameness," even an innovative one.

This call for self-creation is a strategy Foucault employs to deal with the problematic of identity. He does not intend to exclude identity, but he rejects it as a universal reality attached to a hidden truth or essence to be uncovered. Identity as a useful concept must be understood as a game or procedure, being in relationships which are fluid, contradictory, and plural. Sharing Smith's (1996) suspicion about the very term "identity," Foucault nevertheless elaborates a double-faced subject which constantly constitutes itself—actively works on itself—beyond its constituted self. The effort to abandon the concept of self versus other is displaced into a new ontology of self that exercises its freedom at the border between social construction and individual creativity. Foucault refuses to provide any *a priori* theory of the subject; through destabilizing identity, he opens a space for transforming the subject through a continuous process of formation and reformation. When the notion of the essence of the subject is at stake, the subject is no longer discovered but is created—not out of nowhere, though, but out of the complex web of historicity, sociality, and individuality. The purpose of the care of the self in the Greco-Roman tradition, for Foucault, is not to maintain sameness but to free differences. The care of the self itself is a practice of freedom, an ancient practice Foucault draws upon to construct new forms of subjectivities, which I will discuss next.

## The Care of the Self and the Ethos of Freedom

> There are times in life when the question of knowing if one can think differently than one thinks, and perceive differently than one sees, is absolutely necessary if one is to go on looking and reflecting at all.
>
> (Foucault, 1985, p. 8)

Foucault's studies on the relationships among power, knowledge, and subjectivity pave the way to understanding the human self as both constructed and constructive angles of self-self relation. In his later works, he "felt obliged to study the games of truth in the relationship of self with self and the forming of oneself as a subject" (1985, p. 6). In other words, he shifts his attention to the relationship of oneself to oneself, i.e., how one constitutes oneself as the subject of one's desires and thoughts, an ethical subject. He defines how the subject constitutes and transforms itself as "technologies of the self":

> Technologies of the self permit individuals to effect by their own means, or with the help of others, a certain number of operations on their own bodies and souls, thoughts, conduct and way of being, so as to transform themselves in order to attain a certain state of happiness, purity, wisdom, perfection, or immortality. (Foucault, 1982b, p. 225)

To explore these technologies of the self, in *The Use of Pleasure,* Foucault (1985) investigates how individuals formed themselves as subjects of desire in antiquity, through dietetics, marriage, and erotic relationships with boys. In *The Care of the Self,* Foucault (1986) turns to the Greco-Roman notion from which the book takes its title to analyze the evolution of self-cultivation. As "one of the main principles of cities, one of the main rules for social and personal conduct and for the art of life" (Foucault, 1982b, p. 226), the care of the self in the Greco-Roman pagan tradition contrasts with early Christianity and its practices of self-cultivation. While on the one hand he points out certain common themes between Greco-Roman principles and Christian notions, such as the prevalence of self-mastery, he painstakingly analyzes how a rupture forms between the two, a rupture that does not exist within the evolution of pagan thought. Such a genealogical analysis aims to "learn to what extent the effort to think one's own history can free thought from what it silently thinks, and so enable it to think differently" (Foucault, 1985, p. 9).

Foucault makes it clear that in his return to the notion of self-cultivation in the Greco-Roman tradition, he does not intend to outline an alternative as a model to the modern subject. His efforts to understand the historicity of the human subject disrupt the myth of progress, and make it possible to think difference. As Mark Poster (1986) points out, Foucault's genealogical analysis questions the implicit universality of the present through tracing the differences of the past and opening up a space for thinking differently, thereby transforming the given.

According to Foucault (1986), the care of the self in the Greco-Roman tradition is embedded in the idea that one ought to attend and constantly return to oneself and care for oneself so that one's soul can be perfected by reason. The care of the self, *epimeleia heautou,* is a concept dating from about the third century B.C. and continuing until the second or third century A.D. This tradition has several principles. It is a rational mastery of the self regarded as an object to be reflected upon and transformed. It is valuable for everyone but particularly necessary for people who rule others, whether in family or in society. It is a soul-oriented activity conducted throughout one's life, without exclusion of the body. It is the practice of freedom through mastery.

In the tradition of the care of the self, one is called upon to take oneself as an object of contemplation and knowledge and to follow the principles of rational conduct in correcting one's faults and perfecting one's soul. Seneca used the Roman Stoic Sextius' questions for reflection upon his soul before retiring for the night: "What bad habit have you cured today? What fault have you resisted? In what respect are you better?" (Foucault, 1986, p. 61). Here self-mastery is in accord with reason. Man regulates his food, regimen, pleasure, and relations with others, such as in marriage and with boys, so that moderation can replace excess for the perfection of the soul. Moderation in its mastery of emotions and regulation of desires is a virtue that enables man to exercise his power over both self and others. Meditations, readings, notes, recollections, letters—all these exercises of the self serve this purpose of living a mode of life that requires one "to act upon himself, to monitor, test, improve, and transform himself" (Foucault, 1985, p. 28). The importance of rationality is unmistakeable.

The care of the self is a valuable style of life that everyone can choose to follow. Actually "everyone" refers only to every man, and, further, only to every free man. In other words, it is an exercise for those people who are already in power and required to rule others. In *The Use of Pleasure*, Foucault (1985) points out that moral reflection upon an appropriate use of pleasure is a male ethic that excludes women. Such an elaboration of masculine conduct invites man to be actively engaged in forming himself as a subject. This style of life, although privileged philosophically and existentially, is not a universal norm. It depends upon one's personal choice of lifestyle. It is not difficult for us to see, however, that the claim of personal choice cannot mask the fact that only privileged people can enjoy the choice, the choice of ruling others through ruling self. In the case of the love of boys, the boy is supposed to assume a passive not active role in relationships with older men. This situation forms the problematic of the "boy" in ancient Greece, as the boy is in the process of becoming a subject himself and thus enjoys a different status from either slave or woman. The masculine dilemma of activity over passivity is highlighted here. The ancient love of boys is distinctively different from contemporary homosexual relationships, and Foucault makes clear his distaste for this ancient practice.

The care of the self, "more than an exercise done at regular intervals … is a constant attitude that one must take toward oneself" (Foucault, 1986,

p. 63), an attitude that suggests a lifelong project of creating an ethically and aesthetically pleasing life. It is never too early or too late to start caring for the soul, and such caring encourages one to be engaged in a ceaseless process of self-transformation.

In this tradition of caring for the self, there is a certain ambivalence concerning the role of the body. On the one hand, self-cultivation aims at caring for one's soul and imbuing it with reason and, as a result, the concern with the body seems not very important. On the other hand, intense attention to the body and the circulation between the body and the soul makes the care of the self closely related to that of the body. The disturbances, excesses, and ills of the body can communicate themselves to the soul and cause its failings, while the bad habits of the soul can result in disease and bodily dysfunction. Due to such interplay, it becomes necessary to pay attention to food and health regimens, and any disturbances of the body influence the practices of the self. Here again, the excesses of the body must be modified to make the virtue of the soul possible. While the body is still under the rational regulation of the soul, the modern dualism between mind and body has not yet formed. In Foucault's vision, the body can become the site for creating new subjectivities. Especially in his later interviews, speaking about "becoming a gay"—speaking against regarding homosexuality as secret truth about the self—Foucault believes that with sexuality, through bodily pleasures, we can create new forms of relationship, new forms of thought, new forms of life, new forms of self. An interesting question to ask here is how the Greco-Roman tradition of the body under the regulation of the soul is transformed into a new ethic of the body as the site for self-creation. We will return to this issue later.

The care of the self is a practice of freedom. In *The Use of Pleasure* and *The Care of the Self*, Foucault (1985, 1986) discusses the notion of freedom in the context of Greco-Roman culture. This notion does not aim at achieving the autonomy of the subject, the independence of a free will, or liberation from oppression. It is characterized as the exercise of self-mastery and the governing of pleasures and desires by an active individual who practices moderation, rationality, and wisdom to achieve a state of beauty in his existence. It is a freedom first exercised over oneself, which refuses the enslavement of the self by oneself or others or institutions. At the same time, it avoids the exercise of abuse of power over others. While recognizing its hierarchical nature, Foucault believes that the care of the self as a practice of freedom can become a way of limiting, regulating, and controlling the domination of power because "it is the power over oneself that thus regulates one's power over others" (Foucault, 1984b, p. 288). In ancient ethics, individual freedom is closely related to the freedom of the polis. When individual males cannot take care of themselves through appropriately exercising their power, the city or the state will be at stake. It is clear that individual freedom cannot be separate from collective freedom. Yet the starting point is with the self rather than with the polis. As a practice of freedom, the care of the self also emphasizes one's independence from the external world in order to focus on the cultivation of the soul. Such a turning away from the external to a retreat into oneself is a personal choice of abstinence and moderation in the exercise of active freedom.

Such a notion of freedom is distinctively different from the modern ideal of universal freedom. Foucault does not define freedom in any systematic or general sense, and his meanings of freedom shift in different contexts. In ancient sexual ethics, freedom is based upon rational self-mastery; in nonidentity politics, freedom is a form of resistance against social domination; in the new ontology of the self, it is embedded in a "limit attitude" which valorizes transgression against historical limitations, emphasizing the creativity of producing new existential possibilities. However, there is a certain thread through his different versions of freedom. Foucault believes that the space of freedom is "a space of concrete freedom, that is, of possible transformation" (1983a, p. 450). In other words, freedom is contextualized rather than abstract or universal; freedom releases differences through an ongoing process rather than staying within the given truth; freedom is an exercise of going beyond limits rather than "an attribute or a transferable possession of the subject" (Ziarek, 2001, p. 8). This process-oriented sense of denormalized transformation as the ethos of freedom can be traced back to Greco-Roman ethics. Foucault states: "In the Greco-Roman world, the care of the self was the mode in which individual freedom—as civil liberty, up to a point—was reflected [*se réfléchie*] as an ethic" (1984b, p. 284). When self-creation as an ethical relationship, rather than a universal demand, is situated in an ongoing process of engagement with transformative activities, according to Foucault, specific and diversified change can occur at the level of both the individual and society. This generative possibility of freedom (both against constraints and toward creativity) goes hand in hand with Foucault's localized and productive view of power. To transform oneself, to surpass oneself, and to know oneself: such are the principles of the practice of producing oneself as the ethical subject that actively constitutes itself.

Foucault acknowledges such practices of self-care as having pedagogical functions. James Marshall (1996) argues that freedom as an exercise of the self is obtained through a "personal philosophical and educational enterprise" (p. 80). Such an enterprise requires a different vision of education from that of modeling an individual student with the purpose of producing docility and engineering selfhood. Any normalizing and universalizing mode, even with the intention of liberation, reinscribes the power of institutions, teachers, or parents on students. Students no longer exercise "the care of the self" if they follow the orders of others. In education for freedom, the main practices are critique, transformation, and creativity. Transformation is made possible by open-ended inquiry, not by the imposition of any grand schema. Thinking differently leads to new modes of pedagogy generating the lived experience of curriculum. Drawing upon the Foucauldian notion of the self, Justen Infinito (2003) argues that education is the vehicle both for understanding our cultural and social conditioning and for promoting the creative capacity for self-formation and reformation. In providing spaces for alternative selves, constructing knowledge of multiple worlds, and cultivating the spirit of critique for inventing new existential conditions, education is engaged in and transformed by the everyday practice of freedom. As a daily practice, freedom is both the means and the end of self-cultivation and education.

Occasionally Foucault directly comments on the problematic of sexual ethics in the Greco-Roman tradition. He is adamant that sexual relationships must be based upon mutual pleasure. However, he leaves unattended the gaps between his own vision of self-creation and that of Greco-Roman tradition. The masculine duality of subject over object, activity over passivity, and reason over emotion can be discerned clearly from the rationale and practice of the care of the self. But, as Poster (1986) points out, Foucault does not ask "the interpretation question of why that was so" (p. 213). We will return to this issue later. Part of the reason that Foucault does not elaborate how the ancient practice can be transformed anew for our contemporary life lies, I believe, in his refusal to present Greco-Roman self-care as an alternative model to follow, and in his rejection of providing a general and universal notion of the subject. Part of the reason lies as well in his effort to contrast pagan traditions with early Christianity—to which I will turn next—in an attempt to perform historical ruptures; part of the reason might be his early death, which left his own project unfinished.

According to Foucault, the Greco-Roman tradition contrasts with early Christianity. He traces the evolution of self-cultivation from Greek, Roman, and Christian thought into the modern subject. From the Greek into the Roman imperial period, there is already an increasing anxiety over pleasure and "a certain strengthening of austerity themes" (Foucault, 1986, p. 235). Such preoccupations anticipate later moral systems. However, Foucault makes a great effort to analyze how such a change within the Greco-Roman tradition does not constitute the same radical rupture as the one between the pagan tradition and the Christian confessional practice of self-salvation, and later, the modern science of the subject.

Through genealogical analysis, Foucault (1986, 1997) shows how the Greco-Roman notion of the care of the self as a positive precept was converted in early Christianity into the negative posture of renouncing one's self in order to obey God's will. In the process, the injunction to "know thyself," initially as a consequence and a part of the "care of the self," became dominant, so that the question of truth came to occupy a central position in the formation of the modern subject. Foucault (1981) calls this technique of the self "the spiral of truth formulation and reality renouncement," since "the more we discover the truth about ourselves, the more we must renounce ourselves; and the more we want to renounce ourselves, the more we need to bring to light the reality of ourselves" (p. 178). Moreover, the Greco-Roman care of the self is more of a management and administrative practice of self-improvement, while Christian self-examination is more of a juridical system of imposing normalizing practices. As a result, the purpose of self-mastery in the former is self-transformation; in the latter, the point is to renounce sin and evil presumably hidden in the heart, in order to purify one's soul. The turn from a holistic notion of the self (with rationality privileged) to a Christian devotion to absolute truth is an inward turn toward a more normalized self.

In the Christian confessional practice of self-examination, thoughts and desires, rather than behaviors, are the primary focus, with the purpose of finding faults, recognizing temptations, and discovering the truth hidden deeply within oneself. Foucault analyzes two techniques of self-examination in early Christianity: *exomologesis*, public recognition of faith which "rubs out the sin and yet reveals the sinner" (1982a, p. 244), and *exagoreusis*, the verbalization of one's thoughts in the renunciation of one's own self. As a result, "knowing thyself" becomes crucial in deciphering and discovering the truth about oneself. Self-knowledge also occupies a strong position in the Greco-Roman notion of care of the self, but it is achieved by care of the self. In other words, the principle of knowing oneself is subordinated to the principle of the care of the self. Moreover, the Greco-Roman practice of self-examination focuses on action, not on the renunciation of the self. Discussing the Stoic Seneca's practices of self-examination, Foucault (1986) writes:

> The purpose of the examination is not . . . to discover one's own guilt, down to its most trifling form and its most tenuous roots. If "one conceals nothing from oneself," if one "omits nothing," it is in order to commit to memory, so as to have them present in one's mind, legitimate ends, but also rules of conduct that enable one to achieve these ends through the choice of appropriate means. The fault is not reactivated by the examination in order to determine culpability or stimulate a feeling of remorse, but in order to strengthen, on the basis of the recapitulated and reconsid-

ered verification of a failure, the rational equipment that ensures a wise behavior. (p. 62)

Important differences between Greco-Roman and Christian self-examination are clarified here. Without the purpose of discovering a secret truth, the care of the self, in the Greco-Roman tradition, aims at adjusting and regulating acts through recollecting what has been done, remembering the rules of rational conduct, and reevaluating what needs to be done in the future. Its purpose is to rid oneself of bad habits, correct faults, and perfect one's life. Unlike the Christian demand for complete obedience to God, Greco-Roman care of the self emphasizes self-reliance, self-regulation, and personal choice. By contrast, Christian confession is a practice of normalization achieved by self-sacrifice[1] and self-punishment, practiced to expel the inner shadow, disclose the self, and purify one's soul. It is a practice of channeling everyone into following only one path for self-salvation. Furthermore, the Greco-Roman focus on action unfolds a process of engagement—Foucault notes that this process further has *undefined* ends—while the Christian emphasis on turning toward the absolute authority defines the only legitimate end state of self-cultivation.

The demand for normalization and the search for hidden truth are also inherent in the claim of universality for the modern subject. However, for Foucault, such a pursuit of absolute truth is actually a mechanism of moral and social control. Moreover, "by emphasizing the self as some deep, mysterious, essentially stable and selfishly desirous entity, we have become obsessed with trying to understand that self rather than seeing the self as something we have a choice in, and seeing the world as something other than 'fixed'" (Infinito, 2003, p. 163). The mission of the knowing subject is to discover and realize the "normal" self rather than to transform and re-create the self. Foucault (1983b) also believes that Descartes separated truth from ethics and located the founding role of the subject in its access to knowledge through scientific evidence. This is contrary to the Greco-Roman tradition in which the ethic of the self is closely linked to the capacity for knowing the truth. As Foucault unmasks the disciplinary face of the modern subject based upon scientific knowledge, the relation one has with oneself is transformed into a creative activity: "From the idea that the self is not given to us, I think that there is only one practical consequence: we have to create ourselves as a work of art" (Foucault, 1983b, p. 262).

Greco-Roman self-care, Christian self-salvation, and the modern universal self produce temporary configurations that characterize the Western individual. These configurations, embodied in different practices of the self, present a mobile and plural construction of the subject which cannot be confined to the modern claim for universality. As a practice of freedom, the care of the self, according to Foucault, encourages one to pass beyond the given, to transform the horizon of what one sees and how one acts, and to become free of oneself in order to invent new subjectivities. Such an practice is embedded in a process of emergence and becoming, a process which can inform—but not model—our present search for alternative structures of the self. In both *The Use of Pleasure* and *The Care of the Self*, Foucault (1985, 1986) suggests that one has to give oneself up in order to *become*. He also comments that his writing (writing is one technique of the self in the ancient Greek tradition) triggers his own transformation (Foucault, 1997). Intellectual work, for Foucault, is a practice of self-creation, a venturing into worlds different from one's own. The process of surrendering oneself in order to transform the self is close to that of aesthetic experience. Here the ethic of the self becomes the aesthetic of existence.

## Possibilities of Self-Creation:
## Identity Politics through Aesthetics and Ethics

Critics of Foucault's notion of self-care accuse it of blurring boundaries among politics, aesthetics, and ethics (Schrag, 1997; Wolin, 1986). In other words, how can politics exist in a work of art? How can ethical values be embedded in aesthetics? As a person coming from Chinese culture, one which does not draw clear distinctions among the three, it is actually not a problem to me. Justen Infinito (2003) explains the relationships among these three realms in the Foucauldian subject: "The ethical is always political and vice versa; both the ethical and political are achieved through the aesthetic; and when ethically informed, the aesthetic leads to human freedom" (p. 155). This act of boundary crossing and blending defies the arbitrary lines by which modern science divides humanity and thus opens up space for thinking differently. Foucault draws upon the critical function of aesthetics to convey a sense of "limit attitude" so that political and ethical relationships are destabilized. However, this reliance on deviant postures of art tends to romanticize aesthetics as necessarily having the potential of going beyond social constraints. But art is hardly free from historical, cultural, and institutional influences. For instance, the Chinese aesthetics of harmony in differences is distinctively different from the Western aesthetics as norm disrupting, due to historical and cultural differences in philosophy, way of life, and notions of the self. In other words, aesthetics is also socially constructed and suffers its own limitations. My concern is to make self-creation possible through *critical* aesthetics and *relational* ethics. How can we make this possibility available to those who are not privileged? But before I consider this question, I would like to focus on the possibilities Foucault tries to open up through the aesthetics of self-care.

By "arts of existence" Foucault (1985) means "those intentional and voluntary actions by which men not only set themselves rules of conduct, but also seek to transform themselves, to change themselves in their singular being, and to make their life into an *oeuvre* that carries certain aesthetic values and meets certain stylistic criteria" (pp. 10–11). Here aesthetic values in the Greco-Roman tradition refer to the beauty of both the soul and the body in harmony. Both ontological order and beautiful shape are maintained in such a life. Certain stylistic criteria structure the art of the everyday existence of man in his relationships with his body, family, and eroticism. Proper relationships obtained by self-restraint are usually maintained by struggles in establishing a mastery over self. Here, the ethics of self-conduct and the morality of constituting the subject become an aesthetics of existence. Different from a narrow sense of aesthetics, the intention of art in this case is not to create or appreciate an object but to work on one's life and invent new modes of being. Such mingling between ethics and aesthetics is grounded in transformative experiences through which an individual can craft his own existence to achieve a certain fulfillment. Such a crafting leads to ruptures between oneself and tradition so that new forms of the self can emerge. For Foucault, the power of aesthetics lies in transforming one's life and one's self. One's identity, in this sense, has no inherent structure to which one must cling; it is set in motion in a process of continuously opening to new possibilities.

The aesthetics of the self are imbued with power relationships and, as a result, are political by nature. The care of the self requires one to form a political relationship first with oneself. This act is political in the sense that one attempts to master one's desires so that one is not a slave to oneself but actively practices self-regulation. The power one exercises over oneself is closely related to the power one exercises over others, so that one's relationships with others are always present in the ethics of self-care. However, Foucault (1984b) claims that "care for others should not be put before the care of oneself. The care of the self is ethically prior in that the relationship with oneself is ontologically prior" (p. 287). For Foucault, when the care for others becomes the main point in an ethical relationship, the care of the self is diminished. Foucault suggests that the appropriate exercise of the self upon the self is intended to transform and renew one's self in its relationships with others, but without self-sacrifice and self-renunciation. One needs to build one's own ethics based upon social and cultural practices, but not be constrained by these practices. Historical, cultural, and social understanding of the situated self is the beginning point—not the ending point—for initiating one's own creative activities. "People have to build their own ethics, taking as a point of departure the historical analysis, sociological analysis, and so on that one can provide for them" (Foucault, 1982c, p. 132).

This vision of the self is also compatible with Foucault's notion of power relationships as localized in networks rather than universalized, decreed from authority, enacted in everyday practices. When a power relationship is contextualized through a concrete individual situated in life history, culture, and society, transformation is the practice of freedom in everyday life. Political change in society starts with reform within the self, which disperses reform outward, throughout social networks.

For me, the priority of self-care over the care of the other, as masculine as it is, becomes an important moment in establishing my identity as a woman—as important as the moment of being able to care for others. I had long believed in and practiced care for others, as many other women do, forgetting how the care for others depends on the care of the self. Without self-affirmation, care for others cannot reach the depths of my own heart to transform myself. When giving is not reciprocal, the flow of energy between self and other is blocked. Without attending to her inner voice, woman is susceptible to others' gaze, and she speaks others' languages. To open up an enclosed internal horizon, the nurturance of her inner self and a certain sense of turning away from others in order to cultivate her own space become crucial: "a room of one's own" (Woolf, 1929). As I will argue later on, Foucauldian self-care needs to be accompanied by simultaneous relationships with others so that the hierarchical priority of self-care over concerns for others is dissolved to a certain degree. Still, to reappropriate this ethics of self-care based upon a gendered analysis, we must address women's concerns about identity politics. Paradoxically, such a tactical move for building women's sense of the self is related to the masculine ethics of self-care, which must be questioned before any strategic reappropriation can occur.

Foucault points out that care of the self implies care for others, since a complex and critical relationship with self cannot be achieved without relationships with others. The care of the self is "an intensification of social relations" (Foucault, 1986, p. 53), by which, in the practice of self-care, one seeks spiritual guidance from another person. This exchange is transformed into a shared experience so that reciprocal friendships and obligations are established. When power is abused and exercised for the purpose of dominating others, it is precisely because one does not take good care of the self. One becomes the slave of one's desires. Foucault (1986, 1997) also points out that the techniques of the self are not purely individual inventions but can be found in social and cultural practices, which suggests that self-care is not exercised in isolation but is obtained through relationships. A new ethics of self-care, Foucault suggests, "permits all possible types of relations to exist and not be prevented, blocked, or annulled by impoverished relational institutions" (1982d, p. 138).

The relationship between care of the self and care for others is implicated in the call for "care about the care of others" (Foucault, 1997, p. 287), especially by philosophers, such as Socrates, who is committed to this "caring about care." A certain element of awakening is evident here, as the philosopher calls upon us to wake up from the taken for granted, to think the unthought, and experience the unspeakable. If the role of the philosopher is primarily one of awakening others, this ethics and aesthetics of self-creation already imply the affirmation of others' engagement with their own self-creation: "How can one make allowance for the other's freedom in the mastery that one exercises over oneself?" (Foucault, 1985, p. 252). While the other's freedom is affirmed, the care of the self as a practice of freedom engages both self and other in transformative, even transgressive, experiences. Is this not a powerful concept for teachers to rethink their role as educators who care about the care of students? Do not women teachers play the role of the philosopher in their (feminist) pedagogy, through which students are encouraged to find their own voices and expand their own limits? In this way, women teachers no longer only serve the interests of others but, through relating to students, are affirmative of both self and other in "an engaged pedagogy" (hooks, 1994a).

For Foucault, the critique embedded in the aesthetics of existence is closely related to the interrogation of a universalized notion of individuality in the contemporary age. No matter whether this notion is situated in religious demands of self-discovery and self-salvation, or in scientific explorations into the truth of the self, or in the contemporary "cult of the self," its motive is to uncover and fulfill the universal essence of the self. The normalizing technology of modern power behind the abstraction of individualization "categorizes the individual, marks him by his own individuality, attaches him to his own identity, imposes a law of truth on him which he must recognize and which others have to recognize in him" (Foucault, 1982e, p. 212). Such a codification of individualization is not about the originality of a concrete person. In this sense, Foucault's ethics and aesthetics of the self are simultaneously a politics of the self against submission, and against an essentialized subjectivity, for a politics of self-creation, to think, perceive, and live otherwise.

Derrida calls us to a sense of responsibility without a universal foundation (Derrida, 1995; Egéa-Kuehne, 1995; Doll, 2001), while Richard Rorty (1999) elaborates an ethics without normalizing principles. Such an emphasis on contextualization rather than abstract universality is echoed in Foucault's refusal to found the ethics of the self upon any essentialized basis. Instead he appropriates the critical potential of aesthetics to encourage the individual toward conduct according to one's own self-surpassing and self-creation. Acknowledging Foucault's ethical–political project of moving beyond limits to expand possibilities, Richard Bernstein (1991) still asks *which* possibilities and *why* it is desirable. I believe that the undecidability of affirming change without affirmative norms is a paradox of human life that we must encounter if we are willing to risk experimentation. Our responsibility is to live with this paradox in an effort to build bridges to new worlds while remaining connected to our own world. Neither by flying into the utopia nor by being locked in our own world can we shoulder the burden of the present while opening new pages of human creation. Foucault's suggestion is a philosophical ethos of permanent critique as aesthetic invention, making "his body, his behavior, his feelings and passions, his very existence, a work of art" (1984a, p. 312).

In Foucault's vision, the body can become the site for an aesthetics of existence. The care of the self in Greco-Roman ethics is mainly concerned with the perfection of the soul, and the body is primarily instrumental to nurturing a beautiful soul. Foucault takes steps to imbue the body with generative and inventive possibilities, especially in his later works. Those "docile bodies," of his early works, produced by discipline and bio-power, are later transformed through experiments with what he calls the "desexualization of pleasure" (Miller, 1993), thereby inventing bodies beyond disciplinary control. An experiment with bodily pleasures not confined to sexual desires can move one to the edge of dissolving the (Cartesian) ego, so that the border of the self can be exceeded. Just as the soul is socially produced, the body is also not only physiologically but also culturally and historically constructed. Foucault construes the body as the site for "limit experiences" with transgressive potential. In his later interviews, he comments upon how bodily experimentation can lead to new forms of relationships and new modes of thought. Intensification of pleasure exceeding sexual norms points to the emergence of a new culture. Sexuality is not so much about our secret desires as about new possibilities for creative life. Foucault is fascinated by what spaces of freedom and pleasure can be brought forth by the shattering of the body (Miller, 1993). Judith Butler (1997) suggests that in the Foucauldian subject, the body plays the role of the psyche in its alterity to the subject, and in such an opening to nonidentity, the body "exceeds and confounds the injunctions of normalization" (p. 94). If the body is registered with what is different from the subject and thereby mobilizes the subject with a potential of going beyond the control of the soul, Foucault moves away from the ancient Greek practice and vision of the self.

While some scholars criticize Foucault for reducing ethics to an amoral aesthetics (O'Farrell, 1989; Wolin, 1986), I would argue that it is his deep distrust of an essentialized notion of the self in metaphysics that makes him enter the realm of aesthetics to release the power of creativity. Such an entrance into aesthetics is not amoral but an attempt to elaborate an ethics of problematization rather than universalized solution, a politics of differentiation rather than that of identification. This is a road less traveled, but the risk is worthwhile so that new paths may emerge.

The question that remains to be answered concerns to what degree this identity politics is useful for people who traditionally stay at the margin, since, after all, the male version of freedom is privileged in the Greco-Roman tradition. Can women reappropriate such an ethics and aesthetics of self-creation to expand their own spaces of freedom? Can a simple affirmation of personal choice against universalized principles elude the complexity of identity politics, whose openness to the possibility of self-creation is very much dependent upon a careful consideration of the relationship between self and other? What do we need to do with the male version of self-creation before articulating women's search for freedom? Attending to women's voices, I will turn now to a gendered critique of the Foucauldian subject.

## Whose Freedom with/out Other?

Foucault is quite clear that the Hellenistic and Roman world was "very strongly marked by the central position of the male personage and by the importance accorded to the masculine role in sexual relationships" (1986, pp. 34–5). Consequently, the care of the self was a practice reserved for privileged Greek free adult males (father, husband, tutor, ruler, etc.) in control of family and society. However, Foucault does not explore in depth how we can transform this male ethic and aesthetics so that women, for instance, can create their own spaces in sexual relations. This elitist and male-dominated ethic, in its notions of rational self-mastery, active subject versus passive object, and the predominance of care of self over care for others, must be reexamined before it can inform feminist identity politics in our contemporary age.

Foucault (1985) attempts to rethink the aesthetics of the self by expanding art beyond the boundary of high culture into everyday life, so that the realm of creativity and imagination, traditionally reserved for artists, can be extended to anyone who is interested in crafting one's own life as a work of art. Foucault asks: "Are we able to have an ethics of acts and their pleasures which would be able to take into account the pleasure of the other? Is the pleasure of the other something that can be integrated in our pleasure, without reference either to law, to marriage, to I do not know what?" (1983b, p. 258). Foucault finds the exclusion of the other in the ancient Greco-Roman male virility "disgusting." Reluctant to resort to law, marriage, and institutions, however, Foucault leaves the problematic of sexual ethics as an open question. Perhaps the issue is not a technical one of how, but an aesthetic one, of whether we can utilize the ancient ethic to free differences without first questioning its basic assumptions.

Foucault (1985) comments that in ancient Greece self-mastery, as active freedom to maintain moderation, is a man's virtue and thereby a masculine principle. Such a relationship with oneself, as an object to elaborate and craft, is "isomorphic with the relationship of domination, hierarchy, and authority that one expected, as a man, a free man, to establish over his inferiors" (p. 83), such as women, boys, and slaves. Women's achieving a certain virility, featured as a combination of strength of character and submission to the man, appears as a serving rather than a ruling virtue. The masculine structure of self-mastery also establishes the opposition between activity and passivity, with the former relating to masculinity and the latter relating to femininity. The boy's passive posture in sexual relationships with adult males is characterized as "feminine." Interestingly, passivity is also considered immoderation, given that the inability to master one's desires properly means one cannot establish a virile attitude toward oneself in the exercise of active freedom. What is at issue here are hierarchical oppositions between subject and object, between being active and being passive, along with an established inferiority of femininity to masculinity. As McNay (1994) points out, Foucault's turn to the aesthetics of Baudelaire to elaborate modern ethics reaffirms, rather than critically encounters, notions of masculine self-mastery and self-determination. Encountering such a male ethic without vigorously questioning these oppositions begs the question: how can we make self-care available to others who are usually situated as objects in a passive position? Can this masculine structure of rational conduct be transformed simply by saying we need also to consider the other's pleasure? Is there not an implicit danger in promoting such an active freedom in a hierarchical relation with oneself and with others? Whose freedom is privileged and whose freedom is at stake? Can the call upon everyone to create one's life as a work of art address this question?

As Poster (1986) points out, the masculine distinction between activity and passivity is ambiguous from the beginning, even between boy and man, especially when emotions are considered. I would argue that passivity, when understood as receptive and responsive, does not necessarily have a negative consequence. In a caring relationship, Nel Noddings (1999) believes, through receiving and respecting the other, the one who cares influences, rather than controls, the other. Both parties' being receptive in caring makes the relationship possible. Here the boundary between activity and passivity is blurred through their mutuality and changeable positions. Noddings also asserts "the essentially nonrational nature of caring" (p. 48) because it occurs not by rules but by attending to the concrete person. Obviously this ethics of care is distinctively different from the ancient Greeks' privileging of activity, rationality, and mastery. Noddings believes that caring forms a central pedagogical relationship. William Pinar (1999) underscored the gendered nature of caring, with its emphasis on feelings, relationships, and receptivity. Women's understanding of caring is different from the Greco-Roman ethics of self-care in that the differences within the self and between self and other are not objectified for the sake of self-mastery. Differences in the other are attended to, and voices of the other are heard, with compassion, pain, and pleasure. Woman's freedom through her relationships, imbued with emotion, becomes one central thread to undo the masculine model of rational self-mastery.

The relationship between self and other is an unstable theme in Foucault's, a fact not unfamiliar to his readers. In Foucault's earlier works, he traces historically how the subject of universal reason has regulated and controlled the other, such as criminals, the sick, or the mad. When an essentialistic notion of the other is rejected, Foucault initiates a movement which destabilizes identity formation. On the other hand, however, when Foucault shifts his attention to the self, which again is not essentialized, the struggle of the other becomes shadowed within the privilege of self-care. As Ewa Ziarek (2001) argues, this ethic reaches its limit without addressing nonappropriative relationships of the self to the other. It is interesting to note, though, that Foucault (1975) actually claims the other in a surprising way when he regards the memoir of Pierre Riviere's murders of his family members (written by Riviere in prison) as singular, extraordinary, and glorious. He believes that such a double subject of the crime and the text shows "how *men* have been able to rise against power, traverse the law, and expose themselves to death through death" (p. 206; emphasis added). Yes, indeed, men.

While I do not want to go as far as Miller (1993), who claims that Foucault regards Riviere's murders as a work of art, I find here an interesting twist that the other—a mad (not indisputable) criminal—is actually transmuted into a self who is capable of creative activity. What are the implications of such a transmutation for the aesthetic relationship between self and other? Can we take it as suggesting that the self/other relationship can be transformed into a subject/subject relationship? Actually bell hooks (1994b) does claim an ethics of "subject-to-subject encounters" based upon the recognition of the other's alterity; however, Foucault is not explicitly interested in linking his ethos of freedom to such encounters.

For Foucault, care for others is already implied in care of the self. As exemplified in the role of the philosopher, he who has an intensified concern for the self consequently also cares for others, including both the citizen and, especially, the ruler, such as the prince. In this case, the care of the self is expressed in the concern for others; it is closely related to the freedom of the state. As self forms a proper relationship with oneself, one's relationship with others will proceed properly. However, how well can one who takes oneself as the object of elaboration—in a relation of domination over oneself—handle the violence of objectification in his relationship with others? In other words, how can the split between subject and object in the ethics of self-care not project objectification upon others?

Sharing Foucault's idea about selfhood as an unending process of creation and re-creation, Mikhail Bakhtin (1993) situates self and other in a relationship of simultaneity in difference. For Bakhtin, the "I-for-myself" does not really exist; the self is coauthored with others. Discussing the relationship between author and hero in polyphonic novels such as Dostoevsky's, Bakhtin (1984) argues for a new authorial position, to permit the independence and freedom of the hero to answer back and surprise the author. Such a relationship between self and other enables both to become active consciousnesses, to address the other as other. Polyphony also happens within the self and invites the reader to enter into the dialogue. In this way, relationships and individuality are both claimed and transformed through open-ended interaction.

Obviously, Foucault is also concerned about differences and individual originality, but his ethics of the self fail to directly address how to work through differences within and between self and other without doing violence to either. Is Smith (1996) not right in claiming that the decentering of the subject without giving up the duality of subject and object is still another form of self over other? While both Bakhtin and Foucault reject essentialistic notions of the self, Bakhtin's notion of the relationship between self and other deals more successfully than does Foucault's with the duality between subject and object and activity and passivity. To allow the other to assume the position of an active subject, Bakhtin works through the violence of objectifying others/otherness to create new forms of inter/subjectivity.

The duality of subject and object in Foucault's work is hardly compatible with feminist critiques. Historically, in Western thought, men as rulers were subjects, while women were objects in obedience, a fact Foucault himself also recognizes. To challenge such a tradition of the subject acting upon an objectified world, it is not enough to relocate women's status as subjects so as to create a more generative intersubjective space. The domination of the subject may still choose another target to objectify, even if it is not woman. The shift from a subject/object split to a subject–subject relationship seems no longer satisfactory if we do not interrogate the very dualism between subject and object with the subject as the controlling party. Can we rethink the relation between the two, not in a sense of domination, but as an intertwining space so that self, other, and the world can be engaged in a process of co-emergence, co-becoming and co-transformation while claiming their respective independence? Can we break through the confinement of object, dominated by subject, in thinking about human relations? Is not the objectification of the world what we need to break away from in order to become a responsible self, not only for itself, but also for the cosmos of which we are an organic part? Feminist critique searches for an expansive and expanding space not only for women, but also for a more sustainable and reciprocal relationship with the world.

As early as 1959, when Huebner (1999) elaborated on education for wonder and awe, he already asked us to see butterflies, rainbows, and fellow travelers not as objects, but as subjects so that "I/It" relationships could be transformed into "I/Thou" relationships, so that we may recognize the mystery and amazement of what is in front of our eyes. Such a relational, rather than objectifying, understanding of the subject shows us a different picture of the human self in its relationships with the world. In articulating a feminist ethics of difference, Ziarek (2001) attempts to redefine freedom in relational terms. She situates transformative experiences in both the transgression of limits and in the responsibility for the other. bell hooks's (1994a) feminist vision of education as a practice of freedom also shifts the location of freedom toward communal inquiry. Teaching to transgress is based on a mutual challenge between teacher and student to go beyond the institutional constraints implicated in sexism, racism, and colonialism. This relational politics of freedom is affirmative and thereby enabling for both teacher and student.

After all, one cannot really be free and feel free without being *with* the other and in the world in a reciprocal way. Education is necessarily a relational enterprise. Such a relation "with" already implies movement beyond objectification toward that sense of "interbeing" Thich Nhat Hanh (1993) identifies, an interbeing between self and other, and between human and non-human worlds. When cosmic generative forces are acknowledged and we give up the controlling position, we will be able to get in touch with and further bring out our own creative potential.

The duality between rationality and desire is another interesting thread in Foucault's theory. The modern dichotomy between reason and emotion is one target of feminist critiques. Although the Greco-Roman tradition has a much more affirmative posture toward body, emotion, and desire, the duality of soul over body is still an important fact for the care of the self. Foucault argues that the regulation of desires and sexuality in the Greco-Roman ethic does not resort to universal law, the deciphering of truth in the self, and its presumably purifying hermeneutics. However, without being strictly codified, and without the necessity of being judged as evil or bad, the body is still under the gaze of the soul. It is clear that the rational control of desires and conduct is a preferable principle for a fulfilling life. Without sufficiently problematizing the ancient notion of rationality, without rearticulating the relationship between body and soul, Foucault takes a difficult step toward a new self born from experiencing and experimenting with (queer) eroticism.

Foucault is explicit about his preference for pleasure over desire, as he is always suspicious of the search for the inherent secret of desire. Yet the complexity of feelings in sexual relationships can hardly be conveyed when pleasure is split from desire. The emotional aspects of sexual ethics—except his preoccupation with pleasure—are barely addressed in Foucault's theory. Needless to say, the body, in Foucault's depiction is, more often than not, male. This gender blindness has been noted by many feminists (McNay, 1992; Hekman, 1996). If the body is socially constructed, gender difference is an important issue that cannot be avoided. Perhaps understanding women's experiences of their own bodies is a task that women have to undertake by themselves. Julia Kristeva takes the uniqueness of womanhood in pregnancy and childbirth and woman's intimacy with the semiotic (which I will discuss in Chapter 4) to understand the subject as one among many efforts to address how the fluidity and plurality of the female body disrupt masculine binaries (Bordo, 1993; Butler, 1990; Cixous, 1994; Irigaray, 1985; Rich, 1984).

After analyzing the problematic of self-formation in male ethics and making a gendered questioning of the relationship between self and other, I argue that Foucault's privilege of self-fashioning can still be rearticulated for women's self-reclamation. Historically, self-sacrifice and dependence were women's virtues; taking care of others was women's obligation. To break with such a chain of submission, can we *transform*—not merely *extend*—the Foucauldian ethics of self-care into a gendered ethics of identity building? Considering the influence of gender on the aesthetics of existence, can we construct women's versions of self-creation without abandoning a relational view of the subject? Foucault's focus on the work that one does on oneself is useful for understanding how important it is for women to turn to themselves for transformation.

But such an intensified relationship with the self, for women, must consider the hierarchical social contexts in which women are situated. In this sense, the struggle with the self in gendered self-care involves taking the self as the site for registering and contesting social injustice. Due to the cultural demand for feminine invisibility, woman does not really have a self. But when she begins to create her own sense of self, she participates in initiating social transformation. To be able to do so, the male version of freedom, subjectivity, and rationality must be displaced into a process of interacting with the feminine through its own *differences* to create a third space in which the gendered double can be mutually engaging.

## Can "I" Become Somebody Else?

There is always within each of us something that fights something else.
(Michel Foucault, quoted in Miller, 1993, p. 278)

The main interest in life and work is to become someone else that you were not in the beginning.
(Foucault, 1988, p. 9)

The ethics of self-creation make it necessary to break with one's traditions and one's self. Although valorizing the central location of the self, such a rupture requires an aggressive tearing away from both institution and oneself. The image of a transgressive self against the conservative and normalizing culture and institutions is conspicuous in Foucault's discourse. Foucault's reference to Riviere's text asks us to rethink the relationship between self and institutions. Is it necessary for the transgressive self to break away from institutions? Should juridical rules necessarily be negated? Can popular practice beyond juridical proceedings replace law and the state to provide more protection for individuals, as Foucault seems to claim (see Miller, 1993)? Are institutions, created and formed by individuals, necessarily antithetical to an individual's creativity? If we situate the transgressive potential of the self in a dynamic interplay between constituting and constituted aspects of the Foucauldian double-faced subject, can we expect the self to go beyond social institutions and the totalization of individuality without fully breaking with either? I argue that a full break is not only impossible but is unnecessary, as the self is situated in social contexts and the relationship between self and society is nondualistic. However, when Foucault talks about the decriminalization of sexuality, the power of mass justice, and the glory of murder (see Miller, 1993), he indeed seems to be promoting a self *against* institutions, rather than a more dynamic relationship between the two. His argument for the decriminalization of all sexual conduct, including rape, as necessary to freeing sexuality from the control of the state is an outrageous claim that arouses strong feminist objections. Such an effort to decenter sexuality, as McNay (1992) points out, overlooks the fact that "violence in rape is fundamentally derived from the asymmetrical construction of sexual relations in modern society," and such a treatment "would further legitimize the sexual oppression of women" (p. 45). Actually, law is not necessarily bad and, indeed, provides certain protections for individuals, and the struggle for legal rights was an important part of women's movements to counteract female subordination. Foucault's dualism between self and society forms a contrast with the Confucian self, which I will discuss in the next chapter.

In Foucault's later works, the rejection of external control is transfigured into a rupture with oneself and a consequent conversion of that self. In several interviews, he claims repeatedly that he writes in order to become somebody else (see Miller, 1993). Such an enthusiasm for something completely new, absolutely other, and utterly beautiful, underscores the complicated link between the Foucauldian subject and the Romantic notion of an original and singular self. According to Charles Taylor (1989), the modern sense of the self is greatly influenced by the aesthetic expressivism initiated by Montaigne, who emphasizes the unrepeatable differences in each individual's original self-exploration and self-discovery. This idea is echoed in Foucault's deep concern with unique individuality, free from control of the state and from the totality of individualization.

However, it is clear that two assumptions of aesthetic expressivism are rejected by Foucault. One is the assumption of an essential and unitary self presupposed by the search for self-discovery and self-expression. Foucault is more concerned about self-creation than about searching for a nonexistent essence of the self, even in its particularity. The other is the obligation of turning inward to reach self-knowledge. In Foucault's ethics of the self, with acknowledgement of the role of self-knowledge, an intense interiority of self-examination for truth has been transformed into outward efforts toward self-stylization. Despite the complex link between Foucault and the Romantic epoch, Foucault's promise that we can work on ourselves to create and re-create our bodies, our souls, and our selves often grips the imagination.

I often have this fantasy: If only I could go to a different place where I knew no one and no one knew me, I could have a new self out of such utter nonidentity. I did move, from one city to another city to yet another, from one country to another country, and I did change, but I could never become "someone else," however much I wanted to. To reintegrate the dissolute self may help me reach another level of the self or add another layer of the self, but I can never be totally different from what I have been. More often than not, when I meet my old friends I haven't seen in quite a while, they exclaim: "Hi, Hongyu, you are still the same!" Still, my mother and Chinese advisor have directly commented about my change—personal and intellectual—since my journey to the United States. Such a coexistence of nonchange and change characterizes the dynamics of the self, making it both impossible and unnecessary to claim a totally new self.

Following the evolution of his discourses, I often can understand Foucault's theory of knowledge, power, and subjectivity in a more complicated and interconnected way. However, if I focus on his works in a certain restricted period of time, I might become quite puzzled. When I want to make a general claim, I often pause and think: "Wait a minute! He says so and so here, but he says otherwise in other works." Considering his commitment to analyzing the historicity and social construction of the self, the claim of becoming someone else seems paradoxical. Maybe both are true, in different contexts. Foucault is certain that "what must be produced is something that absolutely does not exist, about which we know nothing . . . the creation of something totally different, an innovation" (quoted in Miller, 1993, p. 336). Such a hope, to some degree, is consistent with the Western concept of creation *ex nihilo*, in contrast to the Chinese notion of creation in a continuum of flow. Can we create ourselves as utterly different? Is it possible for anyone to create a completely "different kind of person with a different kind of soul and a different kind of body" (Miller, 1993, p. 345)?

In Foucault's analysis of the care of the self, there is a peculiar paradox. On the one hand, he emphasizes that self-mortification is not the cultivation of the self; the self must not be shadowed by sacrificial ethics. On the other hand, his call for tearing away from oneself in order to become a new person necessarily requires a certain sense of self-negation. Between the two there is an ambiguous zone in which the individual can decide his style of life only in an uncertain way. Perhaps Foucault's protest against self-renunciation is not against self-sacrifice per se, but against what self-sacrifice is associated with in confessional Christianity: unconditional obedience to the absolute rule of authority and the demand for revealing the truth. In fact, he speaks about the affinities between self-creation through writing and ancient asceticism.

I suspect, in the desire for becoming somebody else, there is a certain element of self-denial, which in my case is gendered (and also cultural; see the next chapter). My first encounter with Foucault carried me away, fascinated by his aesthetics of imagination and creativity and his promise of becoming different. Rereading him this time, though, leaves me more skeptical. The time period in between coincided with my struggle to search for a path rising from the deep valley in which the self is dissolute. Only when I do not have that fantasy of becoming a completely new self can I gradually accept who I am, embrace the wonder and mystery of the valley, and climb the mountain to become more than what I am. Perhaps self-negation is something many people have to face one way or another. So the issue is more about how to deal with self-denial and transform it toward creative directions rather than about simply rejecting its existence.

I am now more willing to say that I write in order to become myself. And this term "become" already implies an open system in which "somebody else" is always present. Do I need to become somebody else before I can be myself, or do I need to become myself before I can be somebody else? Perhaps there is no rigid "before" and "after" in a simultaneous and intertwining process of becoming that never unites self and other. This is the paradox of the self in its double gestures of affirming singular responsibility through aporias. In Foucault's longing to become someone else, the theme of self and other is again touched upon, but not fully elaborated. It is Kristeva's notion of psychic alterity that will take us on a tour through the stranger inside: We are becoming ourselves more fully in understanding somebody else within the self.

Problematizing Foucault's approach to an ancient male-dominated ethic of the self in its duality does not mean dismissing its great potential for providing insights to address feminist concerns about identity and politics. Foucault's simultaneous emphasis upon the priority of self-formation and the destabilizing nature of self-creation points to new directions for women to affirm their identities, while at the same time construing this affirmation as a continuous journey of the self. McNay (1992) argues for taking Foucault's discourse as a challenge to rethink a gendered self:

> [I]t is more fruitful not simply to accuse Foucault of a straightforward 'gender blindness' in his ethics of the self, but rather to invert the problem and ask how his work presents a challenge to feminists to think of an ethics which does not rest on a fixed or naturalized notion of 'woman.' (p. 112)

This poses a difficult task for women, as self-affirmation is crucial for the feminist project. However, we need to consider that what is imposed upon women by a patriarchal society is precisely a fixed identity in the first place. To defy such an externally imposed identity while searching for yet another essence of woman does not escape from the very logic used against woman. As Jana Sawicki (1991, 1994) points out, the history of feminism has already shown that the search for the essence of femininity fails to consider differences across class, race, ethnicity, and sexual orientation and that this leads to new forms of exclusions and repression. If the image of an essential woman—whatever it may be—no longer dominates, as Foucault's challenge asks us to envisage, woman no longer needs to identify with any ethics imposed by others, but is left with the task of creating her own singular ethics of the self. According to Foucault, this process of destabilizing the self releases plural and diverse points of resistance, and contests the socially defined category of the normal individual. Refusing to be a "normal" woman, compliant to the gendered rule of law, we may attempt to register diversified, multiple, and fluid forces of contestation for "a patient labor giving form to our impatience for liberty" (Foucault, 1984a, p. 319). Without a stable foundation, such a project of becoming a unique woman on winding paths is ambiguous and uncertain. But the efforts to push the limits of body, knowledge, and subjectivity to claim her self, while not contained within the boundary, must be open-ended. She does not need to become somebody else, but she is challenged to create her own womanhood, constantly at the edge of becoming different.

In short, to utilize Foucault's ideas for feminist identity politics, I would argue that women need to rethink the dualities already encoded in the Greco-Roman traditions. In promoting a transgressive self, Foucault implies a dualistic view of self and society. Such a posture is not the one women would prefer to adopt if they want to acknowledge how their search for the self goes hand in hand with the transformation of society. The purpose of incorporating gendered reality is not to turn the duality upside down, but to address issues of self, other, and differences in new ways. While the self is privileged in Foucault's discourses, the "other" loses its concreteness in its differences with the self and its own alterity within. The call from the (feminine) other becomes silent. Paradoxically, Foucault's vision of self-creation is not without self-negation in his displacement of self/other relationships, in inviting one to become someone else. How can woman release the other from the confinement of the self to rearticulate a new relational ethics of the self that valorizes differences? How can woman negotiate a space between self-affirmation and self-displacement? How can woman's gendered body register a politics different from her male counterpart? These are all questions that we need to investigate further.

Foucault is a highly complicated thinker. These gendered critiques from a woman's perspective run the risk of reducing the richness of his theory into a one-sided view. But for the purpose of *experiencing* thoughts in order to pave a path for my self-understanding, I prefer an incomplete reading—if not skewed—picking up a theme not fully complete itself, if partly due to Foucault's early death. The theme of care of the self is simultaneously appealing and unsatisfactory to me. As I attempt to analyze the inner contradiction and ambiguity of Foucault's works, I am also grappling with my own inner conflicts as a cultural and gendered "other." Therefore, my reading of the Foucauldian subject is not for any abstract systematic study, but for my own self-reflection, and it is necessarily partial. My partial readings of Confucius and Kristeva have similar motives, as we will see in later chapters.

Foucault's discussion of ancient ethics in Western civilization brings me back to the other side of the ocean: How is the Chinese self constructed? What can the relational notion of the Chinese self compared to Western self-cultivation tell us? How does the notorious sexism, with its culmination in footbinding in China, play out its own drama? Are gender biases such as the Western duality in its correspondence with sexual differences applicable to other c–ultures? What can the Foucauldian subject offer to the Chinese, and can the Chinese provide any possibility for rethinking Western dualism? I move to the Confucian self through a cross-cultural (and intercultural) inquiry in the next chapter and, later, I will journey back to the issue of woman's subjectivity through Kristeva's theory to address the problematic of gendered self.

## Note

1.  Is self-sacrifice necessarily negative? I would argue not, as long as it is not a blind obedience to laws and authorities. Without considering specific religions, I will briefly comment on the cultural and gendered consideration of self-sacrifice. The Chinese self is always related to others, and a relational notion of the self asks one to give up certain aspects of oneself to be able to connect to others. Sometimes such self-sacrifice is necessary under the limitations of living resources and spaces. Self-sacrifice for children and family is part of women's lives. Does simply putting self-care over concerns about others (Foucault's argument) give enough credit to women's own ways of thinking and living? I believe that the potential of self-care for women attending to their own personal cultivation is more likely to be realized without setting up the dichotomy of self-sacrifice and self-creation.

# Chapter 3
# Back to the Root: The Confucian Self and an Ecology of Personal Cultivation

As an undergraduate, I had a professor whom students affectionately called "a great Confucian." He taught me about Confucius as an educator, and I wrote a long paper on Confucius and education in his class—my first serious academic work. Whenever I had confusions or doubts about my studies, I would turn to him for guidance. Every time, he would tell me in his uniquely calm way to keep going and cultivate a rich inner life, regardless of the turbulent external world. Before I left for Shanghai to pursue my graduate studies, I went to his home one night to say good-bye. When I walked down the stairway in the darkness, he was holding a flashlight behind me to light the path under my feet. Light. Held by a Confucian for me, for my future. This is a powerful image I have always kept deeply in my heart. Somehow this image gradually became vague during my journey to the West—until one day, in the middle of my struggling with Confucianism in the United States, this image suddenly returned. I knew at that moment that, despite all odds and difficulties, I was going to carry and renew this light. It is a light within, shining on a continuous path of an old civilization that could be rejuvenated, a part of me already existing long before I was born.

In this chapter I discuss the notion of the Confucian self in its communal and cosmic relatedness. In tracing the historical ruptures between classical Confucianism and Neo-Confucianism (Cheng-Zhu branch), I analyze the impact of moral reason on diminishing the potential of the relational self, particularly woman's self. The chapter also initiates a dialogue between the Foucauldian subject and the Confucian self so that a cross-cultural third space can be articulated.

## Confucianism: Personal Cultivation in Relationships

[I]n Confucianism . . . the identity of each person is not in his or her independent existence, but in his or her relations to the cosmic principles, to other people, to social
communities, and to his or her own moral cultivation by which the self is brought
into maturity.

(Yao Xinzhong, 1996, p. 83)

The return to Confucianism is an ambivalent project for me, not only because
Confucianism has long been condemned for the failures of Chinese culture,
but also because it is so notorious for suppressing women. As a woman constantly struggling to gain and regain a certain sense of the self, why do I not
just take an easy flight away from it? Why do I bother to initiate this unexpected return? Why does the Western critique of the modern self lead me to
reclaim this part of my tradition? Is Confucianism as father somehow transformed into mother due to a complicated interplay between East and West?
Or is it still alive in my heart, calling me to listen carefully? Is there any potential within Confucianism that has been ignored while Chinese people have
been preoccupied by the modernization of both nation and culture (defined,
by and large, by the West)? If what is strange to the self could be the otherness of the self within, what is familiar to the self has the potential to be regenerated into something new. Michel Serres (1997) asks, "Does one only
invent something new when it issues from the deepest roots?" (p. 96). Carrying my own puzzlement, I venture into the paradoxical, the ambiguous, and
the unexpected of my own traditions.

The effort to reclaim the Confucian self in its human and cosmic interconnections as different from Western individualism is hardly my own idea.
Scholars in many different academic disciplines, Chinese or Westerners,
make such a call (de Bary, 1991; Munro, 1985; Tu, 1979, 1985a; Yao,
1996). Interestingly, scholars in mainland China (Jin & Liu, 1984; Xu, 1994;
Zhuang, 1997) are much more critical toward Confucianism, while scholars
in Hong Kong, Taiwan, and overseas (Lin, 1983, 1986; Liu, 1989; Muo,
1997) are much more optimistic about the possibility of its renewal. The editor of a book series, *Culture: China and the World,* Gan Yang radically
claims, "The best method to carry forward traditions is anti-tradition"
(quoted in Zhuang, 1997, p. 197). On the other side of the ocean, Tu Wei-
ming at Harvard University painstakingly attempts to reconstruct Confucianism on a worldwide basis.

I am deeply suspicious of any efforts to break with the past completely.
On the other hand, Tu's intention to reconstruct a metaphysics out of Confucianism is also problematic to me. What I am concerned about here is how to
conduct genuine conversations both within and between cultures in order to

refigure the portrait of the human/woman self. Conversation, reflection, and critique are much more crucial for constructing new landscapes of humanity than a simple "antitradition" or another mode of metaphysics. How can we reclaim our own traditions in such a way that transformation of the past can be risked to create new forms of life? How can we open up our own horizons to the otherness and to the strangeness of different cultures in such a way that the fullness of the self can be brought into shared understanding? How can we regenerate our traditions through conversations with other cultures, but without assuming that our way is the only path leading to new possibilities in life? How can we share with, interact with, and learn from each other and from the past without doing violence to either side? Perhaps one way is to join in the complicated curriculum conversation to open new horizons of understanding.

My own return to Confucianism actually occurred during my reading of Foucault's genealogical analysis of Western self-cultivation. But it was the Chinese scholar and novelist Lin Yutang's book *From Pagan to Christian* (1959) that led me into the door of Confucianism. I still remember the moment of encountering his statement that self-cultivation lies at the heart of Confucianism. "How could that be?" I asked myself aloud. I never really thought that in Confucianism there was any notion of the self! As I toured with Lin (1959) through "the mansion of Confucius," "the peak of Mount Tao," and "the dissolving mist of Buddhism," I realized how much homework I needed to do with my own traditions. When I first traveled back to China, observing the Chinese way of life from somehow an outsider's angle, this urge to go back to my own spiritual roots was intensified. With a newly discovered enthusiasm, I plunged into both the classical literature and contemporary studies of Confucianism. The more I probed, the more I was amazed by how much we Chinese are still embedded in this tradition, no matter how many times during the last one hundred years we have witnessed anti-Confucianism. If it cannot be killed, is it possible to replant the seed in a more nurturing environment to grow new forms? Yet, renewing a tradition, as I have already mentioned, must be based upon historical analysis, reflection, and critique.

How has the original idea of Confucianism turned into a dogma which has suppressed individual freedom for so long? What role does the institutionalized practice of Confucianism play in obscuring Confucius' thoughts on personal cultivation and social order? How can we regenerate this tradition without being caught in its shadow? What can the Confucian self offer to contemporary life? I became intrigued by the development of classical Confucianism into Neo-Confucianism in the context of the institutionalization of Confucianism and how this evolution suppressed the transformative

potential of Confucian personal cultivation in its communal and cosmic relatedness. Foucault has taught me that history can be read in a discontinuous
and nonlinear way and that the points of discontinuity register the possibilities of change. More often than not, scholars, whether they hold positive or
negative attitudes toward Confucianism, talk about classical Confucianism
and Neo-Confucianism as one. I argue that it is the discontinuity between the
two—without denying continuity—that provides the promise of regenerating
the Confucian self for rethinking the issue of identity politics. Let me start
with classical Confucianism.

## Personal Cultivation as a Situated Journey

In *The Great Learning*, one of the four Confucian classics (the other three
are *The Analects*, *Mencius*, and *The Doctrine of the Mean*), it is clearly stated
that "from the emperor down to the common people, all must consider the
cultivation of the person as the root of all. It cannot be that, when the root is
neglected, what springs from it will be well-ordered."[1] For Confucius (551–
479 B.C.), personal cultivation[2] is fundamental to the development of both
individual and society, and social reform must be achieved through personal
transformation. When personal cultivation as the root is firmly planted, harmonious human relationships and social peace grow naturally. Here Confucius does not bother to formulate an abstract idea of the self or an
essentialistic view of human nature to uphold his scheme for personal cultivation. He is much more concerned with how to bring out the best in humanity by education than he is with metaphysical speculations about human
nature. This link between morality, politics, and education through the focus
of personal cultivation becomes a cornerstone of Confucianism.

As Hall and Ames (1987) suggest, in contrast to Western transcendental
traditions which support a substance view of the self, the Confucian self is
based upon an ontology of events, not of substances. While transcendental
principles define the Western nature of the self, the Confucian immanent
view of the world situates the self within its concrete interactions in particular settings. As a result, the Confucian self is an interactive process, dependent upon specific events which both determine and are determined by
contexts. In such a process, one's disposition, character, and behaviors are
cultivated and transformed toward the full realization of hum*an*ity.

Confucian selfhood is a lifelong project which is always yet to be
achieved, an unfolding process of continuous transformation and becoming. One of Confucius' favorite disciples, Zeng Zi (Tseng Tzu) once exclaimed that the task of fulfilling humanity is so heavy because it is a
ceaseless journey which never ends before death (*The Analects*, 8.7). There
is an often-quoted saying in *The Great Learning*: "If you can renovate your-

self one day, then you can do so every day, and keep doing so day after day."[3] Such a journey of personal cultivation as an everyday and persistent exercise is echoed in the Greco-Roman tradition of the care of the self.

This journey can be undertaken as only a process of proper cultivation and nurturance. It cannot be hurried. An interesting fable in *Mencius* (3.2) describes a farmer who was so eager to harvest his crops that he pulled all the shoots one by one to help them grow. As a result of his efforts, all the shoots withered. Like the planting of crops, personal cultivation follows its own growing rhythm, and the attempt to get on with it quickly, without everlasting and consistent effort, cannot work.

Confucius himself sets up an example of lifelong devotion to the realization of the Way: "At fifteen I set my heart upon learning. At thirty I established myself [in accordance with ritual]. At forty I no longer had doubts. At fifty I realized the Mandate (*ming*) of Heaven. At sixty I was at ease with what I heard. At seventy I could follow my heart to do whatever I wanted to do without transgressing what was right" (*The Analects*, 2.4). This is not a model for everyone to follow because the paths of self-realization and self-transformation are varied. But it does clearly show Confucius' commitment to constantly cultivating the self. His ideal of achieving freedom in harmony with one's own action and desire through realizing the Way indicates a version of "freedom" different from Foucault's transgressive concept.

Confucianism believes that everyone has the capacity to become a sage, and the Confucian confidence in the human capacity for personal transformation through education makes many Confucians well-known educators as well as thinkers. A highly revered educator, Confucius insisted that education is for everyone, not just the elite (*The Analects*, 15.39). In his early twenties, he had already opened his teachings to students who were willing to learn, charging whatever fees each of them could afford. Another Confucian master, Mencius (372–289 B.C.) commented, "Good government cannot reach people's hearts so much as good education" (*Mencius*, 13.14). Both Confucius and Mencius believed that education was crucial to a person's inner transformation; both were teachers.

Education is about cultivating students' own moral sense, but it is also about how to contextualize morality so that proper behavior may have different concrete manifestations. Students are guided into taking different actions, all embodying the same Way. Confucius was an artful teacher in situating pedagogy in students' different personal qualities. Some stories recorded in *The Analects* vividly depict how Confucius responded differently to the same question from different disciples. For example, both Zilu and Ran You asked whether they should immediately carry into practice what they heard. Confucius answered yes to Ran You but told Zilu that his father and elder brothers must be consulted first. Confused by Confucius' different answers, another disciple, asked the reason for the apparent inconsistency. Confucius explained, "You is retiring and slow; therefore, I urged him forward. Zilu is too audacious; therefore, I kept him back" (*The Analects*, 11.22). What is shown in this story is Confucius' wisdom in bringing out the best part of his disciples by forming an interactive relationship with each disciple. Such a contextualized mode of teaching is compatible with his philosophy of cultivating the self in its concrete and particular situations. Throughout *Mencius*, "situational flexibility"—as Tamney and Chiang (2002) call it—is evident, and abundant examples show how different *junzi* (translated as noblemen, gentlemen, superior men, men of perfect virtue, or exemplary persons) respond to similar situations differently, yet not failing to realize the Way. This pedagogy of responding to differences also indicates that the Confucian Way is not a fixed principle but, instead, is situated.

## The Process of Personal Cultivation

In *The Great Learning*, the eight steps of personal cultivation serve as a general scheme for the moral and educational development of individuals and for subsequent social well-being and harmony:

> When things are investigated, knowledge is achieved. When knowledge is achieved, then one reaches sincerity of thoughts. When one reaches the sincerity of thoughts, the rightness of heart comes. With the rightness of heart, the person can be cultivated. When the person is cultivated, the family life can be regulated. When the family life is regulated, the State can be rightly governed. When the State is rightly governed, the whole world can be made peaceful.[4]

The process of personal cultivation outlined in this passage begins with understanding the world by investigating things and extending knowledge. It centers around personal and moral cultivation inward, and extends outward to regulate the family, the state, and the world. This is an ideal for cultivating one's humanity by assisting all people to accomplish their own perfection. As a result, personal cultivation cannot be separated from social participation and public responsibility. The road to personal cultivation is based upon ever-enlarging social and cosmic relationships and involves the development of the whole person in terms of intellectual, emotional, moral, and spiritual cultivation. These steps also imply, as Tu (1998) argues, the necessity of going beyond selfishness, nepotism, parochialism, ethnocentrism, nationalism, and anthropocentrism. The ideal of the union between person and universe—which will be discussed later—constantly pushes the self to go beyond the limitations of any bounded circle to reach a cosmological state.

Confucian personal cultivation conveys an organic and interconnected sense of the self. Rightness of heart cannot be achieved without knowledge and thought, yet thinking is not for representing an objective reality, but for engaging in practical activities which unite emotion and intellect, fact and value, and knowledge and action. The Western dualism between subject and object, and mind and body, can hardly be seen here. The translation of heart (*xin*) as one Chinese character into English is a puzzle; some current translations use mind-heart to indicate the sense of union between thinking and feeling. Literally, the Chinese characters for personal cultivation (*hsiu-shen*) refer to the cultivation of the body, which makes explicit the unity between body and mind (see Ames, 1984, for a discussion of the classical Chinese concept of body from both a philological and a philosophical analysis). The project of personal cultivation outlined by Confucius begins with poetry, establishes itself through ritual, and achieves its fruition in music (*The Analects*, 8.8). The study of poetry provides stimulation for the mind, guidance for harmonizing emotions, and opportunities for self-contemplation. The establishment of ritual cultivates one's character, directs human emotions, and accepts social responsibilities in the context of human-relatedness and cultural values. The fruition of a long process of personal cultivation is embodied in the flowing harmony of music, which symbolizes achieving the unity of the whole person in oneness with the world.

## Social Relationships and Independent Personality

The relationship between self and other is crucial to understanding Confucian personal cultivation because of its moral and relational nature. This is an area arousing great debates. Critics of Confucianism often point out its hierarchical and authoritarian nature, while other scholars, such as Tu Wei-ming (1985), argue that the Confucian self/other relationship is an open system in which both self and other can be generated anew through mutual engagement. However, in negotiating between these opposite claims, one thing is clear: the Confucian self does not exist in isolation and must form relationships with others. Zeng Zi asked himself three questions for daily self-examination: "Whether, in transacting business for others, I may have been not faithful; whether, in interaction with friends, I may have been not sincere; whether I may have not mastered and practiced the instructions of my teacher" (*The Analects*, 1.4). It is obvious that the focus of Confucian self-examination is almost exclusively on the relationships between self and other, a focus different from the Greco-Roman tradition of self-examination, although both aim at self-transformation.

In *The Analects*, Confucius' response to the question about what principle one should follow throughout one's lifetime is, "What you do not want done to yourself, do not do to others" (*The Analects*, 15.24). To state it in a positive sense, "The *junzi* wishing to be established himself, seeks to establish others; wishing to be enlarged himself, seeks also to enlarge others" (*The Analects*, 6.30). Such a rule might not be much different from the Christian Golden Rule (Reid, 1999, p. 244): "Do unto others as you would have them do unto you; for this is the law and the prophet." Yet within the similar principle of reciprocity, the focus of the two is different somehow: In the Confucian self, the emphasis is on relationships (albeit starting with the individual), while the Christian self puts more emphasis on the individual (albeit following God's calling).

Speaking of relationships, Mencius defines five human relationships which become moral rules for Confucians:

> Between father and son, there should be affection;
> Between ruler and minister, there should be righteousness;
> Between husband and wife, there should be attention to their separate functions;
> Between old and young, there should be proper order;
> Between friends, there should be faithfulness. (*Mencius*, 5.4)

It is not difficult to notice that in each relationship both parties have obligations to each other. For example, affection is what binds father and son: father should be kind and son should be respectful. Both ruler and minister are committed to what is right, in contrast to the common belief that the Confucian minister should be obedient to the ruler. While there is a certain reciprocity and mutuality in these pairs of moral principles, there is not much room for equality. Only the last pair, between friends, has the potential of equality. Equality still depends upon the context, though, since age is an important factor in deciding "proper order." Interestingly, woman's role explicitly appears only as wife, occupying a lower position in her pairing with husband.

While recognizing a hierarchical nature in Confucian relationships, we also need to understand the inherent claim of independence in the Confucian self, a factor which is usually ignored by contemporary commentaries, especially in the West. Relationships must be sustained by an independent sense of *ren* (translated as benevolence, humanity, reciprocity, or love) and righteousness. To criticize the ruler when the government deviates from the way of *ren* is the obligation of *junzi*, since Confucius advocates the realization of the Way rather than loyalty to rulers. Confucius also says, "A *junzi* seeks harmony but not conformity. An inferior man seeks conformity but not harmony" (*The Analects*, 13.23). This refusal to conform is also echoed in Mencius' criticism of consenting to the current customs in the dark age (*Mencius*,

14.37). Their claims urge Confucians to cultivate an internal sense of what is good and right and to make a commitment to independent directions regardless of whatever is popular belief and practice. "Harmony" here means negotiating between the Way and current circumstances, with balance at heart. To claim that "the importance of harmony has made criticism an act of disloyalty" (Tamney & Chiang, 2002, p. 43) does not reveal an in-depth understanding of the Chinese notion of harmony. Harmony is contrary to, rather than compatible with, conformity. Harmony is not achieved by agreement, rather, criticism is necessary for reaching harmony. For Mencius, overthrowing a government that violates the will of the people is achieving harmony. For Confucius, the purpose of criticizing rulers is to urge them to follow the Way of harmony. True loyal Confucian ministers are willing to sacrifice their lives by criticizing a government that does not practice *ren*. Although Confucianism was the official ideology for centuries in ancient China, rulers of various dynasties never did fully embrace Confucianism in its independence, its rebellious spirit against autocracy. Instead, rulers appropriated the principle of reciprocity to reinforce their government, whatever it might be.

Confucians usually have a strong sense of a personal, moral mission even in conditions of poverty, hardship, or adversity. The Way is not externally imposed but must be realized from within. It requires a person to cultivate an inner sense of morality, coping with all kinds of difficulties or resisting the temptation to seek only external rewards. For Confucius, as long as a scholar follows the Way, harsh and miserable circumstances cannot prevent him from enjoying what the Way can bring to him (*The Analects*, 6.11 and 7.16). Mencius points out that *ren* and righteousness are the way of morality, not instruments for practical usage (*Mencius*, 8.19). He comments: "Wealth and honor cannot confuse my heart, poverty and lower status cannot change my aspiration, power and force cannot bend my integrity" (*Mencius*, 6.2). Actually, Confucians can regard poverty and exile as opportunities to nurture their personal character in solitude. The plum blossom, orchid, bamboo, and chrysanthemum, called the four noblemen in traditional Chinese painting and poetry, symbolize the inner power of the person to maintain moral integrity by overcoming the adversity of the environment. The ability to keep pursuing the Way is prerequisite for personal transformation. Maintaining an independent personality is a cherished virtue that a Confucian must be able to preserve and pursue. Taken to the extreme, such an independence can be embodied either in open rebellion against despotic rule or in silent retreat into the self to cultivate one's own inner life. The theme of struggles within to search for inner light is supported by a sense of personal integrity and dignity, similar to the Greco-Roman tradition of battling with the self to achieve a fulfilling life.

There are different opinions regarding the purpose of Confucian personal cultivation. Is it for the harmony of society, or is it for self-fulfillment? Recognizing how situated Confucian "personalism" is in the context of tradition, community, and natural environment, de Bary (1998) challenges the idea that Confucian personalism has the intention of "performing for others, fulfilling a social role, or conforming to the values of the group" (p. 25). I would add that, especially when the group does not follow the Way, it becomes imperative that personal cultivation aims at nurturing individual integrity in order to subvert collective intentions. The common belief that "self-cultivation is a means used to create a strong group" (Tamney & Chiang, 2002, p. 53) is also disputed by Tu Wei-ming (1985), who elaborates on Confucius' comment, "In ancient times, men learned for the sake of the self. Nowadays, men learn for the sake of others" (*The Analects*, 14.24). Learning for the sake of the self rather than the approval of others implies that self-cultivation is an end in itself and that self-realization is immanent in every person's effort to achieve humanity.

To debate the Confucian destination, we need to consider the historical time in which both Confucius and Mencius lived. It was one of the most turbulent periods in ancient China, as separatist rulers continually warred among themselves and people led precarious lives of daily danger and insecurity. The link between the individual and society was imposed more explicitly than in other, more peaceful, times. There was no guarantee of individual freedom in a war-torn society, and an individual could be easily submerged in the turbulence. Confucius and Mencius proposed the idea of government by *ren* and righteousness with the intention to *transform* society. The continuity between self and society in their political ideal was sustained by a dynamic notion of harmony culminating in the notion of "sageliness within and kingliness without," which centers on personal cultivation.

The Confucian Way comprises both individual and social transformation. Interestingly, the thoughts of Confucius and Mencius were not adopted by any ruler of their time; the elevation of the Confucian moral order to an official ideology occurred after China was unified during the Han dynasty (206 B.C.–A.D. 220). If we recognize the connection between self and society in Confucianism, we don't need to locate the end of personal cultivation as either self or as society. This interdependent relationship between self and society for transformation contrasts with Foucault's vision of self *against* society for creativity. Needless to say, the postmodern condition of simultaneous fragmentation, multiplicity, and totalization differs from the condition in ancient war-torn China. Still, the mode of *with* versus *against* implies a different civilizational orientation toward subjectivity and society. Objectifying others, society, or nature is not intrinsic to Confucian thought. Confucius regards "freedom" as harmony *with* the Way, not a rupture with the society.

## Unity between Humanity and Universe

The concept of self as relational is further expanded by the notion of the unity between humanity and the universe. Unlike the Western tradition of creation *ex nihilo*, classical Chinese thought conceives of the universe as spontaneously self-generating (Tu, 1985a), with humanity and divinity organically related to each other along a shared continuum. Through attuning itself to the spirit of the universe, the self is simultaneously dissolved and enlarged by participating in the transformation of the ever-expanding cosmos. The self becomes a part of the creative cosmic processes. In traditional Chinese landscape paintings, human figures, if there are any, usually appear as a small, vague, and sometimes almost invisible, sketch, symbolizing the embeddedness of humanity within nature. Many ancient academies of classical learning were established on famous mountains by water so that students could experience the union between nature and humanity throughout their education.

Strangely, it is in another country where I experience this power of immersion in nature in a dramatic way. When in crises, I often go to the university lake for walks at night. Walking barefoot in the sand, looking up at the night sky, I am touched, even overwhelmed, by the mysterious power of the universe. The moon with its tender light, stars with their blinking eyes, clouds with their fractal shapes, all send me messages from nature in their beauty, complexity, and fluctuation. Looking around at night lights from surrounding houses, I can almost see smiles and tears, and hear sighs and laughter, with their own rhythms, flowing out of the buildings into the ripples of the lakeshore. Embraced by the breeze from the lake, awed by the inspiration from the stillness of the beach, I feel myself becoming a part of the night landscape and the night sky becoming a part of me. Every detail of the universe—a piece of green leaf, a tract of meadow, a bunch of wild flowers, or a car passing by with its lights on, now, in my eyes—tells its own story about the omnipresent power of life, and unfolds mysterious interconnections. The darkness of the night becomes intimate, gently embracing my tense body and calming my racing mind. I return to my apartment to resume the daily routine—with its sighs, struggles, and pains. However, it no longer feels crushing; I fall asleep soundly, to dream my dreams. Rereading Confucian classics brings these memories back to me.

As Zi Si (Tsesze, grandson of Confucius) says, "To arrive at a true understanding by realizing one's true self is called [the way of] nature. To realize one's true self from understanding [of the universe] is called [the way of] culture. Who has realized his true self gains thereby understanding. Who has gained a [complete] understanding finds his true self."[5] By this way, the organic growth of humanity is in accordance with the fulfillment of the way of the universe. According to *The Doctrine of the Mean*, another Confucian classic, people who can fulfill their own natures can fulfill the nature of creatures and things, and, furthermore, help nature to nourish and sustain life. As a result of this expansive realization, the self forms a trinity with earth and heaven. This organic process, as Yao Xinzhong (1996) points out, requires bringing "all emotions and feelings and actions into harmony" (p. 189). Here harmony is obtained by dynamic interconnections (not necessarily devoid of conflicts) within and without. Therefore, personal cultivation ultimately achieves unity between the earth, heaven, and person (the self) through transformation and harmony, rather than in a static state and through conformity.

## Confucianism as the State Cult, Neo-Confucianism, and the Critique of Moral Reason

With its emphasis on extending the self through social and cosmic relationships to embrace humanity and the universe, Confucianism pays more attention to the commonality of humanity than to its differences. As a result, it has a certain tendency to suppress individuality and promote social hierarchy. It is also a patriarchal discourse in which women are inferior to men. Confucius has a famous dictum: "Only women and inferior men are difficult to deal with" (*The Analects*, 17.25). Scholars attempt to argue that here the term *women* does not refer to all women; however, throughout the master's teachings, there are few remarks about women, and in these remarks, Confucius (and Mencius) comments on women's inferiority and obedience. Theoretically, personal cultivation, as in the Greco-Roman notion of the care of the self, is available to everyone, women as well as men. However, cultural contexts and social practices make such a possibility slim, even though a mother plays an important role in a son's education. The elitist tendency in the Confucian self is also reflected in the educated and passive role of the people (Dawson, 1993), in contrast with the educative and participatory role of the intellectual. As a note, the Confucian elite were not born, but had to achieve their status through education and personal cultivation, which, not unlike the American dream, promised everyone who was willing to try a chance to become an intellectual/official. But the cultural myth of people rising from low status to become important government officials—although it did happen once in a while—masked the inequality of the social structure.

The patriarchal and unequal tendency in classical thought was pushed to its extreme with the institutionalization of Confucianism and in (Cheng-Zhu) Neo-Confucianism, with its metaphysics of moral reason. Sexual inequality was already well established in the Han dynasty; it was further intensified in the Song dynasty (A.D. 960–1276). According to Bettine Birge (1989), women's status declined during the Song dynasty, due to the influence of the new, Neo-Confucian doctrine, which imposed upon women more severe forms and practices of subjugation as the way of heaven. Chiao Chien (1992) also argues that the doctrine of Neo-Confucianism increased the emphasis on the importance of female chastity and made the code of female chastity much more specific, rigid, demanding, and coercive. Such an ideology of gender inequality became more persuasive in the dynasties following the Song dynasty, when Neo-Confucianism obtained its official status.

In Confucius' own day, his was only one of many schools of thought (the so-called hundred schools of thought) influential at the time, and his teachings about government and morality were, for most of his life, not accepted by rulers. But during the Western Han dynasty, Confucianism became the only official ideology, serving the purpose of establishing a central autocratic government. Dong Zhong-shu (Tung Chung-shu) (177–104 B.C.) suggested that Confucianism be respected exclusively, with the expulsion of other schools of thought. The emperor Han Wu Di readily accepted this suggestion. It signaled the beginning of Confucianism as the state cult (136 B.C.) of China. Dong further argued for the Three Standards as the unchanging way of heaven. These are: (1) the emperor is the standard of the minister; (2) the father is the standard of the son; and (3) the husband is the standard of the wife. As the dogma of Confucian ethics, it firmly established the absolute authority of the ruler over the ruled, the elderly over the young, and men over women. Furthermore, the ethics was politicized to serve the state.

As I have already pointed out, Confucius' intention was not to exercise moral control in the service of government, but to transform politics through the "law" of the heart, and thereby achieve social harmony. Unfortunately, only one side of Confucius' teachings about the interdependence between self and society was encoded in the institutionalization of Confucianism. This control of the state and the family over the individual in general, and over women in particular, has become one of the main sources of Chinese tragedy.

The relationships between ruler and ruled, father and son, husband and wife, as Confucius envisioned them, are indeed hierarchical, but Confucius also vigorously urged that the ruler must practice a government of *ren*, and that fathers should be affectionate to their sons. Besides, the nature of the relationship between the ruler and the ruled, and between the father and the son, makes it difficult, if not impossible, to have an equal stance in a general sense. (The relationship between husband and wife is another story.) In Confucius' ideal, these relationships keep certain elements of mutuality although not equality. This mutuality was largely lost in Dong's interpretation and in the later development of Confucian doctrines in which unilateral obedience was emphasized. After the Northern Song dynasty, the central autocratic system became highly developed. A highly politicized and "metaphysical" interpretation of Confucianism called Neo-Confucianism emerged during this period. As Xu (1994) points out, the rise and fall of Neo-Confucianism paralleled the climax and decay of the central autocratic system. It might not be an exaggeration to say that the degeneration of Confucianism into an ossified dogma, employed exclusively for official control, contributed to the fall of ancient China.

Though Confucius was himself not interested in metaphysics, both a metaphysical foundation and a rational basis were established when classical Confucian thought was developed into Neo-Confucianism. As a master of Neo-Confucianism during the Song dynasty, Zhu Xi (Chu Hsi) (A.D. 1130–1200) formulated Principle (*li*) as the foundation of everything, including truth and values. Principle exists in all things, even before an object comes into existence: "In the beginning, when no single physical object yet existed, there was then nothing but Principle" (quoted in Fung, 1983, p. 535). Principle also constitutes human nature and is the source of moral virtues such as *ren*, righteousness (*yi*), propriety (*li*), wisdom (*zhi*), faithfulness (*xin*). Principle as the way of "above shapes" is eternal and universal and determines *qi* (*ch'i*, energy), the instrument of "within shapes," whose movement makes up all things. John Berthrong (1998) regards the separation of principle and *qi* as "quasi-dualistic," since principle is above *qi* but must be actualized in *qi*. As a result, the separation between the two is not complete. The Supreme Ultimate (*Tai-ji*) consists of the principles of all things in the universe and is the highest and most generalized principle. Principle not only generalizes the totality of the universe but is also immanent in every individual human being or thing.

The central concern of personal cultivation in the Neo-Confucianism of Cheng-Zhu is the realization of Principle. For Zhu Xi, the investigation of things and the exercise of reverence are necessary for personal cultivation. The goal of investigating things is to seek the principles of things in order to extend knowledge to the utmost, as an exhaustive knowledge of the principles of external things is the way to achieve understanding of human nature and of heaven. The exercise of reverence refers to one's efforts to free oneself from distractions and to concentrate on achieving Principle. When one is watchful over oneself in the pursuit of mind, the virtues of *ren*, righteousness, propriety, wisdom, and faithfulness, become manifested in one's efforts. The moral nature of reverence is explicit here. These two aspects of personal cultivation are also intimately related to each other: The exercise of reverence provides a mental attitude in which the investigation of things can be effectively carried out. Only when one attends to and regulates one's emotions and actions can one's intellectual pursuit lead to the realization of Principle. Meanwhile, the effective investigation of things and extension of knowledge is a process of strengthening one's inner control according to moral reason to achieve understanding of the principles of things.

Underlying both the investigation of things and the exercise of reverence is the effort to "preserve Heavenly Principle and extinguish human desires." *The Doctrine of the Mean* defines the state of mind as *equilibrium* before feelings of pleasure, anger, sorrow, or joy arise, and as *harmony* after these feelings are aroused but act in their due degree and meet right occasions. Zhu Xi takes another dramatic step in defining emotions and feelings as manifesting *qi*; according to his theory, whenever emotions are in excess, they become the source of evil. Therefore, to realize Heavenly Principle requires the harmonious control of emotions. As Lo Ping-cheng (1993) argues, the dualism between Heavenly Principle and human desires is not ontological, since Zhu Xi admits that some natural human desires are of Heavenly Principle. Zhu Xi uses "human desires" interchangeably with "selfish desires" and "material desires," to specify excessive or improper desires rather than all desires. For example, the desire for food is of Heavenly Principle; the desire for delicious food is of human desire. For Zhu Xi, human nature is originally clean, but human desires renders it a pearl immersed in impure water. To make human nature lustrous again, human desires need to be under the control of Principle. The purpose of education is to recover the goodness of human nature and restore its inherent *Tai-ji*. Thus, the ability to conquer self becomes essential to personal cultivation in Neo-Confucianism.

The process of investigating things involves dissolving human desires to realize Principle. Complementary to this process of externally harmonizing the mind with things is the exercise of reverence, which keeps human impulses under control in order to achieve internal equilibrium of the mind. Regarding the relationship between self-conquest, extension of knowledge, and exercise of reverence, Zhu Xi (1990) makes a vivid analogy:

> If we liken the "extension of knowledge," "inner mental attentiveness" [reverence] and "subduing the self," these three matters, to a house, "inner attentiveness [reverence]" corresponds to the man who guards the door, "subduing the self" corresponds to warding off the robber, and the "extension of knowledge" corresponds to investigating the external affairs that affect one's home. (p. 119)

The metaphor of reverence as a watchman who decides what can come inside the mind and self-conquest as resisting evil vividly shows the importance of moral control in the process of personal cultivation. As Julia Ching (1986) suggests, self-vigilance in the practice of reverence has some parallel to the technique of the self in Western confessional Christianity. What is different is that, in the Chinese context, there is no demand to detect and expose sin in order to follow the order of God for spiritual salvation. Confucianism holds a more positive view of human nature. But in terms of exercising mental discipline and self-conquest, they are quite similar, and Principle plays a role analogous to God in guarding the mind against evil. When imposed upon women, Zhu Xi's ethics of self-conquest and self-sacrifice intensified their subjugated status. If, as Foucault argues, the Greco-Roman tradition of the care of the self is obscured by Christian self-knowledge and the quest for spiritual salvation through self-sacrifice, I would venture to say that the Confucian classical notion of personal cultivation is shadowed by Neo-Confucian metaphysics.

Zhu Xi's Heavenly Principle is universal, moral, and rational. Mencius believed that the mandate of heaven is not immutable, but Zhu Xi approaches Principle as unchangeable and universally applicable. The moral nature of Principle is explicit not only in its constitution in humanity and virtues, but also in the purpose of knowing things as extending morality. Objective reality in the Western scientific sense does not exist in Zhu Xi's theory. Zhu Xi's metaphysics is based upon moral reason instead of scientific reason. The rationality of self-conquest in Zhu Xi's Principle makes it not surprising that one of his disciples would comment on the master's notion, "The mind is master of the body" (quoted in Berthrong, 1998, p. 135). Zhu Xi epitomizes the thought of Neo-Confucianism and reformulates the classical theory by responding to the challenge of Taoism and Buddhism. His system of thought is comprehensive and complicated. His discourse on cosmology is much more mature than classical thought. While not going into the details of his achievement, let us especially note that Zhu Xi's theory is not as transcendental as Western metaphysics, and that he preserves the Confucian tradition of contextualization, as Principle can be actualized only in concrete things and events through the movement of *qi*. It is this interplay between Principle and *qi* that is usually lost in the institutionalization of Confucianism, which underscores the rational control of Principle.

Zhu Xi's doctrine of "preserving Heavenly Principle and extinguishing human desire" is developed from Confucius' notion of subduing one's self and returning to propriety (*The Analects*, 12.1). However, it bases rational self-discipline upon a metaphysical Principle and extends it to the extreme, which leaves it vulnerable for conversion into a tool for suppressive moral control. While, in modern Western thought, a transcendental self located in universal scientific reason plays a negative role in the full development of humanity, a relational self based upon universal moral reason in Zhu Xi's metaphysics, casts shadows on efforts to nurture individuality. This suppression of individuality is shown even in a double sense. The Confucian emphasis on the commonality of humanity through relationship is pushed further by Zhu Xi's subduing one's self within an all-encompassing Principle and his privilege of rational self-conquest in the process of personal cultivation. His distinction between Heavenly Principle and human desire and his privileging of knowledge obscure Confucius' more dynamic and interactive notion of self and can too easily be turned against humanity itself. If it can be said that Confucius' notion of self in its expansive relationships starts with the self and is open to its own emergence, Zhu Xi's notion of self dominated by moral reason is more controlling. Institutional use and interpretation of Neo-Confucianism has intensified this theoretical tendency: those in power define "Principle" and "human desires." In order to release the potential of the Confucian notion of a relational self in its connection with the other and with the universe, Zhu Xi's metaphysical foundation must be challenged. The effort to regenerate Confucianism cannot take flight into the metaphysical.

Through this historical analysis of Confucianism and Neo-Confucianism, I conclude it is the historical rupture produced by the *metaphysical* elevation of an embodied and relational worldview that is precisely what we need to attend to in order for Confucianism to offer its best for our simultaneously fragmented and globalized contemporary life. With this attention to Confucius' original thought, I now discuss how the Confucian relational view of the self can converse with the Western subject.

## Unity between the Universe and the Self, and Dichotomy of Subject and Object: An East–West Dialogue

Heaven is my father and earth is my mother and even such a small creature as I finds an intimate place in its midst. That which extends throughout the universe, I regard as my body and that which directs the universe, I regard as my nature. All people are my brothers and sisters and all things are my companions.

(Zhang Zai, quoted in Berry, 1988, p. 14)

The pure wind makes me chant poems.
The bright moon urges me to drink.
Intoxicated, I fall among the flowers,
Heaven my blanket, earth my pillow.

(Yang Wan-li, in Chaves, 1975, p. 91)

Unity between *tian* (heaven, universe, or cosmos) and *ren* (man, humanity, or self)[6] is a common theme throughout Confucian literature, although different thinkers have interpreted the relationship differently. The theme of oneness between heaven and man reaches its maturity and culmination in Neo-Confucian thought. While it offers insights for rethinking the contemporary endangered relationship among humanity, nature, and cosmos, Neo-Confucianism's metaphysics of moral reason is problematic. For the light to break through its confinement by moral Principle infused by heavenly destiny, let me start with Confucius again.

As scholars (Hall & Ames, 1987; Meng, 1997) have noticed, Confucius is not explicitly concerned with the question of *tian* and seldom mentions it. However, he says that "at fifty I realized the *ming* [mandate, fate, or destiny] of *tian*" and insists that "a person who does not understand *ming* has no way of becoming a *junzi*" (*The Analects*, 20.3). In *The Analects*, his comments on *tian*—when they appear—are elusive. It is sometimes described as the creator of sages; sometimes as the provider of health, status, and wealth; sometimes as a superior power bestowing the vocation of becoming a *junzi*; and sometimes as a source of all phenomena, including natural processes of change. Without a stable definition, *tian* is not a predetermined order or a transcendental principle independent of humanity. This continuum of universe and humanity leads to Mencius' dictum about understanding *tian* by understanding *xing* (human natural tendency), which forms the ancient notion of the unity between universe and humanity. Here, *tian* represents the cosmos through *Tao* or Way,[7] and *xing* refers to humanity, while *ming* connects *tian* and humanity. What is implied in this relational way of thinking about the self and the universe is that the *Tao* of the cosmos is implicit in humanity and the Way of being a human can be achieved by understanding the universe. The distinction between the self and external objects is vague and permeable, a distinction which characterizes ancient Chinese thought and which differs from the Western subject/object dichotomy. Furthermore, Confucius believes that the *ming* of *tian* is only possible for those who have already achieved the quality of *de* (virtues, morality), which gives the *Tao* a certain sense of morality. In other words, the *Tao* of cosmos is imbued with moral values and meanings for humanity, a fact which makes the sharp distinction between the knowing subject and the objectified external world even more impossible.

It is important to understand *ming*, *Tao*, and *xing* as changeable, transformative, and creative in classical Confucianism, as Hall and Ames (1987) argue in their criticism of Tu Wei-ming as imposing Western transcendental concepts upon the early Chinese traditions. I have similar doubts concerning Tu's reconstruction of Confucian metaphysics as an alternative to Western individualism. Early Confucian thought concerning the interactive relation between the *Tao* of the universe and the *xing* of humanity do not assume an absolute, independent, and superior principle above human experience. *Tao* is not an externally imposed absolute standard; it emerges out of the interaction between humanity and environment. It is a result of events and activities. Confucius says, "It is the human being who is able to extend *Tao*, not *Tao* that is able to extend the human being" (*The Analects*, 15.29). Here Confucius emphasizes the active and creative role of humanity, not only in keeping *Tao,* but also transforming and broadening *Tao*, a role that is often ignored in criticisms of Confucianism. Human participation in *Tao*, rather than blind obedience to predetermined law or truth, is the key to the unity between the universe and humanity. In a similar manner, *ming* is not predetermined; *xing* is not something unchangeable either. That is one reason that education and personal cultivation play such important roles in the Confucian self. Confucians not only follow *Tao* but also actively engage in co-creating *Tao* with *tian*, so that the union between the universe and the self is dynamic. In this sense, to approach the Confucian self merely as "on the path" to self-realization can capture only part of the picture. The transformative potential of becoming a Confucian *junzi* is another intertwined aspect of the process. The Confucian self is simultaneously preservative and creative.

While Confucius' thoughts about *tian* are generally implicit, Mencius clearly brings forth the unity between *tian* and man. He says, "Knowing his nature, he knows *tian*" (*Mencius*, 13.1). Heaven, earth, and all kinds of phenomena and things are all unified with man, whose nature is basically good. Good human nature coming from *ren, yi, li, zhi* is endowed by heaven, and understanding human *xing* is intertwined with understanding heavenly *Tao*. By defining human nature in this way, Mencius is more essentialized than Confucius who does not define human nature as good or bad. But it is through the later developments of Confucianism that the generative potential of Confucius' interaction between *tian*'s *Tao* and humanity is lost. When Confucianism became the official ideology under the Han dynasty, Dong Zhong-shu suggested that heaven is the creator of everything and that the Three Standards—notorious as hierarchical ethics—are heavenly principles for everyone to follow. Here the intention of (moral) heaven controlling humanity becomes very explicit. Confucius' transformative *Tao* disappeared in Dong's argument for an unchangeable heaven and Way.

The tendency of heavenly *Tao* to suppress human nature was particularly developed in the Cheng-Zhu branch of Neo-Confucian moral metaphysics.[8] Cheng Yichuan (A.D. 1033–1107) established the fundamental role of Principle as heavenly *ming*, the source of everything in the cosmos. As the master of the Principle branch of Neo-Confucianism, Zhu Xi developed Cheng's perspectives into a more systematic and mature theory. He interpreted Prin-

ciple as metaphysical *Tao* that is the sum of *ren, yi, li,* and *zhi.* Man comes
from the integration of Principle and *qi,* human nature (*xing*) is from Principle, and moral consciousness in human nature comes from Heavenly Principle. To become unified with Principle—the key to the unity between heaven
and man—one must start with subduing human desires, since circulation of
*qi,* if motivated by human desires, results in evil.

Confucius' refusal to take up metaphysics is finally reversed in Zhu Xi's
theory of Principle. Confucius' concern over personal experiential transformation is displaced, as I have argued before, by Zhu Xi's focus on the role of
rational control. De Bary (1991a) argues that Confucian personalism, as it
developed in the Cheng-Zhu Neo-Confucian school, is closer to Western individualism; however, it is indeed this metaphysical closeness between Zhu
Xi's self-realization and Western individualism that bothers me. This parallel
between the Western scientific reason/self and the Neo-Confucian moral rea-
son/self is something we need to reflect on critically so that a more relational, experiential, and generative sense of the Confucian self—not loaded
by moral metaphysics—can come forward.

## A Third Space: A Cross-Cultural Perspective

According to Zhang Shiying (1995), traditional Chinese philosophy and
modern Western philosophy follow two different paths regarding the relationship between human beings and the world: oneness between heaven and
man versus the subject/object dichotomy. He further argues that the lack of
the concept of subjectivity in Chinese cultural traditions leads to the suppression of humanity by heaven, while the Western absolute "self" mystifies an
abstract, independent, yet decontextualized self at the expense of an individual's concrete life. For me, both paths have limitations regarding how to respect others' differences: Confucian relationships can easily submerge the
other's alterity within the social and cosmic nexus, while the Western self
can easily objectify the other and impose its own framework. Zhang believes
that the postmodern turn in the West is not fully applicable to the Chinese
situation. For him, a more creative, dynamic sense of unity depends upon the
separation between subject and object. Contrary to his claims, Meng Peiyuan
(1997) believes that the traditional Chinese way of thinking has its own subjective principle situated in the network of humanity and nature; subject and
object are unified instead of dichotomized. It is not an objective epistemology, but a subjective axiology. Looking upon world, nature, or self as an object of knowing is absent in Chinese subjective traditions.

The term Zhang uses, "oneness between heaven and man," already implies his critique of the Chinese sense of oneness. I doubt that Chinese
thought must go through the Western subject/object split before reaching

another level of maturity, as he suggests. Since the path of the subject/object dichotomy is not promising, why cannot we construct another road? While Zhang's vigilance against a conservative return to traditions is admirable, I would like to think about a possible third space, instead of following the path already trodden. I agree with Meng that subjectivity should not be exclusively defined by Western modern philosophy, and I do discern a certain sense of subjectivity in Confucian traditions. However, Meng does not address the historical and the theoretical failures of these traditions. Without the sharp edge of serious critical elaboration, the Chinese relational ideal cannot be renewed.

My own experiences of walking into the "West" have persuaded me to look for a third space beyond self and other, especially if both stay at the level of ideal. In crisis, the moment of feeling union between self and world was also a moment of self-dissolution for me. My wandering into a knowing and adventurous subject defined mainly by the Western ideal was also a failure. Only when I could situate myself on the boundary, at the border, and at the edge of the double and the multiple, was I able to detour around the dead end of "either/or" in various forms to come out anew. My cross-cultural and intercultural encounters and conversations both within the self and with others and with texts have given me a new eye, a "third eye" (Tyler, 2001) enabling me to see both worlds differently. This third way of perceiving East and West is necessary in order to create new spaces of individuality, subjectivity, and relationality, spaces in which curriculum and education can be envisaged differently.

Donna Porche-Frilot (2002) makes an insightful critique (from an African-American perspective) of my use of the stranger metaphor. She points out that there is a potential danger of the stranger's dominating the self. Wanting to enter into a third space, I advocate a mutuality of self and stranger in generating new spaces, acknowledging the unbalanced power relationships of East and West. At the same time, I dramatize intentionally the differences between two worldviews—thus the necessity for the metaphor of the stranger—in order to let mutual respect for otherness to come forward. Already consciously resisting assimilation and refusing the position of the cultural superiority of the West—in other words, carrying the assumption of cultural equality—I aspire to a third space. I often feel the tensions of an in-between space, filled with clashes of dramatically different orientations, not necessarily structured by a power struggle (especially defined in its traditional sense). These tensions and conflicts are what push me to search for alternative directions in a third space in which both affirmation and critique of self and other are necessary. Perhaps the power dynamics of approaching the stranger as an outsider (a Chinese encountering the United States) and an insider (an African American facing the racism of the United States) cannot be the same. As a result, the search for a third space in any particular context must consider concrete power circulations and their impacts on the relationship between the self and the stranger.

It is simplistic to define Chinese thinking as relational and Western thinking as dualistic. Historically, some important nonmainstream thinkers held opinions different from the dominant modes of thinking on both sides of the ocean. Still, different orientations regarding the relationship between the self and the external world and subject and object in Chinese and Western philosophies are not difficult to discern. Even Foucault, a rebel against modern Western traditions, does not directly challenge the duality originating from the Greco-Roman tradition, the priority of self over other. The reversal of the mind-body dualism in the case of the body in his later works does not deconstruct the dualism itself. Isn't the body as the site of creating new subjectivity, in contrast to the soul as the locus of spiritual cultivation, still located in duality itself? The destabilized Foucauldian subject takes "oneself as [the] object of a complex and difficult elaboration" (Foucault, 1984a, p. 312) to invent new modes of subjectivity. Complicated, yes, but one's self remains an object, nevertheless.

Understanding nature is different from understanding humanity. The interaction between the two is important, but there is no interaction if the two are unified. The cosmological principle is not human nature, although the two are intertwined and overlapped. The call to situate the self in a communal, ecological, and cosmological network is ancient—yet also contemporary—but to answer this call in our time, we must understand how complex and multilayered this network can be and how crucial the independence of each participant is to its dynamics. Unity may suffocate internal differences if this network is not dynamic, transformative, and creative. Relationships without enough differentiation, as the evolution of Chinese thought has already shown, cannot make us listen attentively to the voices of the other. The spontaneity and independence of the other cannot be brought forth if it is not given enough space to grow.

Without maintaining a certain degree of detachment from both self and tradition, we cannot engage in productive self-reflection and social critique. As a result, we may be submerged by whatever tradition we have already had. We can keep a constructive connection with the network only by participating in its renewal and regeneration. On the other hand, when the distance between subject and object is increased to the level of dualism, the objectifying control by the subject brings disaster, not only to the other but also to itself. The contemporary ecological movement has shown that this dualism is not only destructive to both the natural environment and human society (Berry, 1990), but the objectification of the other unconsciously turns this violence back onto the self (Pinar, 2001). Derrida's deconstruction of dualism, including that of the subject/object dualism, indicates that hierarchical violence is inherent in it.

How can the alternative ways of East and West in dealing with dualism and unity be negotiated in a new space in which new paths of individuality and sociality can be opened up? Can the violence of dualism be resisted without abolishing the conceptual distinction between subject and object? Is there a way to destabilize the boundary between the subject and object while maintaining a certain distance between self and other? Without referring to the self as the object of personal cultivation, can the self be engaged in activities of self-examination, self-reflection, and self-transformation?

My hope is to answer all of these questions affirmatively. What is important here is to build connections and relationships in such a way that differences and the alterity of both self and other can be respected and even promoted under certain conditions. I am searching for a third space as a result of this intercultural conversation, a space in which self/subject, other, and universe co-emerge based upon differentiation instead of nondifferentiation between subject and object, together yet apart, a space in which individuality and sociality are engaged with each other in a journey of constructing new forms of life.

The universe/self unity and the subject/object dichotomy provide double directions for entering into a third space. To venture there, we can start from either Chinese relationality or Western differentiation, but the creative transformation of both through one's engagement with the other is crucial. The conflicting directions of connections and individuality must be addressed through dynamic interaction in one's own local context to generate a cross-cultural third space, which is embodied differently for each participant, whether culturally or personally.

Related to the duality between subject and object, the relationship between self and society is another theme on which the Confucian self and the Western subject—specifically as Foucault theorizes it—diverge. Actually, both Confucius and Foucault share suspicion of juridical authority: Confucius and his followers didn't believe that written laws and courts can bring forth a good society; Foucault did not trust justice by law. However, Confucius relied on morality and education, while Foucault encouraged the critique of almost all aspects of sociality. While the Foucauldian subject is basically ruptured from society, the Confucian self is more in continuity with society, in their mutual transformation. The Foucauldian project of selfhood focuses more on discontinuity, resistance, and fragmentation. The Confucian self is much more unitary and focuses on consistency. To objectify society as being

suppressive of individual creativity is a Western dualism in which one is superior to the other, no matter which side is chosen. Such dichotomous thinking is not present in the Chinese tradition. Can Foucault's transgressive self
and the Confucian transformative self approach each other, not necessarily to
meet in the middle, but to create a third space in which both rupture and continuity can stage various performances of subjectivity? Can we envision a
self in which a strong sense of Confucian relationality is carved by the sharp
edge of Foucauldian creativity?

There are common themes of self-cultivation in both traditions: affirmative themes such as lifelong commitment, critical self-reflection, and personal integrity; and destructive themes such as elitist and patriarchal
tendencies. Even the transgressive edge of the Foucauldian self is not completely lacking in the Confucian sense of subjectivity. The Confucian respect
for traditions is also not without reservation. Mencius comments: "It would
be better to not have the *Book of History* than to believe it completely" (*Mencius*, 14.3). On the other hand, Foucault suggests a nonviolent relationship
between self and other, through a reciprocal respect for the self-creation of
others. His proposal for creative individuality is not devoid of social relations, either. In an interesting way, the other part of Confucius and the other
voice of Foucault, to a great degree, lurk within themselves without being
noticed. Through this intercultural conversation, is it possible to redraw the
other faces of both so that intercivilizational stories about both conflicts and
intersections can be told?

In contemporary China, there has appeared a renewed search for the individual self as a counteraction to a long history of collectivism. However,
this search is sometimes reflected in contemporary "vanguard" literature in
the image of an individual male hero (Lu, 1993) striving for his freedom.
This movement toward Western individualism forms a "conspiracy" with
capitalism and leads to the erosion of communal values. To become engaged
in a dialogue with the West in a creative way, it is necessary to reclaim the
Confucian value of relationality while, at the same time, searching for new
ways of promoting individuality. Therefore, to negotiate a dialogue between
the Foucauldian subject and the Confucian self in a third space of mutuality
and transformation, I believe that we need to generate a new sense of relational individuality, situated in dynamic and complex cultural connections,
social interactions, and cosmic processes. Such individuality can be transformed into a fuller and deeper sense of self. Such selfhood is constantly created and re-created in richer and more open interconnections in which
individuality can be expressed, supported, and transformed. The more profound one's participation in dialogic encounters across differences with
others and with the world, the more deeply and creatively one's own indi-

viduality evolves. The more unique and particular each individual's contribution to the whole, the more complex and generative the web of relationships and connections that can emerge. Through this dynamic interaction between individuality and relationality, the creative potential of the self is constantly called into existence. This new sense of the self also calls upon a renewed sense of community that is more open to differences and supportive of personal creation. The web of connections and relationships brings out an interactive wholeness, simultaneously in harmony and in tension. Creativity comes out of the interplay between unmerged union and constructive dissipation in a shifting intersubjective space. The co-emergence and co-creation of self, other, and world must be based upon mutual respect for the alterity of the other. As a result, this strong principle of subjectivity is not separate from the world and is constantly regenerated through the creative social, historical, and cosmic network in which the self is situated. Such a third space would have different expressions when situated in the West or in the East, as mutual transformation does not aim at universality, but attempts to bring forth the creative imagination of each party, depicting new sceneries of the self while contributing to the other's own self-creation.

## A Third Space: An Educational Consideration

A creative cross-cultural space based upon relational individuality generates different pictures of curriculum contextualized in local situations. The heated debates regarding multicultural education in the United States ask us to understand the central issue of identity and education from a new subject position. To challenge the myth of individualism, we must first recognize how an individual is situated in social, racial, cultural, religious, and sexual contexts. Yet, the notion of the socially constructed self is a difficult concept for mainstream students and teachers, given that they often (unconsciously) feel threatened by socially constructed *differences* which were invisible before. The traditional central position of being the subject objectifying a minority other—such as people of color, women, the poor, and homosexuals—is no longer secure, and "subject-to-subject encounters" call for new human relationships. In the process of repositioning, the subjugated perspectives of the marginal members of the classroom get recognized. In other words, subjectivities of the other people's children are respected, and genuine mutuality between self and other is pursued.

On the other hand, teaching about social constructions of race, gender, class, and sexuality in a third space does not intend to fix any individual to any static identity, but to reach another level of individuality which is both socially situated and personally generative, creating new layers of the self defiant against social injustice. Only when social and cultural limits are understood can a person choose how to play with them. In this way, creativity dwelling in contexualized individuality can bring forth new modes of relationship and sociality. Feelings of being threatened can be transformed into an expansive reaching out toward the other and returning to the self with something new. In this local context, education dealing with diversity issues must first recognize the importance of the socially constituted nature of reality and the relational nature of the self.

In the East, Chinese education has begun to bring diversity to the attention of the public, but in a different way. The challenge is to cultivate and encourage individuality, which has been suppressed by sociality and collectivity. The Chinese focus is more on the individual and one's own uniqueness beyond institutional constraints. This call for creative individuality and a personalized curriculum and teaching, rather than a standardized national system, has been heard in Chinese education for two decades. The advocacy of personal and independent singularity and a creative spirit (a reclaiming of the Confucian tradition) does not intend to negate the importance of relationality, but is an effort to release the full potential of an individual to build a more constructive connection. Socially issues such as gender and urban/rural inequality, which have been downplayed officially, are also a part of every student's daily life. They need to be addressed. In this context, education for social transformation starts not with sociality but with individuality.

It is not difficult to notice that in a third space of curriculum and pedagogy, every engaged culture moves in a new direction, albeit in its own mode. Both sides of the ocean are dealing with the issues of individuality and relationality, but their moves toward relational individuality or individualized relationality are not going to be alike: even if we see that they are moving toward each other, each dance has its unique style. Such is the creative potential of a shifting third space which spins each participant into her/his own new realm of life.

A third space in which both individuality and relationality interact with each other is also a gendered space, turning woman's deep sense of connection into the site for self-creation. Before I address this issue (in the next chapter), let me analyze to what degree women can claim themselves in the Confucian relational self.

## Gender Analysis of Confucianism and Neo-Confucianism: Do Women Have More Space in a Relational Self?

Dragons and tigers are dispersed,
Winds and clouds have vanished.

A thousand years of sorrow—
To whom can she tell them?

(Wang Qinghui, 1270, in Chang & Saussy, 1999, p. 113)

Against all shackles and fetters, the Chinese woman has exerted herself and achieved for herself a place in the family, in society, and in history.

(Hu Shi, 1931, p. 15)

One of the projects of feminism, especially in the West, is to resituate the self in social and cultural relationships as an alternative to the paradigms of male heroic self. Due to this concern, some feminist critics turn to Eastern thought, including Confucianism (Li, 2000), for other possibilities. I am deeply skeptical, however, about efforts such as Li's to search for a common ground between Confucian and feminist ethics. I do not think that the relational nature of the Confucian self, though seemingly compatible with the Western feminist critique of reason, can divert our attention from Confucianism's patriarchal character. Using Western feminist concerns to analyze the gendered nature of Confucianism is, to a great degree, a decontextualized project. If the axis of reason versus emotion is one of the major tools in the exclusion of women in Western culture, the lack of "reason" in classical Confucianism by no means implies the lack of patriarchal thinking, which can come from different sources. Although, as suggested by Hall and Ames (2000), Chinese sexism can be understood through a correlative model which is more fluid and less stable than Western sexism with its dualism, it can also bring a greater degree of suppression under a hierarchical system. The evolution of Chinese patriarchy is too complicated for me to explore here, but I will trace how Confucianism developed into a rigid dogma wherein women began to have diminishing space to breathe and live.

"Of all people, women and inferior men are the most difficult to deal with. If you are close to them, they lose their humility. If you are distant from them, they are discontented" (*The Analects*, 17.25). Confucius' remark in *The Analects* is often charged with being an expression of the master's sexism. While Paul Goldin (2000) attempts to argue that Confucius does not mean that women are "incapable of moral self-cultivation" (p. 140) and that cultivated women are no lower than cultivated men, there is not much doubt that women's moral cultivation, if it existed, was mainly intended to teach them "suitable" virtues—suitable to maintaining a system in which men were in charge, intellectually and morally.

I believe that classical Confucianism, from Confucius on, has already planted its patriarchal seed. It is interesting here to notice how the cornerstone of Confucian thought, *ren*, evolved from its original meaning. As Brooks and Brooks point out (1998), in archaic usage *ren* had no moral connotation and referred to the virile and manly manner of a hero. Confucius gave it ethical and moral meanings, indicating a moral relationship with both self and others. The original maleness in this basic Confucian ethical rule is clearly conveyed. However, Chinese women, throughout various dynasties, did utilize the general orientation of personal cultivation to expand their own lives, and numerous ancient Chinese women acted as diplomats, politicians, and generals without contradicting Confucian ethics. There is a certain flexibility that allowed women to play their roles in the public sphere due to the permeable distinction between "inner" and "outer," as Goldin (2000) argue. Morality, ethics, and politics flow from the inner to the outer, which makes women's positions important in terms of both personal cultivation and the public good. Occasionally women's stepping outside of the family is acceptable to Confucians, and there is no objection to women's participation in their husbands' public work. I agree with Goldin that the later manifestations of sexism and misogyny in imperial times established much harsher and stricter standards of obedience for women to follow. Lin Yutang (1936) refers to Neo-Confucian ethics for women as "puritanico-sadistic" (p. 36), having lost the humanism and tolerance of Confucius.

As I have mentioned, during the Han dynasty, state Confucianism emphasized social order along with increased government centralization. The Three Standards as women's ideal demanded women's blind obedience and submission to men. Tales of how women could corrupt men's hearts by their special powers and charm began to flourish. As a response to the myth of destructive feminine power, much more restrictive control was imposed. Interestingly, even during this period of state Confucianism, women exercised a certain flexibility in pursuing more equal relationships with men. The so-called Confucian model wife (Peterson et al., 2000), Meng Guang, declined her father's arrangement of marriage to select her own husband, Liang Hong, and went through many hardships together with him. She set up a model of a harmonious, respectful relationship between husband and wife. Another fascinating female figure during this period is Ban Zhao (A.D. 49–120), the first female historian of China. She not only completed her *History of the Han Dynasty*, but also utilized a new style of writing history as biography that was adopted by subsequent dynasties. Women's virtues can lead women into their own intellectual, political, ethical, and artistic creations when such virtues are reappropriated and reinterpreted at the edge of, rather than within, sexism.

Women's freedom, if there was any, was largely limited, starting from the Song dynasty, during which Neo-Confucianism had begun to be formulated. Following Mencius' principle of "separate functions between husband and wife," Zhu Xi strengthened and developed the unequal gender roles in these classical teachings. For him, women do not have the intellectual ability to understand the metaphysical Principle that men should pursue and promote; women's activities should be confined to the home. According to Zhu Xi (1990), such a differentiation is the basis for proper relationships with children, practicing filial piety, pursuing righteousness, and performing rites. Zhu Xi reiterated the inferior status of women and further ossified the ethics of women's obedience. According to Birge's (1989) studies of Zhu Xi's writings for funerary inscriptions of women, Zhu Xi's ideal of womanhood included serving her parents-in-law diligently (without any complaints), following her husband's orders, keeping harmony among family members, taking good care of the household in a frugal way, and educating her children for their moral cultivation. There is no place left for herself: Women are supposed to sacrifice and devote themselves to others and the family. The feminine virtue Zhu Xi praises most is the endurance of hardships, difficulties, physical sacrifice, and even death. While hardly a demand only for women, their self-sacrifice and, even, self-mutilation is much more intense. Prior to Zhu Xi's time, it was not uncommon for widows or divorced women to remarry. But Zhu Xi made chastity and absolute loyalty to one man important, remarriage meant a loss of one's virtue.

Footbinding began to gain popularity during the Song dynasty. From a psychoanalytic view, Julia Kristeva (1977a) believes that footbinding could have been an act of relieving fear and anxiety over female power. The fear of woman's seductive power was incorporated into popular culture from the time of the Han dynasty, but the anxiety over maternal reproductive power was even more ancient. Women were made less threatening when they could be kept away from the public sphere, by confining their bodies. The morality that Neo-Confucianism advocates undoubtedly contributed to this cruelty. According to Howard Levy (1966), Zhu Xi is said to have introduced footbinding into the southern part of China to promote women's chastity and to teach the separative functions of men and women. Zhu Xi's moral prohibition against the remarriage of widows condemned women to the status of men's property. The suicide of women following their husbands' deaths, became, strangely, the highest point of women's loyalty and chastity. This cult of widow fidelity reached its peak in a later dynasty: the Ming dynasty (A.D. 1368–1644).

In this context, Lu Xun's (1918) well-known outcry against traditional Chinese ethics as "eating people," became more precisely an ethic of eating women. Lu comments on women's chastity: "The earlier her husband dies and the poorer her family, the more chaste it is possible for her to be. In addition, there are two other types of chaste woman: One kills herself when her husband or fiancé dies; the other manages to commit suicide when confronted by a ravisher, or meets her death while resisting. The more cruel her death, the greater glory she wins" (quoted in Chiao, 1992, p. 142). Lu's irony vividly shows how cruel the code of female chastity became. I am aware that "placing the blame on Neo-Confucianism has been a convenient way for modern writers to condemn patriarchy in China without condemning Chinese culture as a whole," as Patricia Ebrey points out (1993, p. 6); however, I believe that the development of Chinese metaphysics in Neo-Confucianism did make women's situation much worse and that revealing this historical evolution can plant seeds for cultural reconstruction.

Even during this reactionary period, there were outstanding women who went beyond the Confucian line to create their own womanhood. Li Qing-zhao (A. D. 1083–1151), a well-known poet, writer, musician, and painter, invented her own style of writing through *ci* poetry. Her style of *ci* is called by her literary name in the history of Chinese literature. Escaping from "foot binding as well as the institution of concubinage" (Peterson et al., 2000, p. 273), Liang Hongyu (A. D. 1100–1135), was a general and a national heroine, demonstrating marvelous bravery and executing brilliant tactics. Both women were well known for their equal and affectionate relationships with their husbands. But our admiration for these exceptional women cannot replace our understanding of how ordinary women, including mothers, wives, and daughters, expanded their horizons of life through seeking certain spaces within the Confucian tradition.

As Ebrey (1993) argues, scholars of women's history tended to focus on outstanding women who gained power in male-dominated worlds of political, military, diplomatic, or literary accomplishment. But they neglected the everyday lives of ordinary women. Such is, a strategy, I would argue, consistent with the traditional, male way of searching for individual historical heroes. The acknowledgment and recovery of our heroines must be coupled with the more difficult work of understanding ordinary women's lives in their own fluidity, complexity, and ambiguity. Ebrey's (1993) remarkable and scholarly effort to explore how ordinary women, not as victims but as capable persons, managed to accomplish much in the Song dynasty challenges taken-for-granted assumptions about women, especially Chinese women. Women in ancient China who belonged to the lowest class created women's script (Zhao, 1995), a recent discovery of an ancient "fact," the origin of which is unclear. We do know that a new language, different from "men's" language in both spoken and written form, was created by ordinary women.

Motherhood was a very important part of ancient Chinese women's identity. More often than not, motherhood became an effective realm for women's expansion of Confucian traditions, creating more room to challenge hierarchy. There are many touching stories describing mothers' influence on their sons through personal example and verbal instruction, enabling them to become great people with lofty ideals. Mother Meng (ca. 400–350 B.C.) is one such mother. She not only taught her son, Mencius, the virtues of scholarly persistence and personal integrity, but she also criticized him for not giving his wife the right to act at ease with herself when alone. She saved her daughter-in-law from a "disgraceful" divorce. Mother Meng's teaching about Confucian virtues was quite original at the time, especially in terms of the relationships between husband and wife.

Cheng Yichuan also praised his mother, Mother Hou (A.D. 1004–1052), for her education. In his reflection, he mentioned how Mother Hou treated servants, the orphaned, the poor, and the sick in caring ways and she urged her children to do the same. In a highly hierarchical society, such respect for people of inferior status was unusual. However, Cheng Yichuan reappropriated his mother's concern for people in unfavorable conditions as feminine devotion to others rather than as a call for equality. How I wish these Confucian masters had been more loyal to their mothers' teaching! These mothers' courage to question social hierarchy demonstrates that women can carry forward the reciprocal side of Confucianism, reappropriating the relationality of the Confucian self to challenge social inequality. They also passed this heritage along to their daughters through education. The accomplishments of women in ancient China cannot be overemphasized in our efforts to understand Chinese sexuality and gender politics.

In contemporary China, motherhood is still an important stage for education. My own mother has been a key teacher in my life. An outstanding professor herself, well loved by her students, she dared to challenge authorities. She did not hesitate to struggle for both her own rights and social justice. I vividly remember how she, a diminutive woman, argued forcefully with a businessman (much larger in stature) to return the money he had cheated from people in the countryside. This sense of social sympathy is intricately connected to her caring relation with others and her strong principle of personal dignity. Her courage, her distaste for various kinds of hierarchy, and her laughing spirit are always an inspiration to me. Particularly her faith in my intellectual ability and her respect for my own mode of understanding have traveled with me into worlds I could never have imagined, cultivating in me the determination to follow my own path no matter what difficulties I may encounter.

Strongly influenced by my mother's faith in women's capacities, and growing up in a period that officially proclaimed that women and men were equal, I have traveled a long road to understand the gendered nature of reality and my own life. Traveling along a highly competitive academic road, I worked with my male counterparts without bothering to think about my gendered identity. But when I chose education as my career, my mother was bitterly disappointed. She must have known that I had chosen a road full of ambiguities, paradoxes, and traps for a woman; she was quite reluctant to let her own daughter follow a path that women have traditionally taken. However, at the time, with inexperienced naiveté and youthful passion, I thought that as a teacher I could teach love and help create a better and more caring world. I truly believed the tenet "To give is better than to receive" without questioning its gendered self-sacrifice. Nor did I know that Zhu Xi, a master of patriarchal ethics, clearly stated that the highest human virtue of a woman is her ability to love, because she does not have any intellectual potential. Even in today's China, the image of teacher—a women's profession—as a candle that fires itself in order to lighten the lives of others is a common metaphor. Such an ethic of self-sacrifice in the educational profession, in conflict with my own desire to claim the self, has brought me moments of turbulence, even crisis. Yet, at the time, I was not really conscious of the gendered aspects of these conflicts. I was bothered, perhaps, by the paradoxes that women throughout Chinese history have encountered when they did not want to confine themselves within conventions. Now, reflecting the journey I have taken, I realize how subtly and unconsciously cultural traditions can shape one's identity, and how complicated and ambiguous is the journey for a woman in the quest for self.

My analysis of the patriarchal nature of Confucianism and, especially, Neo-Confucianism, attempts to show that a relational self, as an alternative to the Western modern self, is not necessarily compatible with feminist projects unless we first deal with the problematic of the relational. In the Chinese relational self, woman is not the other in the Western objectified sense, but still an inferior, who does not have equal intellectual capacity to cultivate herself, and a stranger who holds mystifying power which must be under the control of man. In this sense, Chinese women are also a "second sex," though more in an upper–lower sense than in subject/object dichotomy.

Chinese sexism points out that the link between women and an ecological sense of the cosmos, or the connection between women and a relational understanding of the world, is not necessarily essential. The ecology of the Confucian self, however relational and cosmic it is, cannot offer women a space of their own. The Confucian self does ask Westerners to rethink the issue of identity beyond the dichotomy of subject/object and self/other, while its own patriarchal and hierarchical nature must be challenged.

Creating woman's language and woman's subjectivity, we need to be engaged in a communal journey of "creating spaces and finding voices" (Miller, 1990) in order to attend to erased songs and invisible paths. Those other voices inaudible in the "patriarchal wilderness" (Pagano, 1990) need our loving ears, and the shadows under the daylight need our insightful eyes. Neither Foucault nor Confucius thought through the issue of the other, especially the feminine other. The relationship between self and other through differences cannot be fully articulated without understanding woman's otherness. Julia Kristeva claims the feminine other in the depth of the human psyche. Following her lead, I suggest that the psychic transformation of the personal is key for rethinking gender issues in rearticulating woman's space. A philosophical inquiry of the self needs to be complemented by a psycho-analytic analysis of gendered subjectivity in order to understand woman's alterity. Kristeva provocatively affirms that the way we form relationships with others is intimately linked to the ways we deal with our own (feminine) otherness and strangeness within. Can we reclaim our womanhood without sacrificing a relational and ecological sense of self, reality, and life? Can we shape the world differently by releasing the power of femininity that is also in the process of creation and re-creation? Can we imagine new visions of humanity and cosmology through listening to the call of the stranger that is woman? My cross-cultural inquiry of the self, without being fulfilled in male versions of the self, takes me to Julia Kristeva's discourse for an in-depth analysis of woman's strangeness, woman's creativity, and woman's self. Let us next listen carefully to ourselves through Kristeva's voice.

## Notes

1. *The Great Learning*, 1. These four Confucian classics, called the Four Books, were compiled by Zhu Xi, a Song Neo-Confucian master, who downplayed other classics.
2. I prefer to use the term "personal cultivation" rather than "self-cultivation," although both can be the direct translation of the ancient Chinese. I believe "personal cultivation" reflects better an embodied and holistic view of Confucianism, while "self-cultivation" has a trace of confining Confucianism within the Western framework of the self.
3. *The Great Learning*, 3.
4. *The Great Learning*, 1.
5. Quoted in Lin Yutang, *From Pagan to Christian*, p. 82. When translating ancient Chinese into English, sometimes I use translations made by Chinese scholars, which I feel are more suitable than mine, since my classical Chinese can fail me. When you notice the "quoted in" format introducing Chinese classical writings, it means that I have used another person's translation.
6. "Man," "woman," and "*ren*" (person/human being) in Chinese characters have different shapes and pronunciations. Sometimes I use "man" purposely to indicate the patriarchal implication of *ren*, especially in Neo-Confucian thought. The English terms "human" and "man" may have similar connotations.
7. I usually use the term "Way" instead of "Tao," referring to Confucian principle, in order to distinguish the different natures of Confucianism and Taoism. Taoists regard *Tao* as

more natural and cosmological, not ontologically related to the human; Confucians regard Way as more moral and imbued with human virtues. Here, because I am talking about the cosmological principle of union between self and universe, I use the term "Tao," although it is still not the same as in the Taoist *Tao*.

8.   Neo-Confucianism includes two branches, one focusing on Principle (*li*) and the other on Heart (*xin*). Both are new interpretations of Confucianism based upon morality and ethics. In this book, when I talk about Neo-Confucianism, I refer to the Neo-Confucian theory of Principle culminating in the Cheng brothers and epitomized in Zhu Xi.

# Chapter 4
# Woman as Stranger:
# Can Her Call Be Heard?

Water drained river             Lady in the woods
His exiled home                 Blessed by trees and birds
Building a wood cabin           Her laughter flows in the air
He is locked by the shadow      Tears are hidden
The smell of chocolate          Tears hidden, milk is bitter
Is so far away, untraceable     A flower lover
The taste of chocolate          She does not know how to balance
Is unreachable, forbidden       Sunshine to grow her own flower
The tyranny of the permitted    Without the spinning plate
The lure of the unknown         The alchemy of chocolate is gone
                    Tears of candle
                    Lighten the path
                    Traces of birds' songs
                    Linger the urge to fly beyond
                    The magic of chocolate
                    Through teacher's
                    Nourishing wor(l)d
                    Spinning play
                    Opens fountains inside of children
                    Flow out
                    Cries, laughter
                    And a new language
(Written after watching the movie Chocolat while reading Kristeva)[1]

The paternal and the maternal flow into the third, the psychic third, the social third, and toward a pedagogy through the third. The possibility of the loving third, however, depends upon the return of the repressed maternal—the stranger within the self—to vitalize (paternal) symbolic structure. Julia Kristeva asks us to hear the call from the feminine located at the boundary between body and language. When woman's estranged voices are expressed and heard, the world can be different. This chapter will use Kristeva's psy-choanalytic metaphor of the stranger to analyze the dynamics between the semiotic/maternal and the symbolic/paternal, and to understand the Kristevian subject in its fluidity, relationality, and creativity. I will also initiate a polyphonic dialogue with the psychoanalytic subject from a cross-cultural perspective. The chapter will end with a brief discussion of the impossibility of synthesis among Foucault, Confucius, and Kristeva.

## Between the Semiotic and the Symbolic: The Subject in Process

[L]et us know ourselves as unconscious, altered, other in order better to approach the universal otherness of the strangers that we are—for only strangeness is universal and such might be the post-Freudian expression of stoicism.

(Julia Kristeva, 1993a, p. 21)

Theory can "situate" such processes and relations [the semiotic and the symbolic] diachronically within the process of the constitution of the subject precisely because *they function synchronically within the signifying process of the subject himself.*

(Julia Kristeva, 1974, p. 29; emphasis in original)

If anything, psychoanalytic theory should point out how strange we are.

(Marla Morris, 2001, p. 56)

As an exiled intellectual and woman in France, Kristeva is concerned with the issues of stranger, foreigner, and estrangement throughout her works, either explicitly or implicitly. Her early works on heterogeneous semiotic and symbolic aspects of language already posit "the subject in process/on trial [*en procès*]" (1974, p. 22). This soon takes a psychoanalytic turn to the stranger within the self. While "stranger to ourselves" is universal to the human psyche, Kristeva believes that woman occupies a peculiar position in negotiating the psyche—due to her unique experience of the semiotic and possibly pregnancy and motherhood. She further articulates the role of woman as stranger (Kristeva, 1989, 1991), the singularity of woman-subject (Kristeva, 1995, 2000a), and maternity as an intersubjective and creative act (Kristeva, 1980, 1993b, 2000b). (I will discuss her analysis of woman's role more in detail in the next section.) In her later works, she also explicitly discusses political and ethical implications of the stranger within. These enable us to theorize social relationships, not as antithetical to the self, but as (a hidden) part of the self to lead us to a relationality based upon understanding and love, rather than denial and violence.

From both a linguistic and psychoanalytic viewpoint, Kristeva's formulation of the semiotic and the symbolic is revolutionary in destabilizing the subject through regenerating the crucial role of the maternal for the human psyche. For Kristeva (1974), the signifying process of language is composed of two inseparable elements: the semiotic and the symbolic. The semiotic refers to bodily drives, such as tones, rhythms, and traces, which are characterized by movement and instability. The pre-Oedipal, preverbal semiotic function of language is feminine and oriented to mother's body. On the other hand, the symbolic refers to the structure, grammar, or syntax of language. The symbolic function of language points to judgment and communication, which is necessarily social and historical. In contrast to the semiotic, the symbolic is characterized by structure and stasis. It is linked to the social order and, in psychoanalytic terms, paternal law.

The relationship between the semiotic and the symbolic in language is dynamic. The semiotic challenges the symbolic, while the symbolic regulates the semiotic. Interestingly, Kristeva interprets the semiotic as "soma-social" instead of "solely biological" (1974, p. 167). In other words, our earliest preverbal experiences are already situated in social and historical relationships, although these unspeakable experiences are not yet marked by words. Such a link is important for understanding how the semiotic participates in translating sensations, emotions, and feelings into signs. In her later psychoanalytic works, she (1995) reiterates that bodily drives always already carry meanings. The traditional dualism between the biological and the social is challenged here. By bringing the body back into language, Kristeva posits a fluid and relational subject.

In *Revolution in Poetic Language* (1974), Kristeva already links her semiotic and symbolic interpretations of language with psychoanalysis: "Our positing of the semiotic is obviously inseparable from a theory of the subject that takes into account the Freudian positing of the unconscious" (p. 30). The semiotic is the repressed, unconscious other, which has the potential to transgress the symbolic order—which is conscious social contract—by motility and polyvalence. Even though the semiotic is repressed, one's gestures, tones, tears, and laughter can indicate ineffable feelings and sensations unavailable to consciousness. To translate the semiotic into words or signs—as poetic language can accomplish—helps one to be in touch with the unconscious so that something innovative can be introduced into the symbolic.

The transition from the semiotic to the symbolic (Kristeva calls it "the thetic break"), as both Freud and Lacan theorize, is made possible by separation. However, for Kristeva, the thetic phase, has already happened in the pre-Oedipal situation in which bodily structures of separation precondition the child's entrance into language. Before infants reach the mirror stage or Oedipal struggle, their bodily experiences of expulsion and their first utterances, saturated by the semiotic, have already prepared them for a symbolic separation from the mother through language. "The child's first so-called holophrastic enunciations include gesture, the object, and vocal emission.... They are already thetic in the sense that they separate an object from the subject, and attribute to it a semiotic fragment, which thereby becomes a signifier" (Kristeva, 1974, p. 43).

In this way, Kristeva brings the semiotic into the psychic process of separation, which challenges the traditional psychoanalytic picture of the child's entrance into language and the social world as only a loss of connection with the maternal. On the other hand, she does refer to the ending of the thetic phase by separation from the maternal and transference of the "semiotic motility onto the symbolic order" (1974, p. 42). Undergoing the Oedipal stage of identity formation, the self usually suppresses the semiotic in order to move away from the maternal body and enter into the realm of the symbolic order. In this sense, the interplay between the unconscious and the conscious parallels the interaction between the semiotic and the symbolic.

As the semiotization of the symbolic, Art—poetry, music, dance, theater, literature—can play a role in connecting social structure and subversive mobility. Through a particular position of "within and against the social order" (Kristeva, 1974, p. 81), poetic language seeks to transform the very structure of the symbolic through the semiotic flux. Poetic representations are situated at the intersection between the body and the social, and they become one of the important bridges conveying human creativity into existence.

*Exhausted but sleepless, I am lying on the sofa. The soft music touches my face gently. Memory of the university lake whispers into my ears through the breeze. Images come and go. Words of books fade away into the shadow. But my own words come back, flowing through the intensity of the body, moving onto a blank sheet of paper. I love ancient Chinese poetry. The sound. The rhythms. The imagery. The mood. Yet I never really write any poetry in Chinese. Does my Chinese permeate through the movement of English which I am trying to speak? At the crossroads of two languages, the voice of the poetic emerges.*

The dialectic and interactive relationship between the semiotic and the symbolic, which Kristeva attempts to maintain, is complex, and her emphasis shifts as she describes different stages of self formation. Kristeva believes, the pre-Oedipal relationship between mother and child is something repressed but crucial for meaning making. Due to this necessity to recover affects, drives, and energy, the post-Oedipal stage of the subject can release more creative potential if the semiotic returns to renew signification. She turns to poetic language, psychoanalysis, and maternity for achieving this return. She affirms the necessity of establishing the symbolic to break away from the maternal through "the third party," which is paternal law. Although the semiotic/maternal is important for psychic fulfillment, the privilege of the symbolic/paternal in forming an (Oedipal) identity is indisputable for her. Kristeva's emphasis on the importance of the symbolic in directing and regulating powerful semiotic "horror" also happens coincidentally as she moves deeply into psychoanalysis. However, even in her later works, I would argue that Kristeva's introduction of the semiotic into psychoanalysis and her emphasis on the maternal function in initiating the child into language moves her beyond the traditional psychoanalytic frameworks which, by and large, privilege the symbolic/paternal role in an unproblematic way.

Kristeva (1993b) confronts what she calls "misinterpretation" of her work in an interview with Scott L. Malcomson. She argues: "I never felt that the semiotic and the symbolic could be separated. One cannot exist without the other; they are two aspects that are always combined in a sort of dialectic of mutual contradiction. If you isolate one of them, you have psychosis" (p. 183). While the symbolic structures the semiotic, the semiotic is the subversive and creative side of the symbolic. The split of the two, no matter which one is excluded, leads to psychic destruction. The pure semiotic is destructive because its dispersing energy excludes stability, while the pure symbolic is repressive because its fixed structure excludes fluidity. In her early articulation of the semiotic and the symbolic, Kristeva (1974) already affirms that these two modalities are both diachronically and synchronically situated in the signifying process, with synchronism being privileged. In this way, Kristeva depicts the human psyche as an open system in which the semiotic and the symbolic interact to engage a creative meaning-making process that upholds both structure and surprise.

Kristeva emphasizes the special potential of maternity in women's negotiation between the semiotic and the symbolic. Motherhood brings women's attention to the semiotic—the alterity of the symbolic law—so that transgression of the law becomes possible. The milk and tears of the maternal body "are the metaphors of nonspeech, of a 'semiotics' that linguistic communication does not account for" (1987a, p. 249). Motherhood, as I will discuss, provides a special zone in which women can get in touch with their own pre-Oedipal relationships with mother; yet, at the same time, they need to initiate and enable their children into the realm of the symbolic. The challenge for maternity is a challenge for human imagination and creativity.

*Mother throws herself onto the bed, crying. The first time I see her tears. Crying at her own mother's death. I have never seen any of my grandparents. Too far away. Before I could make it, they died. I did write to my paternal grandmother once to invite her to my parent's house since she was having a difficult time with her other son and his wife. Now Mom's mom passes away and I will never be able to see her. Mother's tears. Sorrowful eternal separation. A schoolgirl, horrified, I do not know what to do. I go over to her and pat her on the back and ask her softly: "Mama, do you want to have some fruit? I can buy some for you."*

Kristeva's discussion of the semiotic and maternal functions invites our efforts to reconceptualize the relationship between subject and other, or between the self and the stranger. When the semiotic as the repressed unconscious, the neglected other, or the rejected stranger returns after (Oedipal) identity, the stability of the subject is challenged. However, such a return is necessary; otherwise, the tyranny of Law would prevail and an exclusive society hostile to strangers—in other words, hostile to selves—would dominate. If, within the self, differences cannot coexist, can there be any possibility of relationships with others through mutual respect? The Kristevian self/other relationship is built upon acknowledging and utilizing the stranger within the self. The importance of the semiotic, however, cannot destroy the symbolic order, without which no society, no community, no loving relationship, no meaning of human life, and, subsequently, no self would exist. As a result, Kristeva is more concerned with the edges between the semiotic and symbolic, between self and alterity, between individual and society. Echoing Foucault's "limit attitudes" from another angle, Kristeva attempts to search for ways of preserving alterity, differences, and strangeness without breaking away from the necessary boundary of identity. The subject is constantly put on trial, and alterity within the subject mobilizes the self. In this process of mobilization, the asymmetrical relationship between the Kristevian semiotic and the symbolic (Kristeva, 1974) implies that what one may encounter in the other cannot be reduced to the sameness of the self, so the other can never be mastered. As Jung Lee (1999) points out, in its multiplication and complexity, the Kristevian stranger appears both within and outside of the self to destabilize the subject from various angles. Or, to use Kristeva's (2000a) own terms, the subject is made possible in "a space of interlocking alterities" and through "plural decentering" (p. 67).

Kristeva (1991) returns to Greek myths and finds that the first foreigner was a woman. Beloved by Zeus, Io was exiled by his jealous wife, Hera. She wandered from Europe to Asia and ended up in Egypt, where she received permission from Zeus to give birth to a son. While pondering whether Io's story is the feminine version of Oedipus' drama, Kristeva traces how her descendents as foreign women—the Danaides—made possible a new social structure (exogamous society) by incorporating strangeness (foreignness). Women as foreigners and strangers expanded the horizon of the ancient civilization. At the same time, however, Kristeva (1993a) argues that women might be strangers to themselves too:

> The idea that the feminine is disquieting and strange is a Freudian idea, in his text on the uncanny. As for me, I've argued that the feminine is an unrepresentable passion, a rebel passion, that it's something uncanny for men *and* for women. Women are wary of their femininity; they have many difficulties in gaining access to their femininity. Even if feminists say, "We are women!" and give their femininity a virile form, it is very troubling to be in contact and in sympathy with femininity—for men and women. (p. 181)

Kristeva emphasizes the difficulty women encounter in getting in touch with their own strangeness. Part of the reason lies in the social contract: men can eroticize the maternal object while women are banned from the maternal body. When woman triumphantly negotiates between the semiotic and the symbolic, however, her coming to terms with the feminine bestows on her "a psychic potential greater than what is demanded of the male sex" (Kristeva, 1989, p. 30). But questions remain: How can we transform this "rebel passion," this disturbing strangeness, into a power to expand (not to destroy) the horizon of humanity? What is the feminine after all?

*As I pursue my path in the academic world, the whisper of a little girl with wide-open, sympathetic, and caring eyes gradually falls into silence. Until I hear her call, until my tears come back to sweeten the milk, ironically, it is still writing, though perhaps in a different style, that can make me feel at ease. But with the return of that tender voice and bittersweet milk, will anything else slip into the repressed? Could I ever know the stranger in me? or get in touch with her? or him? or s/he?*[2]

### Between Matricide and Creative Motherhood:
### Woman, Mother, and Self-Other

> Women have the luck and the responsibility of being boundary-subjects: body and thought, biology and language, personal identity and dissemination during childhood, origin and judgment, nation and world—more dramatically so than men are ....The maturity of the second sex will be judged in coming years according to its ability to...[orient] toward a still unforeseeable conception of a polyvalent community.
>
> (Julia Kristeva, 1993a, p. 35)

> For man and for woman the loss of the mother is a biological and psychic necessity, the first step on the way to becoming autonomous. Matricide is our vital necessity, the sine-qua-non condition of our individuation, provided that it takes place under optimal circumstances and can be eroticized. . . .
>
>                                                        (Julia Kristeva, 1989, p. 28)

Kristeva (1977b, 1993b, 1996) never hesitates to say that there are dangers within feminist movements, although she does not deny that she is involved in feminism from time to time as a woman who envisages the world differently. She outlines three generations of feminism (Kristeva, 1977b). The first generation is the feminism of struggling for equal rights between men and women. While this movement is instrumental in securing women more legal rights than before, it erases women's *differences* by inserting women into men's history. The second generation intends to restore women's differences in order to challenge the phallic order. Though women are recognized for their own sake, there is a tendency toward an essentialized call for the feminine opposite to the masculine. Both are problematic for Kristeva. She insists that the singularity of woman as creator is manifested by her unique reappropriation of, rather than the simple rejection of, the symbolic through a semiotic investment in language.

In her vision, the third generation of feminism, with which she is affiliated, not only provides a generative space for an individual woman's unique expression of herself. It also challenges the very notion of a stable identity, especially sexual identity. So comes her question: "[Will feminism] manage to rid itself of its belief in Woman, Her power, and Her writing and support instead the singularity of each woman, her complexities, her many languages, at the cost of a single horizon, of a single perspective, of faith?" (p. 221).

Kristeva's critiques of the first and second generations of feminism are related to her belief in a balanced relation between the semiotic and the symbolic. Assimilation into the symbolic/paternal law without semiotic motility is as unsatisfactory as the retreat into the semiotic/maternal continent without actively participating in the transformation of the symbolic. Although both movements have indeed contributed to the improvement of women's status in society, both are vulnerable to the possibility of further alienating the feminine. Woman's *simultaneous* investment in her body, language, and imagination is crucial for fulfilling her fluid subjectivity.

Kristeva (1996) believes that the intellectual realm is one in which women can participate and through which they can create "new objects of thought" (p. 124). This is a knowledge which men may have difficulty accessing. This adventure has its own specificity in women's sensitivity to the archaic mother/child bond. Paradoxically, breaking this bond may evoke more violent effort on the part of woman to drive toward the symbolic, although the realm of the symbolic does not necessarily welcome her coming. Woman's marginal position at the intersection between body and language, like the status of a foreigner, exiles her from both paternal law and maternal intimacy. In discussing the intellectual as dissident, Kristeva (1986) describes the peculiar status of being a woman:

> A woman is trapped within the frontier of her body and even of her species, and consequently always feels *exiled* both by the general clichés that make up a common consensus and by the very powers of generalization intrinsic to language. This female exile in relation to the General and to Meaning is such that a woman is always singular, to the point where she comes to represent the singularity of the singular— the fragmentation, the drive, the unnamable. (p. 296; emphasis in original)

Is it possible for woman to overcome her own estrangement to language by embodying the unnamable and reorganizing the psychic structure through a new space of reading and writing? The effort of an intellectual woman to think the unthinkable and represent the unrepresentable takes us toward the unknown—an unknown world of plural singularity. Woman's strangeness inside needs to be recognized by both herself and others so that femininity in society can be transformed into a creative site.

*A literature activity group gathering at school. Everyone gives their own life creed. A caretaker among my peers, I claim that "to give is happier than to take." Applause from everyone (especially my male classmates) except one girl—brilliant and intelligent—who is suspicious. She asks me: "Are you going to remain this selfless?" She goes to a very prestigious university later on. Then I hear that she tried to commit suicide (fortunately without success) because of a reason unknown to me. Has her strong sense of the self bumped into a wall harder than the structure of the wood cabin, or has she lost the magical ability to balance sunshine? Going through my own identity storm, I often think of her and quietly wish her well after her recovery.*

Writing through and about her own passions, desires, and energies rather than cold logic, woman may be able to negotiate her difficult passages between the maternal and the paternal to create new forms of knowledge— artistic or intellectual. Like an artist, woman writes as she paints so that color inspires; she composes so that rhythm flows. While Miglena Nikolchina (1991) argues that Kristeva believes "language is the homelessness of being" (p. 235), I have a different reading due to her efforts to recover the semiotic in language. If body does not have to be an opposite to language, woman's exile from words can be navigated through her sensual bodily experiences toward creating new thoughts. In this way, language is not necessarily homeless but destabilized, a mobile home in a process of reconstruction. To achieve this end, woman can become a "female voyager" so that "her constant moving from place to place that enables her to view everything as strange may actually help her to mediate more productively the relation between body and language" (Smith, 1996, p. 59). Such a journey beyond is not necessarily physical but can be (inter)textual, if we think about how Emily Dickinson created extraordinary poetry beyond the confinement of her time while physically staying at home.

*His tyranny is devastating. Yet He is weak too, powerless. Her power is suffocating. Yet She is loving too, sorrowful. Under the clashes between the two, one may run away, to flee, to seek another world. Yet in another world, He and She do not disappear but multiply. Without belongings, the traveler nevertheless brings the treasures of the study along the road. Writing is neither Hers nor His, so can't one write through both Her and Him to reach a Third? Through absence of both? Challenging the tyranny of the permitted and engaging the alchemy of chocolate, could one ever write through this space of present absence, becoming oneself?*

Woman's close tie to instinctual drives, on the other hand, makes it more difficult for her to work through separation and differentiation in establishing an Oedipal identity. The social taboo against eroticizing mother for women and the implication of certain self-rejection in women's turning away from the maternal create double difficulty. However, regression into the blissful pre-Oedipal fusion with the archaic mother or the inability to mourn the lost mother is destructive to forming one's independent sense of the self. In her studies of female depression, Kristeva (1989) points out how a third party—the symbolic, the father—is crucial for woman to achieve autonomy from mother. So comes Kristeva's "matricide is our vital necessity" (p. 27). (As we will see later on, such a claim provokes strong critiques from some feminist theorists.) Kristeva also suggests that such a matricide must be coupled with the return of the semiotic for the psychic well-being of woman (and man). Woman's simultaneous "identification with and revolt against the symbolic order" (Smith, 1998) provides her a unique strategy for traveling between the semiotic and the symbolic and coming out anew.

The return of the semiotic can be achieved by motherhood. Especially after her son's birth, Kristeva gives maternity a very important position in thinking about creative womanhood. Maternal love which both sustains and destabilizes identity "is at the heart of all loving relationships" (Kristeva, 1996, p. 62). In pregnancy and motherhood, woman's relationship with meaning and the other is transformed by a simultaneous embodiment of the child in herself and attention to the child as a subject. Such an interdependent yet respectful relationship with each other in a new motherhood can become a creative act. The other (the child)'s capacity for surprising and out-growing the mother is not only acknowledged but also encouraged, so that the unknown in the other is not threatening, but presents the potential for the child's authoring of her own life.

The influx of the semiotic experiences in maternity also connects women across generations. Motherhood helps a woman get in touch with her primary memory of, and archaic relationship with, her mother so that resis-tance against the closure and stasis of the symbolic becomes stronger. Through a "reunion" with her mother in pregnancy and childbirth, woman also relives her childhood with her own child through love. Such a notion of the maternal body as the location of creativity and *jouissance* in femininity challenges the Freudian interpretation of childbirth as penis envy, which Kristeva calls male phantasm. Maternity, through its *differences* from the paternal rather than a reduced duplication or imitation of the father, points to women's own potential to create through both union and separation.

For Kristeva, "the maternal body is the module of a biosocial program" (1980, p. 241). Sociality is always already imprinted in the body of a sym-bolizing subject. Contrary to criticisms that Kristeva reduces the maternal to the biological (Butler, 1989), Kristeva suggests that a successful mother is a woman who not only takes care of the child but also has her own "third party," which, in turn, helps the child enter the social realm with less diffi-culty. "If maternity is to be guilt-free, this journey needs to be undertaken without masochism and without annihilating one's affective, intellectual, and professional personality, either. In this way, maternity becomes a true *creative act*, something that we have not yet been able to imagine" (1995, p. 220; emphasis in original). This potential of maternity seems to me, crea-tive as it is, to be greatly constrained by existing social, political, and gen-dered structures. How many women have enough institutional and emotional support to have a successful professional life while being a fulfilling mo-ther?

*Mengmeng, my nephew, likes to play with me. I am not only fond of him but also amazed by him. To watch how he grows from that little creature in the crib fills me with awe, affection, and love. I still remember the moment when I taught him to say "not have" with a big panda toy hiding behind him or showing before his eyes. His sound, so soft, his gaze, hazy but with con-centration, and his imitation, quite accurate and tirelessly repetitive, fasci-nate me beyond what I can describe. When he can speak, he is always eager to tell me something whenever I am around. I listen to him, patiently. I play with him. I tell him stories I have told him again and again lying beside him, and he corrects me whenever there is any inconsistency. He knows when to go down on the floor when I am too tired to carry him anymore: "Auntie, I will walk." He also knows how to upset me when he feels I deserve "pun-ishment." That cunning smile on the face of a little boy! Now Mengmeng's big dream is to come to the United States as a graduate student.*

For Kristeva, separation and bonding are both necessary to form loving relationships: "My knowledge that I can leave is what enables us to be to-gether" (1996, p. 75). This sense of both leaving and togetherness brings a necessary interaction between psychic instability and stability. In terms of maternal love, an appropriate distance between mother and child is impor-tant in order to leave a certain space for symbolic elaboration. Such is the love which the mother offers the child—freedom to explore and growth into independence. Love and freedom can meet each other in a loving maternal relationship, though with much difficulty psychologically, historically, and socially, as with any other form of love embedded in the acceptance of the other's *differences*.

Between matricide and creative motherhood, Kristeva maintains a deli-cate balance. Standing on the tenuous line of this link, she opens herself to strong criticism from feminists who regard the necessity of matricide as po-litically reactionary and the mother ideal as normalizing compulsive hetero-sexuality. In criticizing *Black Sun*, Janice Doane and Devon Hodges (1992) assert that Kristeva assumes that "for women the relation to a primary ma-ternal object is particularly dangerous and an identification with a paternal object is particularly beneficial" (p. 65). I find Kristeva's analysis of female depression cases in *Black Sun*, which always traces the clients' symptoms back to early trauma in mother–daughter relationships, a bit unsettling. Such an analysis not only implies the literal, rather than metaphorical, meaning of the maternal but also leaves out the role of the father, although mother–father interactions in social contexts certainly have an important impact on the way the mother interacts with the child. However, reducing the complex-ity of the issues that Kristeva attempts to address to the simple accusation that she valorizes the paternal while downplaying the maternal is misleading.

Matricide is a metaphorical way of speaking about the necessity of mov-ing away from dependence on the maternal body in archaic relationships—which is not the same as any concrete maternal relationship that a mother has with her child—in order to establish the psychic capacity. It does not imply the devaluation of woman's status. While claiming independence from mother is crucial for both boys and girls, Kristeva does point out the particular difficulty of achieving matricide—a term to which I will return—on the woman's part. But this difficulty is not Kristeva's "creation," I would argue, but is a part of the psychic reality which is embedded in women's *differences* in experiencing sexuality. Claiming these differences can help rather than damage our ongoing efforts to expand spaces for femininity based upon our specificity. In understanding woman's psychic experiences as different from man's, Kristeva quickly draws our attention to the greater psychic power that woman has demonstrated in her struggles to achieve independence. She further points out that woman may have greater potential to renew language than man due to the closer relations that woman has with the semiotic flux. In other words, woman's differences bring both danger and inspiration; danger itself can nourish creativity.

The advocacy of matricide sounds contradictory to the valuation of motherhood, yet, again, the "in between" space as the site for the birth of creativity is Kristeva's concern with, just as she attempts to negotiate the passage between the semiotic and the symbolic. A successful mother builds a bridge between body and language so that both she and the child can travel back and forth. Due to the crucial role of mother at the crossroads, a mother's ability to make it possible to let the child go and let herself grow becomes a creative process. The special status of maternity in Kristeva's discourse, as I read it, challenges us to rethink woman's psychic power in offering an alternative path to symbolic violence. If the traditionally devalued "profession" of woman—motherhood—as "an irreplaceable vocation" (Kristeva, 1999, p. 403) actually offers us a way to transcend "the wholesale automation of human beings" (p. 402) which threatens contemporary society as Kristeva sees it, her intentions of valorizing motherhood are clear. Such a mother is impossible without a working-through of her own loss, or, in Kristeva's terms, matricide initiates her capacity to claim her own maternity. Without cultivating her own independence, a mother may be indifferent to the child, or may be bound too closely to the child, or may hate the child, none of which can lead to creative maternal relationships. Meanwhile, Kristeva's reappropriation of maternity does not lead to compulsory motherhood, as she has affirmed of woman's right to create her own style of writing and living. In her latest efforts to write about female geniuses, Kristeva calls for "feminine specificity or freedom that is not based on seduction—which means not based on reproduction and consumption" (p. 402). Kristeva does not advocate the reproductive functions of mothering, especially when motherhood serves the needs of compulsory heterosexuality and patriarchy. She is concerned with the creativity of motherhood. Between matricide and creative motherhood resides the central issue of claiming both independence and relationality to nurture creativity. Furthermore, if we take the maternal at the metaphorical level, as Kristeva (1996) asserts, I would argue that the potential of maternity can be embodied in many creative activities in which we are engaged—pedagogy is one. We give birth not only to babies.

Reiterating the ideal of motherhood, Kristeva (1996) talks about the relationship between self and other as a space in which loving interdependence

and autonomy interact and transform each other. She also suggests the possibility of a "paradoxical community" in which

> We try to help one another, all. But not a community that unifies and banalizes. We
> recognize one another, as foreigners, strangers. That is to say, as weak, that is to say,
> as potentially sick. And it is by being able to hear the other as tracked by some pa-
> thology, by some anomaly, as I myself am, that I refuse to see in the other an en-
> emy. And this would be a basis for a form of morality. (p. 41)

Such a consciousness of and willingness to be with others through our
own weakness and suffering indicates the ethic of a compassionate self-other
relationship, implied by both a loving motherhood and a singular womanhood, which makes living together less violent and more mutually respectful. In *Nation without Nationalism,* Kristeva (1993a) characterizes this
community as *polyvalent.*

Echoing Foucault's aesthetics of self-care but talking about woman this
time, Kristeva calls for "a permanent vigilance and a constant working on
oneself" (1996, p. 126). Women's struggles to get in touch with their own
femininity as the source of creation are particularly difficult and painful.
However, through pain, weakness, and even pathology, woman as stranger
can be more open to others who are particularly marked by other forms of
strangeness and marginality. In alliance with other minority groups in society, woman has a unique stake in reconstructing society and politics. And
this compassion, rather than hostility, toward the other becomes a cornerstone upon which a community connected by love and destabilized by freedom can be built.

*At school, I had a classmate who was very disruptive to the class. His
tablemate refused to team with him anymore and no one wanted to sit beside
him. (In Chinese classrooms, one boy and one girl are paired to share one
table, resulting in an endless game of the middle line which is not supposed
to be crossed.) As shy as I was, I volunteered to sit with him at the same table, smiling away others' sneers. I simply did not believe that a schoolboy
could be so bad as to deserve to be excluded by others. Though my kindness
softened his temper, he still did not make his way into a privileged high
school. He did manage to enter college though. When he visited me at home
during a college holiday, I was startled: He had grown into a man of intimi-
dating size and shape. However, his manner was much milder and he looked
much happier. He told me with that funny look that he was popular among
his classmates. I secretly asked myself: Would I ever be brave enough to approach him with the same kindness and the same faith in him if he had
turned into a violent and aggressive man? However, doesn't the show of*

*violence and aggression hide the inner softness and the wounded desire for love? And what can the possible repression of one's aggressive drive do to oneself if polite smiles and guarded detachment elude others' attention? Is aggression part of human life not only psychically but also socially? How can we live with it without destruction if we cannot get rid of it completely? Can a simple openness to the stranger inside be constructive enough? Can we create an ethics or morality beyond a mutual acceptance and respect for each other (and internally the self)?*

An ethics of both love and freedom through the strange site of otherness, according to Kristeva, is necessary for a creative selfhood in a global society in which the issue of foreigners must be confronted. In the ideal of "nations without nationalism," Kristeva envisages a new world without rigid national boundaries but does not give up national identity, in which foreigners are not treated as foreigners but their differences can be recognized and accepted. Just like a good mother who respects the fact that her child will become a person she may not expect, one needs to allow the other to surprise, even if the other's otherness does not coincide with one's own sense of the self. Such a relationship between self and other, based upon both compassion and alterity, expands one's psychic space to incorporate differences, enabling one to respond to others in a mutually sustainable way. Envisaging a community in which the stranger within and the stranger without are welcome, the Kristevian self-other relationship is constantly in movement just as the subject in process is engaged in an ongoing creative process.

## Im/possibility of a Loving Third

*Tremble*
*of my heart*
*in touching the returned*
*Moves with your words*

*Freedom*
*of my fingers*
*in writing the unbearable*
*Flows from your smiles*

*Silence*
*of my mind*
*in saturating the courage to speak*
*stirs from your tender whispers*

> *My stranger*
> *traveler's guide*
> *in the distance*
> *yet near*
> *blinks steady messages in the dark*
> *I am led out*
> *through the dark*
> *without much fear*
> *the lure of another horizon*

*The loving third leads me out, brings me back, and meets my eyes gently. She is a man who smiles through words. He is a woman who writes through the loss. She sets foot to venture out but stretches her hands back to connect. He returns but does not stay. Her laughter vibrates through both here and there toward a new space, both yesterday and today into another day. The loving third between the maternal and the paternal. The loving third between the semiotic and the symbolic. Bringing the body into the language, she creates the wor(l)d. Imbuing discourses with affects, he traverses the Law. The stranger sings, luring travelers to journey beyond.*

In *Tales of Love*, Kristeva utilizes the new system theory to understand the heterogeneity of desire and discourse in a stabilizing–destabilizing dynamic between "the chaotic hyperconnectedness of the fusion of love" and "the death-dealing stabilization of love's absence" to sustain the openness of the psyche in its own self-organization (1987a, p. 15). This permanent stabilization–destabilization between the symbolic and the semiotic is made possible through love in general, and through psychoanalytic transferential love in particular. For Kristeva, the function of love is for renewal and rebirth. This loving space as the third, beyond the wrapping of the maternal flux and the rigidity of the paternal structure, is a generative site for inscribing the "complexification" (Kristeva, 2002, p. 268) of humanity through body, soul, and mind.

In *Intimate Revolt,* Kristeva (2002) rearticulates the notion of the semiotic and its relation with language. She uses the term "transverbal" to clarify the confusion caused by the term "preverbal" she first used to articulate the notion of the semiotic. She says,

> I say transverbal, for to say preverbal leads to confusion: the semiotic is not independent of language; it interferes with language, and under its domination, articulates other arrangements of meaning, which are not significations, but rhythmic, melodic articulations. (p. 259)

Referring the semiotic to the translinguistic unconscious, Kristeva reaffirms her position at the border between drives and representation, the unconscious and the conscious, the maternal and the paternal, and biology and psyche in their *interactions* through *both* irreducible heterogeneity *and* connected coexistence. The semiotic is not outside of language, yet it is the force that cannot be mastered merely by significations. It defies normative representation. The semiotic coexists with the symbolic in language, yet it is the *differences* between the two that make the signifying process alive. Between the semiotic and the symbolic, the third space of creativity sustained by both the maternal position of holding and the paternal position of differentiation is made possible through love.

Interestingly, in *Tales of Love*, and in other works, Kristeva attempts to regenerate this loving third in Freud's notion of "the father of individual prehistory" (1987a, p. 22), the imaginary father. This image of father, different from the stern Oedipal father, combines the functions of both mother and father, which Kristeva refers to as "loving father." As the archaic disposition of the paternal function, the imaginary father precedes the name, the symbolic, and the "mirror stage," which "introduces the Third Party as a condition of psychic life, to the extent that it is a loving life" (p. 34). At the same time, the maternal position of directing toward this third party is crucial for the child to enter into the world of discourse. When Kristeva introduces the term "the loving third," she refers to the necessity of moving away from the mother/child dyad. This is similar to her paradoxical ideal of maternity in expanding psychic space while at the same time advocating "matricide." She does bring the maternal function of holding into this paternal image, while at the same time pointing out the link between the Oedipal father and the archaic father:

> The supporting father of such a symbolic triumph is not the Oedipal father but truly that "imaginary father," "father in individual prehistory" according to Freud, who guarantees primary identification. Nevertheless, it is imperative that this father in individual prehistory be capable of playing his part as Oedipal father in symbolic Law, for it is on the basis of that harmonious blending of the two facets of fatherhood that the abstract and arbitrary signs of communication may be fortunate enough to be tied to the affective meaning of prehistorical identifications, and the ideal language of the potentially depressive person can arrive at a live meaning in the bond with others. (1989, pp. 23-4)

In articulating the imaginary father, Kristeva (1987a) points out the multiplicity of fatherhood and further argues that the crisis in paternity is in fact "an erosion of the loving father" (p. 379). By introducing love into paternity, Kristeva questions the whole arrangement of social structure through the paternal and attempts to endow the human psyche with a certain sense of agency through primary identification with the imaginary father. At the same time, parallel with her efforts to regenerate the loving paternal function, Kristeva (2001) reads Melanie Klein's notion of matricide not only as pain (a "depressive position") but also as creativity. The *desire* for knowledge is essentially feminine, and the potential for creating new thoughts is registered in the maternal. In this way, the paternal embraces love while the maternal initiates knowing. In other words, the paternal and the maternal walk toward each other while the conceptual heterogeneity of each prevents them from falling into fusion. However, neither Klein nor Kristeva is ambivalent about the necessity of breaking away from the maternal in order to form one's ego.

Although we can "remain prisoners of the archaic mother" (Kristeva, 1987a, p. 42), I would argue that we can be locked up by the paternal too. The mayor in the movie *Chocalat* (1999) is a good example of a prisoner of the (Oedipal) father. Without having to choose which prison is better, I would like to read Kristeva's loving third as the third beyond—and also embodied in—both the maternal and the paternal. The role of the archaic father as having both maternal and paternal functions in the Kristevian psychic world already asks us to negotiate between the two functions. As Kelly Oliver (2002a) argues, "Kristeva's imaginary father can be read as part of [the] patriarchal tradition; or, as I am trying to do, it can be read against it" (p. 53). Following Oliver's preference for not associating the loving third with the father or the paternal, I will read Kristeva's discourse about the imaginary father as articulating a third space which is both psychic and social, in which the unconscious semiotic and the conscious symbolic, affects and representation, and the somatic and the cultural move toward each other, yet remain apart, in order to make the creativity of both possible. This reading is also an organic part of my search for a third space of mutual transformation to invent new subjectivities. This space is generated by the tensions between the double orientations of the maternal and the paternal and further forms its own creative dynamics. It not only is embedded in the conflicting double but also reaches a new space beyond an in-between position. In other words, both maternity and paternity are valued, but also transcended to reach a third space. Refusing to locate the third in the paternal deprives paternal authority of its founding role.

*My mouth is shut, desiring nothing. The steam of delicious rice makes me nauseous. I can't take it into my body. The stacks of books in the library, like cold clouds, press down on my head. I can't take them into my mind. I want to run away, but I cannot set my feet free. I am bonded. I cannot leave, neither can I stay. Connection is lost. Meaning is gone. Until your gentle utterance shines on me, my loving third, breathing intimate words into the depths of my heart.*

In psychoanalysis, situated at the crossroads of the unconscious and the conscious, transferential love enables the analysand to reformulate his/her psychic structure by working through the suffering of separation. Just like a good mother, or the imaginary father, the analyst lovingly and patiently holds the analysand as s/he painfully becomes conscious of what is repressed, while at the same time the analyst brings her/him to articulate the suffering. There is "not just a suspension of judgment but a giving of meaning, beyond judgment, within transference/countertransference" (Kristeva, 2002, p. 12). This giving of meaning does not (only) refer to intellectual mastery but must connect to the analysand's affects. By building such bridges, psychic rebirth is possible. This dynamic combination of holding and meaning through the endurance of loss, at the borders of the conscious/unconscious, the psychical/biological, the energetic/hermeneutic, drive/representation, time/"the timeless" (sustained in the archaic memory) is the loving third space of analytic work.

Holding enables meaning, which is dramatized at the end of the analytic relationship by the demand that the analysand keeps going by herself. At the same time, meaning is embedded in the bond of love. Without one or the other, it is impossible to reestablish the psychic space. Transferential love as an open system aims to make that which is terminated at the end of the analysis interminable. Kristeva (2002) phrases it as "moving forward in the time of becoming conscious" (p. 40). The disappearance of the analyst leads to, ideally, the emergence of loving relationships re-created by the analysand in living with others. "To recapture memory would be to create it by creating new words and thoughts" (2002, p. 57), which is an endless process of healing and meaning making. Claudia Eppert (2000) also phrases learning practice as "interminable" through one's "responsible engagements with others" (p. 214) and self.

Transferential love, the creative relationships of maternity, or a loving father, as Kristeva shows, has provocative pedagogical implications. In bringing students to the structure of various subjects, can we create a loving third space in which they can connect their desires and command of the subjects? What will be a teaching position that suspends judgment yet still guides students in a journey of meaning making? Is it possible to teach in order not to teach, so that students can travel themselves? What learning can be enabled by a pedagogy of listening through the loving ears and eyes of the teacher? Can we create an educative community in which many of us participate in one another's meaning-making process as the third?

Wendy Atwell-Vasey (1998a, 1998b) calls for bringing nourishing words back to schools from their exile in standards, formulas, and grammar structures. Mary Aswell Doll (2000), Susan Edgerton (1996), and Maxine Greene (1995) all emphasize the role of imagination, aesthetic experience, and narratives in the classroom, reflecting Kristeva's privileging of poetic language in bridging the maternal and the paternal. Kristeva (1996) also discusses the role of the teacher in bringing out the unknown in students. To reflect back to students their own unknown desires and emotions, the teacher encourages students to move beyond the given. This is parallel to what Kristeva refers to as becoming conscious of the unconscious: In attending to the unknown, students' psychic spaces are expanded, while the unknown keeps slipping away and refuses to be mastered. This encounter with the semiotic is an important aspect of educative experience that is usually neglected in our schools and that asks for the art of pedagogical listening. William Pinar (2001) formulates *currere* as "an autobiographics of alterity" (p. 2), which—especially situated in the fabrication of (white) manhood in the United States—calls for "re-experiencing that pre-Oedipal relation with the 'mother'" (p. 12). This reexperiencing of the maternal is a necessary step in breaking down the fixation on paternal authority. The destabilizing power of the semiotic, when it returns through *currere*, moves students (and the teacher) toward the limit of the social and the personal to open new possibilities.

Here the metaphor of the spinning plate, borrowed from the movie *Chocolat*, might be helpful for thinking about how pedagogy negotiates between the semiotic and the symbolic. The spinning plate (inherited from the maternal line) is used by the heroine to "read" the unknown desires of the townspeople who are her customers, so that she can find a particular type of chocolate, "surprising" them with a perfect match. When the plate begins to spin, she asks the townspeople to *articulate* what they see on the plate. Through the unconscious, imagination, and words, they project their feelings onto the plate. According to the images that her customers describe, the heroine matches them to a chocolate. Here chocolate serves as a catalyst, helping people get in touch with what is repressed through smell, color, shape, taste, and the words that are connected to affects. The return of the semiotic eventually moves the townspeople out of their old-fashioned way of life. For me, the spinning plate symbolizes a successful pedagogy, as it opens the semiotic flux within children and facilitates their meaningful play with the symbolic structure. This (spinning) play between the semiotic and the symbolic is what we need to bring into the classroom.

The pedagogical relationships between teachers and students are crucial in building bridges and initiating play. In articulating the ethics of radical alterity and irreducible particularity, jan jagodzinski (2002) draws our attention to "an *asymmetry* in the human relation" (p. 85; emphasis in original). This asymmetrical relationship acknowledges the unknowable so that the other is affirmed through its own alterity and independence. This is similar to what Kristeva argues for psychoanalytic relationships in which the analysand has become able to encounter the uncertainty of life through the analyst's respect for the alterity of the analysand. As jagodzinski (2002) argues, the teacher plays the pedagogical role of a third party which orients students to the alterity of the text, while the teacher persistently "holds" students in their encounter with the newness of the text. During this process, the teacher has to confront his or her own mastery anxiety and fear of becoming *other*. Undoubtedly, this is a difficult position for the teacher—as difficult as, if not more difficult than, the students' navigation:

> We are confronted with an alterity that we are unable to master completely, hence it seems teachers devise all kinds of means to disavow and avoid the possibility of facing this "moment" of alterity, a moment that is fraught with anxiety in the sense that it throws the legitimacy of what we are doing to our students in the name of education into question. (jagodzinski, 2002, p. 86)

What may happen if we let go the efforts to master the unmasterable? What does that demand of the teacher? Can we "hold" students as long as they need us while we ourselves need to be held for our own transformation? Who or what can become the teacher's loving third so that she can sustain this journey of traveling in and through the third space together with her students? As the image of the teacher is, more often than not, associated with women who are still under social constraints, it becomes paradoxical to ask women teachers to dance on the thin line between the maternal and the paternal.

Being an educator in an American university classroom, I have often been struck by a certain sense of helplessness from students who are teachers, administrators, or future professors. Trapped by the current campaign for standards, criteria, and the procedural, they often feel that they can do nothing, as schools are controlled by multiple forces, alien to educative possibilities. While I encourage them to think about how to play *with* rather than merely *within* all kinds of "institutional constraints"—a term Foucault uses—students' profound sense of not being able to move within the current social spaces does raise the question about what can make the loving third psychic space possible, socially and culturally. This is an inevitable political and ethical question, one which might be particularly painful for those who, for some reason, stay at the margin. Their difficult negotiations may be blocked due to the lack of supportive social spaces.

*More often than not, I feel myself in such an antithesis to American culture when I watch TV, at parties, in classes, at academic conferences, in American families. Or when I want to be quiet but am expected to speak, when I am feeling bad but need to say "I am fine," when I am embarrassed but supposed to say "Thank you," when I stay in a big house alone but want some company. I can be bitter, too, as I witness how China is portrayed explicitly or implicitly as an enemy, even in this supposedly post–Cold War age. The United States seems to be constantly at war: not only at war with enemies, drugs, and crime, but also at war with its own schools, its children's academic scores, and environmental issues. However, I am staying here. Can I say that differences can be charming and strangeness can be refreshing, and even antitheses can be illuminating? Youthful spirit. Laughter. Articulate brilliance. Energy. Expressive openness. I remain fascinated, yet with a certain bitterness. I am learning, though, that the enemy is within the self too. When antithesis does not lead to war, I am searching, searching for the impossible possibility of the loving third between where I am from and where I am now, not only psychically but also socially.*

Kelly Oliver (2002a) suggests that the lack of social support makes the split between words and affects difficult to overcome, and maternal depression a social melancholy instead of individual pathology. "There is no social space within which maternal affects can be articulated or heard within a culture that devalues, even abjects, the maternal body" (p. 51). The unspoken is a result of social marginalization. Oliver argues that the sociality of an individual starts with birth, and that the mother/child relationship is always mediated and marked by the social. We can see here the differences between the archaic maternal fusion—which Kristeva claims must be broken away from in order to become an independent person—and a concrete maternal relationship which is already situated in social spaces, although the two are also interrelated. The creative potential of maternity, as Kristeva describes, is difficult, if not impossible, to achieve without social spaces that build the bridges between drives/affects and words/symbols, enabling woman's articulation of her unique experiences.

Oliver's argument for a loving third social space is particularly appealing to me. Although Doane and Hodges' (1992) interpretation that Kristeva blames the mother for social pathology is a misreading, I do argue that Kristeva's analysis of maternal depression as the source of individual pathology needs to be coupled with a social analysis of women and maternity so that what makes the mother become depressive can be brought to light. If the social space does not become the loving third, the struggles of the psyche can only be intensified. The failure of psychic space is already implicated in the failure of social space. When the analysand leaves the analytic relationship, the loving third played by the analyst is no longer present. This absence makes supportive social relationships necessary (which might be lacking for the analysand in the first place), in order to provide the nurturing interdependence for the analysand's independence. Thus social injustice and suffering must be encountered in revitalizing psychic life. Pinar (1991, 2001) understands curriculum as social psychoanalysis in which the human psyche is always implicated in the social and the cultural. In their struggles in "seeking passage" (Martusewicz, 2001) and creating the loving third space for students and with students, women teachers need loving social space which, in turn, sustains their own open psychic space. Paradoxically, social transformation is mutually dependent upon psychic transformation (Kristeva, 1996; Pinar, 2001), which makes negotiation between these two spaces vital, although difficult.

*Exhausted after teaching the night class, I return to my apartment. I know a sleepless night is ahead of me. I pull out a book written in a narrative form about multicultural education and read it through the night, marking pages I may use for the class. My mind keeps slipping away to the class that I just taught. It was a disaster. Why did students have so much difficulty in "seeing" what is in front of them? Did they know or not know what is behind their forceful rational arguments? Narratives did not work for them either. Why couldn't I as the teacher keep my patience in the class, confronting what I would call "American maleness" (without any attempt on my part to make generalizations)? I certainly cannot blame students, but where am I stuck? A lonely night of reading, torn apart by unspeakable pains. How long can I do this? Should I just pack up to get out of here and go back home? How can this help me to negotiate a pedagogical space in which I would like to dwell? Isn't what is provoked in myself by students, something that I need to work through? But where is a possible space which can uphold me in my efforts to stand up where I failed? When the light of the dawn comes to replace the light of the lamp beside my bed, another day of struggle begins.*

Kristeva returns to the issue of ethics and politics in her later writings. In one of her interviews (1993b), she affirms that her intellectual work and her analytic practice are political and moral engagements. Kristeva (2000a, 2002) calls for the necessity of revolt. This revolt, however, is an "intimate revolt," to use her phrase, in which the unspoken and inaudible voices of the body silenced by society return to deconstruct established codes. This revolt challenges social systems through the depth of the human psyche. As Oliver (2002a) points out, "Social revolt and psychic revolt, what Kristeva calls intimate revolt, go hand in hand; one is not possible without the other" (p. 63).

For Kristeva (2002), the intimacy "resides precisely in the heterogeneity of the two sensorial/symbolic, affects/thought registers" (p. 49), and the creation of sensory meaning is impossible without the experience of suffering through the imaginary.

Such a call is a response to contemporary flattened psychic space in social realms, the result of technological and corporate control, consumerism, and globalization (coupled with racism), all threatening one's specificity in meaning making. To resist this invisible tendency to universalize our social and psychic lives, the pedagogical art of listening to what is not spoken by students becomes crucial. Usually the site of silence is where articulation can take a form of social critique. Pedagogical relationships are essentially ethical and political ones which cannot be "mastered." We must confront the "faces" of students "which we will *never* completely know about" (jagodzinski, 2002, p. 86; emphasis in original). The pedagogical act of working through failures provokes and invites the teacher's own psychic transformation. In this relational noncoincidence of encountering the unknown in students (and ourselves), we as educators are called upon to reach out of ourselves in our im/possible meeting with students so that pedagogical potentialities can be realized for us all.

Such a loving third space—both psychic and social—through intimate revolt leads us on *journeys* of inhabiting "the dehabitation" (Kristeva, 2001). In such a process of working through the experience of suffering, our capacity to respond to loss and conflict must be transformed (Britzman, 1998) so that we are able to "stay," to live, with the unstable and the painful. In these journeys out, the mother is met and the stranger is claimed, many times, and in different ways. The "tenderness toward the other" (Kristeva, 2001, p. 240) is pedagogical and asks for the teacher's persistence in supporting students. An encounter of "surprise" (Edgerton, 1996; Eppert, 2000) happens along the way in this tenderness, so that knowing is not able to be colonized within the known. To inhabit the primordial separation in original languages asks for a complicated work of both memory and representation (Morris, 2001), which is an essential site for curriculum transformation.

## Language, the Gendered Self, and Culture:
## A Polyphonic Dialogue with the Kristevian Subject

I only want to walk into a Chinese character,
Over and over again.
    Read
    Write

Life and death.

(Ren Hongxuan, 1988, p. 199)

Kristeva's daring project of rethinking the human psyche through bringing body into language is inspiring. The unique path she draws, leading to human creativity through an interactive relation between connections and differences, challenges the taken-for-granted notions of identity, self, and inter/subjectivity. Her discourses hold out promise for woman to express her individuality and strangeness in new ways. She envisages a paradoxical community with plural singularities. Her reconstruction of self–other relationships based upon the notions of "the strangers to ourselves" and creative maternity as well as her call for a new politics of nation without nationalism point us toward new ethical and political horizons. However, reading Kristeva needs to be accompanied by dialogue, conversation, and contestation.

Mikhail Bakhtin's (1984) notion of polyphonic dialogue influenced Kristeva's early works, which is obvious from the title of her *Polylogue*. Although Kristeva does not really focus on this theme again, her notion of the heterogeneous construction of language, self, and life is not incompatible with this notion of polyphonic dialogue. Polyphony always leaves room for differences, whether in a relationship with self or with others. With the recognition that I am from a very different language and cultural background, I approach the Kristevian subject through this polyphonic space. My encounter with her notion of the subject will be contingent upon *nonconsensual differences* but without assuming that any theory is presumed to cover the whole of humanity across diversities.

Reading Kristeva, for me, as a "foreign" woman, was unsettling. According to Kristeva, the complicated interaction between the semiotic and the symbolic is essential for establishing an open psychic space. I find this a very difficult, if not impossible, task. It is not only difficult in itself, but my resistance also derives from my own background in Chinese language and culture, with their greater emphasis on interconnection and relatedness. One of the challenges I pose is that the Kristevian semiotic/symbolic binary, which sustains the founding moment of identity upon separation, makes creativity through relationships particularly vulnerable. The Chinese tradition of *yin* and *yang* also assumes conceptual differentiation, but there is no demand for an Oedipal break with the semiotic, and *yin* is always infused in the cosmos and throughout one's life. The bridge between the semiotic and the symbolic can be wider than Kristeva's depiction.

Actually, Kristeva does recognize differences between Chinese, as an ideograph language, and phonetically oriented languages such as English and French. Amazingly, she took time to learn to write a number of Chinese characters. Kristeva (1996) is indeed skeptical about whether the Oedipal complex is applicable to the Chinese psyche. However, this does not prevent her from categorizing the Chinese language as demonstrating pre-Oedipal qualities. Even if her categorical assumption is correct, it returns to challenge her very notion of the pre-Oedipal unconscious semiotic as opposite to the conscious symbolic, since Chinese, in its spoken and written forms, embodies both the semiotic and the symbolic. Besides, Chinese myth is less about Oedipus and more about the *Tao,* which is hardly structured by the phallus.[3] To sustain the role of phallic organization, Kristeva comments that "Oriental nothingness probably better sums up what, in the eyes of Westerners, can only be regression [to the maternal]" (Kristeva, 1980, p. 240). The psychoanalytic term of regression to the maternal indicates, traditionally, that the psyche does not reach maturity. But it is precisely through the Westerner's eyes that the potential of the stranger (the Oriental) is reduced within the Westerner's own framework. Ironically, such a reduction of otherness (Oriental holism) to the same (the Western criteria of independence) is what Kristeva argues against. While realizing that what I see through my eyes is situated in my own context as a Chinese woman, I also intend to point to Kristeva's inner paradoxes and conflicting gestures regarding the issues of woman, mother, and femininity and subsequent relationships with their counterparts: man, father, and masculinity.

Oliver (1993) reads Kristeva as "a melancholy theorist longing for her mother-tongue" (p. 16). Actually, Kristeva (2000b) confesses her difficulty in keeping her mother-tongue because, as a language, Bulgarian is nearly dead. So comes the birth of her essay, "Bulgaria, My Suffering." Yet Bulgarian still comes back to her: in dreams, when she loses words or expressions in alien languages; or in trouble, when she is too stressed to calculate rationally.

Understanding the giving up of one's native language as a revengeful matricide, Kristeva attempts to build a new home upon this musical "still warm corpse of my maternal memory" (p. 169), immersed in suffering, above suffering:

> But above this hidden crypt, on this stagnant reservoir that is disintegrating, I have built a new residence in which I dwell and that dwells in me, and in which there unfolds what one might call, not without affectation obviously, the true life of the spirit and the flesh. (p. 166)

The almost-lost mother tongue keeps coming back, "at the outer edge of words set to music and of unnamable urges" (p. 169), bringing imagination to her existence in French, so that she can fly higher, with more strength and freedom. This distant yet nurturing intimacy keeps calling, invisibly, as she travels into a new world.

*At the threshold of fantasy and reality, I knock on the door, willing to go back to the World. The door is closed and indifferent to my call. I sit down and write, casually. Chinese words and English words mingle together, mostly English words, since I have learned to think in English. Reading what I have written down, I feel Chinese and English fit together so nicely, while translation is impossible and not necessary. Chinese comes out naturally when English fails me. English commands me with its own structure and rhythm, but it is more like a game. Before I finish my practice, though, I am back to the World, in which I must express myself either in Chinese or in English. In my mind, however, the two languages are already mingled, sometimes in honeymoon, sometimes in conflict, with, unsurprisingly, many English grammatical errors.*

Listening to the call, Kristeva brings the semiotic back, yet resists being lured back to a childhood mother tongue; she secures the position of the symbolic as crucial for a person's independence through matricide. What I am interested in asking is: If Bulgarian as a mother-tongue were still alive with its own symbolic structure, would matricide be any different for Kristeva? Would this matricide also be necessarily accompanied by an overthrow of native symbolic laws in order for her to enter into another set of symbolic laws? Although the archaic maternal relationships and concrete embodiment of maternity are two different realities, the metaphorical link between the two makes "matricide" an excessive claim, a claim which can be easily assimilated into the control of paternal. Kristeva (2001) once argued for Melanie Klein's position to be read as "a sort of rhetorical exaggeration" (p. 241), for persuasive effect. Does Kristeva herself also engage in this rhetorical excess for the sake of claiming independence, securing the position of the paternal for one's freedom?

Kristeva emphasizes the importance of the semiotic in both the pre-Oedipal stage and the post-Oedipal stages, while she suggests the necessity of establishing the symbolic to break through the maternal relationship by introducing paternal law. While the semiotic/maternal does play a subversive role in mobilizing the static symbolic structure, the traditional privilege of the symbolic/paternal in forming the Oedipal identity is sustained. Psychoanalytically speaking, the maternal and the paternal are both metaphors for psychic representations; femininity, for instance, is available to both women and men. Kristeva (1996) acknowledges this point and notes that the third party, leading the child away from the maternal into the symbolic, can be a woman, a man, or even an institution.

On the other hand, Kristeva claims that father as nurturer in the family "will decimate the paternal function" of separation (1996, p. 118). She attempts to regenerate the "father of the individual prehistory" as a loving father who plays a primary symbolic role. Such an effort holds promising potential for reformulating psychoanalytic theory. However, on other occasions, she argues that the mixing of the paternal and maternal functions in the family can result in more borderline cases (1996, p. 119). While matricide is vital for psychic independence, the archaic father becomes the cornerstone for the possibility of autonomy. Such a privileging of the father makes her ambivalent toward homosexuality. Acknowledging the bond between the mother and the child as always implicated in the social, I prefer to situate a loving third between (and beyond) the semiotic and the symbolic rather than to secure the role of the paternal *as* the third.

I suspect the tensions within Kristeva reflect the crisis of traditional psychoanalysis, especially regarding Oedipal identity in the West. Understanding the self under an emerging, dramatically different picture of family structure will require new vocabularies and new theories which challenge traditional discourses. When femininity and masculinity become sites for contestations and interrogations, what can no longer be obscured is that the very terms "mother" and "father" are socially and historically constructed. As gender is subject to fiction (Munro, 1998b; Pinar, 2001), so are social constructions of father and mother.

*When I write at home on summer holidays, father usually brings me fruit, quietly putting some on my table. I take it quietly. He even transcribes my articles once in a while, to help me keep up with deadlines. We don't talk with each other much. After I became a foreigner, he tells me that he was most close to his grandmother. I have never met my own grandmother, let alone his. But I do remember that faded picture of a smiling old woman that father used to show me and my sisters, and that touch of gentleness and affection in his tone when introducing the photo to us. I wonder, is it through the loving memory of her that the refreshing smell of fruit laced with the fragrance of "chocolate" is passing on to me in an almost untraceable way?*

The term "matricide" is problematic for me, since it implies a full break. Although I understand that it refers to the archaic maternal relationship, why must we break fully away from mother first in order to declare independence, and then painfully reclaim the maternal relationship through recovering the semiotic? Cannot interdependence be sustained at the moment of founding independence? The Western (psychoanalytic) ideal of (psychic) independence by both matricide and patricide (taking over the symbolic from the father) needs to be rethought. Taking a cross-cultural point of view, I want to repeat that the Chinese notion of the self (as we have seen in Chapter 3) is under no pressure to claim its independence by matricide or patricide or both. Interdependence, rather than rebellious independence, is a continuous thread throughout a Chinese's life, sustaining the self. Without romanticizing this notion of the self, it demonstrates that the psyche can be constructed in a different way.

The issues of the semiotic and the symbolic and interdependence and independence take me to Chinese as a language, which exhibits a much more intertwined landscape of the self than the psychoanalytic subject. As I have already mentioned, Kristeva (1981) acknowledges several particular features of Chinese, such as the phonetic and grammatical polyvalence of words, and the intricate relationships between figurative representations and written forms, which modify the pattern of referent/signifier/signified. Meaning/sound/thing are fused into an ideogram. Chinese has many homophones; one word can be used as a noun, verb, or adjective, depending on its context. To isolate the meaning of a thing, a process, or a quality is impossible without approaching it contextually. Due to such an intertwining relationship among the concept, the sound, and the thing, Chinese ideographic writing cannot be confined within the Western framework of the subject/object system. Kristeva also points out that the written structure of one word can be a combination of two or more pictograms. One good example she gives is *hao* (好), the verb "to love" and the adjective "good": It is a combination of the signs for "woman" (女) and "child" (子) or "female" (女) and "male" (子).

Li Leyi's (1993) studies on the evolution of Chinese characters trace their transformation from the pictographic stage to the modern style of writing. His studies indicate that Kristeva's emphasis on the role of mother in Chinese society could be true, tracing the root of 好 (to love; good) to maternal relationships with a nonaccidental (I would argue) observation about the sex of the child: male. Li Xin (2002) points out how Chinese words form terms (two words together to function like one word) and phrases (multiple combinations of words) in a similarly interconnected way. What is also interesting to me is that Chinese terms or phrases made from two abstract characters can convey something concrete, or vice versa, or a mixture of the two. A simple example, 尺寸, which means "the size or the degree," is composed of "feet/ruler" (尺) and "inch" (寸). This is a case in which two concrete words compose one abstract concept. Another term, 东西, means "thing" and is composed of "east" (东) and "west" (西). This is an illustration of two abstract words composing one concrete word. Another example, 空洞, means "hollow" or "devoid of content" and is composed of "empty" (空) and "hole or cave" (洞). This concept is formed from one concrete word and one abstract word.

Sometimes contradictory words are combined to convey one meaning, such as 长短, "length," which is composed of "long" (长) and "short" (短). Many a four-character phrase has an interesting story behind its abstract meaning. Such a mingling of the concrete and the abstract in language and linguistic appropriation of contradictions asks us to rethink psychoanalytic assumptions about language and self. This complicated relationship between meanings and structures of words and phrases in an ideograph, in combination with an intonation system (*hao* as a verb is in the fourth tone and as an adjective is in the third tone), indicates the presence of the semiotic and the symbolic at the same time.

With a certain understanding of Chinese language and her studies of other language systems, Kristeva (1981) nevertheless claims that "the signifying system studied by Freud has a universality that 'traverses' constituted national languages" (p. 272). If this universality can be claimed at the level of acknowledging the existence of the unconscious, cannot the movement of the unconscious have different rhythms due to differences in linguistic and cultural systems? If, as Kristeva suggests, Chinese writing presupposes a speaking and writing individual who stays at a "pre-Oedipal phase— dependency on the maternal, socionatural continuum, absence of clear-cut divisions between the order of things and the order of symbols, predominance of the unconscious impulses" (1977a, p. 56), does this mean that the Chinese self or Chinese culture at large is more marked by "the regression" to the maternal? To understand the otherness of the Chinese, if we do not fall into the claim (which Kristeva contends is racist) that the Chinese self is immature compared with the Western subject, do we need to transform the psychoanalytic vocabulary in order to convey the complexity of self, language, and culture? Even if the unconscious is already genetically proven to be universal (Kristeva, 1981), I still believe that cultural and social transmutation of a universal psychological framework is needed to interpret another kind of self in another kind of language system, in this case, Chinese.

*Chinese students who have just come to the United States are discussing the choice of "leaving or staying." While male students argue about "the mainstream" and "the margin," female students turn to me asking: "What am I going to do with my child if I stay here? How can I keep the Chinese tradition for* ta *[Chinese pronunciation of s/he or her/him is the same]?" What a coincidence I am trying to work though Kristeva's theory about language and maternity! How do I know? I manage to say: "Perhaps you cannot, unless you can manage to make* ta *really learn the language, and bring* ta *back and forth between two cultures." For Kingston (1989), an American-born Chinese who had no experience of China at the time of writing her book* The Woman Warrior, *China hovers over her like a ghost. It could be a bad ghost not only due to mother's distant tales but also due to the implicit influence of the media and politics in the United States. It could be an idealized image, too. One of my friends, a foreign-born Chinese, cried for days about the dissolution of her beautiful dream about China when she went to China for a visit. Without actual encounter with a culture and its people, language itself fails, since it remains at an imaginary level. But what if* ta *stays here and chooses to become an American? What if* ta *resists learning Chinese and prefers English as a mother-tongue? Still, what if the repressed collective unconscious returns anyway, regardless of* ta*'s decisions in life? Perhaps the fluidity of national borders will bring a new type of person and a new identity across the border. I am indeed intrigued by this possibility.*

To recognize the relational nature of the Chinese language, just as in recognizing the relational nature of the Chinese self, does not mean that this relationship is itself free from paternal law and its patriarchal implications. Again, tracing the evolution of Chinese characters can show us how the maternal, while valued, is still inferior to the paternal. For example, the Chinese character "female" (女) comes from a kneeling woman, and "married woman" (妇) comes from a kneeling woman who holds a broom to clean the house, while "human" (人) comes from a standing man (Li, 1993). Kneeling in ancient Chinese rituals indicates respect for the elder and the superior, so kneeling men's figures can also be found. However, after checking 500 characters listed in Li's book, I notice that almost any word whose pictorial representative traces back to woman is marked by kneeling. But characters for "human" or "guest," which are supposed to have both female and male connotations, are pictorially traced back to male figures as the standard.

As Hall and Ames (2000) observe, Chinese characters in which one component is "female" (女) often indicate negative qualities such as 奸 (lewdness), 奴 (slave), 妒 (envy), 嫉 (jealousy), 婪 (greed), and 姘 (illicit sexual relationships). In addition to indicating family relationships, female beauty and charm also make up a major group of words with "female" (女) as a component part, such as 婷 (graceful), 娇 (charming), 娜 (tenderly attractive), and 妍 (beautiful). There are some exceptions, though, indicating positive qualities, for example 始 (origin), 娲 (female creator), 娄 (star, corresponding to female, indicating female creative power), 娱 (happiness), 嬉 (play), and 妙 (wonderful). It is clear that gender biases appear at the linguistic level.

Upon reflection, I cannot hold my previous position (stated in Chapter 1) about social and cultural constructions of language, more than language itself, being implicated in patriarchy. The interactive relationship between language and culture makes it almost impossible to separate the two and their respective influences on gender construction. On the other hand, it would be simplistic to claim that language itself is patriarchal. The coexistence of the paternal and the maternal in the Chinese language, even in a negative sense, again makes the boundary between the semiotic and the symbolic permeable. When the semiotic/maternal is explicitly present in language, the initiation of the child into the language is not necessarily marked by separation from, or at least not a full break with, the mother. Even if the birth of the sign is made possible by the mother's absence, the child's encounter with the sign can be another way of connecting with the mother. The Oedipal founding moment of independence upon separation in psychoanalysis may not be applicable to all cultures. But I have no intention of dismissing psychoanalysis as a way of understanding and interpreting the human self. What I have attempted to do is to bring a sense of cultural interdependence into the framework so that both relationships and freedom can be valued. This is a cross-cultural third space of the human/woman psyche that I am interested in pursuing in my further research.

The problematic of language, the gendered self, and culture retains its polyphonic nature after my encounter with Kristeva. Differences sustain, so further conversation is possible. While I question the binary of the semiotic/maternal and the symbolic/paternal, I appreciate her own interactive and even contradictory postures toward this split and her subversive strategy of bringing affects back into signification. Kristeva's formulation of the semiotic revolutionizes our efforts to understand the human psyche. Her particular emphasis on the significance of the semiotic, even in the process of separation, has transformed psychoanalysis and complicated our discussion about gender. Her unique contribution invites us to engage in a creative journey of selfhood.

## An Impossible Synthesis: Self, Community, and Creativity

Traveling through Foucauldian self-creation, the Confucian relational self, and the Kristevian subject-in-process, one may find it difficult, almost impossible, to live in a space full of ambivalence and contradictions. Perhaps the project of rethinking the human/woman self, as complex and shifting as it can be, is itself unthinkable in any coherent way. As Kristeva notices, Eastern wisdom leaves space for ambivalence and paradoxes. I find it unsettling, yet challenging, to carve out a space for weaving these fragmented threads together, without making a seamless whole. Without any final synthesis, they nevertheless come together in my own lived experiences as a cross-cultural being through space and time. As I will discuss a cross-cultural gendered self in a third space in detail in the next chapter, here I just want to point out certain problematic themes briefly, regarding critical issues of self and curriculum in differences, community, and creativity.

These three thinkers—Kristeva, Confucius, and Foucault—coming from different intellectual and personal backgrounds, focus on the notion of the self from different traditions. Foucault's self-care puts the self at the center of his discourse in his later work, identifying social and cultural constraints as what need to be transgressed by a creative subject. Although Confucius and Kristeva follow a dramatically different path, they both acknowledge that no political, social, or cultural transformation can be accomplished without the transformation of the self. Such a focus on change sets the self into motion, although their approaches to mobilizing the self are hardly the same. Foucault's subject is marked by transgression and endless critique. The Kristevian semiotic constantly subverts the paternal law and invents new words and realities. The Confucian self cultivates inner transformation as a lifelong project with an ideal which never can be mastered.

The subject-in-process is implicated in questioning the norms, with which both Foucault and Kristeva are explicitly engaged. Both of them argue that modern man is losing himself in an overwhelmingly consumerist, materialistic, and technological society. As I pointed out in Chapter 2, Foucault argues that the normalizing disciplinary power of modern society is behind the screen of abstract individualization. For Kristeva (1995), the contemporary age is marked by "new maladies of souls," an age carried away by images without stimulating imagination and consumed by insignificant objects without psychic satisfaction. Confucius has a more uneasy relationship with the concept of norm. While *ren* can be said to be a social and political norm, what *ren* represents is not fixed. Its meaning shifts in different settings, referring to a complicated, multilayered, and nonunitary notion. This difference between East and West reflects a general dissonance in understanding culture and society. For Foucault, culture is more or less a conservative background *against* which new visions of life can be imagined. Kristeva approaches the social as what must be subverted for creativity. The Confucian self, however, values culture as always related to the intellectual, the artistic/aesthetic, and the spiritual, which upholds both continuity and transformation.

Foucault and Kristeva do not head in the same direction either. While Foucault devotes himself to the singularity of the human subject, Kristeva refuses to choose one pole, but takes on both the universal and the singular. While she is committed to going "as deeply as possible into the psychic particularity of sexual and love organization" (1984, p. 338), Kristeva believes that it is the paradox of every human science to attend to both giving meaning to the individual and understanding the deep structure of individuality.

The universal notion that Oedipal identity privileges the symbolic is constantly destabilized throughout her writings by reformulation of maternal and paternal functions. Her consideration of maternity as a creative relationship embodying both self and other is complemented by the singularity of womanhood. Attending to both the universal and the particular, she is constantly lured to either one pole or the other. Refusing to settle down with either, however, she chooses to stay in an in-between space. Perhaps any theory attending to the particularity and uniqueness of the self, while required by the necessity for generalization in theorizing, must compromise between the universal and the singular, as creative potential might reside in the very movement between the two.

Subject-in-process is intricately related to subject-in-relation because the fluidity of the self is enabled by responding to the other. Both Kristeva and Foucault pay close attention to the issue of differences, but Kristeva explicitly elaborates how the differences within can lead to a new sense of community in which differences become generative in forming polyphonic relationships with the stranger. Foucault seldom provides any vision of community, though he implies that there can be a community which enables self-creation of both self and other. Both Kristeva and Confucius think about the relationship between self and other, but Kristeva pays much more attention to alterity, differences, and the deep psychic structure underlying these.

Confucius also pays attention to "the self within," but it is not in a psychoanalytic sense; it is in the sense of an inner cultivation of independent personality situated in the ecology of selfhood. Moreover, the Confucian self is expanded to the other through continuity, similarity, and social structures supporting this relationship. Perhaps without a certain sense of commonality, human community cannot be grounded. On the other hand, without differences, a community cannot exist either (Britzman, 1998). Confucian selfhood locates the self in the center and expands itself outward toward others and the cosmos. The Foucauldian subject disperses the self without making any explicit interconnections, although there are underground channels through which to do so. The Kristevian subject also articulates individual locations of the self, but there are bridges and networks within, between, and among different selves. As a result, the Confucian community is a harmonious community, the Foucauldian community is a transgressive community, and the Kristevian community is a polyvalent community.

As the subject becomes mobile and relational, how can dynamic interconnections be built in such a way that creativity can be released in the relationships of the self with the other, the alterity of the other? For both Foucault and Kristeva, the sharp edge of break and discontinuity is necessary to make creativity possible. While Foucault pays attention mainly to individuality, the Kristevian subject, through loving relationships, indicates the mutuality of creativity. The co-creation of the self and the universe is an important theme of Confucian selfhood. Thomas Berry's (1988, 1990) call for us to listen to the earth, as he himself acknowledges, echoes a Confucian understanding of the trinity between humanity, earth, and heaven. Is not "the dream of the earth" (Berry, 1990) also the dream of an ecology of selfhood? However, on the other hand, can an ecology of selfhood without enough attention to the differentiation of sexuality form an interactive dynamic? How can co-creation of self, other, and the universe be possible without sacrificing their respective independences?

When I started this project, I had hoped that Kristeva could help me weave Confucius and Foucault together, as she is concerned with the issues of both social relationships and individual creativity. To some degree, she does bridge the two in terms of explicitly discussing how the self becomes creative through the relationality of the mother/child bond, and how individual identity is formed through loving relationships. However, this bridge is fragile as she approaches the self's relationship with the other as being built upon a sense of separation and division. Kristeva shares more common ground with Foucault in terms of attending to differences, and, in a sense, she is further away from Confucius' relational self while she probes deeply into the psychic structure objectifying the self. Foucault's philosophical analysis of self-examination and self-mastery without essentialization and normalization, on the other hand, echoes certain themes from the Confucian traditions of self-reflection. While the Confucian emphasis on relationship is an antithesis to Foucault's centering on the self, this emphasis is also an antithesis to Kristeva's paradoxical self–other relationships. Needless to say, Kristeva's notion of creative womanhood is beyond both Foucault's and Confucius' reach and concern. Are these three thinkers complementary to one another, or are they heading in their own dispersed directions without much intersection? There is no single direction that one can take to go out, and while passages can be built among them, dead ends are also evident, demanding detours. Indeed the human/woman self is a labyrinth from which one cannot take easy flight. But, as an ancient Chinese poem notes, when you believe you have reached a dead end, another village is actually ahead of you. Beyond dead ends, another passage, another landscape is coming. Such a difficult journey is labor we need to share with our students.

The emphasis on a transformative and creative self in relation with the other, from three great thinkers across different historical times and cultural spaces, forms a sharp contrast with our current schooling. Almost opposite to this teaching, our schools do not start with the individual person, but with social standards and cultural norms. In China, schools promote an explicit political agenda to unify individual persons into one ideal. In the United States, an implicit normalization process, through media, technology, and culture, makes explicit the advocacy for the individual abstract and untenable (Pinar, 1994). To renew our understanding of self, community, and creativity, complicated by the discourses of Foucault, Kristeva, and Confucius, it becomes crucial to rethink the important issues of curriculum and education. What does the self mean and what does it mean to a curriculum conceived as a journey? What are the relationships among knower, known, and knowing (Pinar, 1994)? Can we cultivate our children through an ecology of selfhood yet, at the same time, release their own "creative energy" (Berry, 1988) through imaginative individualization? Dare we build a school community which strangers/outcasts can join while preserving their own uniqueness? Can interconnected networks through teacher, student, and text (Doll, 1993) be generative enough to meet the child's curious eyes in his/her own strange yet probing way? The shift to the self is an issue that needs to be rethought on both sides of the Pacific Ocean.

Without being able to link a transformative and creative notion of self-in-relation, self-in-process, and self-in-alterity to any fixed position free from conflicts, I intend to conduct a tour of the complicated web of the human/woman self, following interconnected yet fragmented curves to reach beyond predictable paths into unexpected landscapes. This requires a creative translation, not only between Western language and Chinese ideographs, but also between femininity and masculinity—inasmuch as both concepts are "subject to fiction" (Munro, 1996). Such a translation is complicated at the intersection of the multiple. Curriculum as an autobiographical and multilayered journey needs to be translated, too (Edgerton, 1996).

## Notes

1.  Here is a double text again to convey a sense of break as life flows through the text to disrupt its neat structure. Somehow I resist writing autobiographically about psychoanalytic discourse. Perhaps I am bothered by the image of becoming an object of analysis, but stories or experiences are usually richer and more complex than any theoretical generalization.

    Putting the human self as the object of analysis is quite different from the Chinese traditions of self-reflection. As I went to Beijing Library in the fall of 2000, trying to searching for books on psychoanalysis, I could not help but feel disappointed that all the theoretical books at hand were general discussions of psychoanalysis, with comparisons between Freud, Jung, Lacan, or even Kristeva. However, I could not find any theoretical critiques of psychoanalysis from a cultural angle, especially from Chinese culture. Does that indicate an acceptance of psychoanalysis as fully applicable to China? Or does it imply that almost irreducible conflicts between this universal model and the Chinese situation prevent scholars from even making a link? Or is the introduction of psychoanalysis only at the preliminary stage in China? How the field of Chinese psychology approaches psychoanalysis is beyond my speculation, but my own doubt about the generalized model of psychoanalysis, rooted in Western languages and Western cultures, is deepened by this lack of cultural critiques. However, it is almost impossible to read psychoanalytic discourse without evoking personal response. I do not want to pretend to be neutral, but neither do I want to put my autobiographical writing completely under the gaze of psychoanalysis. I choose again to use double text.

Regarding the prose I use for the beginning of this chapter (and the beginning of the third section on the im/possibility of the loving third), I do not intend to claim it as "poetry," since it does not follow the formal structure and rhythm of poetry. It is more of a play with words, images, and thoughts. At best it conveys a poetic voice. Without formal punctuation, it indicates a flow, with pauses indicated by spacing. I also intentionally use the present tense, as you will see in the following italicized writings, to narrate stories, although they all occurred in the past. In the past, however, they still linger in the present. This is an invitation for readers to experience stories as if they happened just around them.

2.  Understanding Kristeva's notion of the semiotic as unconscious, which is related to femininity and the maternal, I do not want to fall into an essentialist claim of femininity. Gender is historically and socially constructed, as Petra Munro (1998a, 1998b) and William Pinar (2001) point out. The Chinese tradition of the masculine in woman and the feminine in man also asks me to approach the notion of 'the stranger' in a complicated way. Especially situated in concrete family life, the stranger could be a "she" or a "he," or an implication of "she" in "he" or "he" in "she."

3.  How the cosmic notion of *Tao* in Taoism and the moral principle of *Tao* in Confucianism interact with each other to shape the Chinese psyche is an issue I have not thought through. However, it does show a somewhat different picture from that of the Western Oedipal complex. The psychoanalytic metaphors of maternal/semiotic and paternal/symbolic may have a certain intersection with the Taoist understanding of *yin* and *yang*. But *yin* and *yang* are much more mutually implicated in each other; as the symbol of *Tai-ji* shows, *yin* is in *yang* and *yang* is in *yin*. Their interaction is not interrupted by any Oedipal break privileging the founding role of *yang* to uphold independence. *Yin* and *yang* are also a much broader concept, not limited to signifying language processes. Moreover, the Oedipal complex is based upon sexuality, while *Tao* shifts as a cosmological energy and permeates not only human relations, but also (erotic) relations between humanity and the universe and relationships within nonhuman existence. How to bridge these two so that independence and fluid interaction can form a constructive relationship to understand the human/woman psyche anew is a project I will undertake in my further research.

# Chapter 5
# The Philosophical Self Meets the Psychic Transformation in a Cross-Cultural Gendered Space

Traveling between and among Foucault, Confucius, and Kristeva, situated in different times and places, I risk reaching a point of losing all those I have taken for granted and having to start all over again without much idea of where I am going. Yet this is a vibrant and pregnant point, full of potential for new directions. So comes the swirling magic of a third space in which the voyager, like a baby just learning how to walk, journeys in an unbalanced balance.

Yet, I dread writing this chapter. Dazzled/puzzled by the light/shadow of an exit, by the im/possibility of coming out anew, I confront this difficult work of connecting bits, parts, and fragments (all are in me nevertheless), a self-imposed effort—mirrored back from the imagined anticipation of my readers—of weaving pieces of the self into a true fiction of a cross-cultural gendered space, an imaginative realm embedded in the undercurrent of un-sayable interconnections. It is a space which one can only poetically experience and where utterances may fail, but about which one must nevertheless try to speak. Before this true fiction finally converges toward a unified self, it diverges toward the multiple; before it multiplies into pure fragments, bits and pieces come together to form a singular rhythm with a universal appeal. So I play with the fiction of the self as I go along.

This writing anxiety reminds me of those days in college when I began to pick up needlework in a panicked effort at—without knowing it at that time—weaving the feminine back into the self which had been consumed by academic studies. While other young women burned their candles for final exams, I stayed outside of the dormitory room under the light in the hallway to work with needles and thread. With the comforting touch of the knitting wool and the silent music of twisting the multiple, my hands quickly adapted to the rhythm of making passages, back and forth, between and beyond, left and right, over and under, within and among, in and out.

Connecting multiple spaces of discourses is different from needlecraft, yet getting in touch with the rhythm is essential to any kind of knitting. My jumping all over intellectual and cultural spaces, the very act of crossing as a prerequisite for creating a third space, is enabled by the invisible threads I do not know by logic but can touch through intuition. In writing what I do not know, I gesture toward a third space yet to be born, and I myself am set into motion. Un/folding the intersections and thresholds of culture, gender, and identity, will I simply add more layers of fragmentation instead of putting the jigsaw of the self together? But if fragments enable the whole and if new threads lead to new designs in the scarf, perhaps the excess of pieces can make possible another pattern at another time. This is a special rhythm of a third space which refuses to stay within any confinement, which even defies the boundary of any exclusive "new."

If writing itself is a process of invention, I venture out and weave back. With the spirit of candle-burning attempts at knitting, I present my autobiographical weaving of a cross-cultural gendered fabric of the self in a loving third space, yet this time without personal narratives. The singular eye/I eluded, I borrow "the third eye" (Tyler, 2001), which multiplies both itself and what can be seen.

## Beyond the Conflicting Double in the Borderlands

To survive the Borderlands
   You must live *sin fronteras* [without borders]
   Be a crossroads

(Gloria Anzaldúa, 1999, p. 217)

A cross-cultural gendered space is a messy space. The paternal benevolence of Confucius smiles like a mother, gestures a loving invitation into the past and into the future. The maternal lyrics of Li Qingzhao utter the inner strength of the feminine beyond the shadow of a confining cabin. The paternal and the maternal change their faces in the complexity of an intercultural psychic space. As we are drawn by the rebelling gaze of Foucault, the hand of Kristeva's "intimate revolt" gently draws us back to touch what is revolutionary within. The philosophy of subjectivity cycling its own subversive potential on the land is destabilized by the semiotic tide which erodes the solid soil. Kristeva's contemporary tales of womanhood connect to ancient women writers in the East, whose stories disrupt the linear notion of historical progress. The other face of Confucius, his claim for independence, emerges through a Foucauldian reading of historical discontinuity. This is a complicated, entangled, and emergent third space which situates singular and multiple stories of the cultural, gendered, and psychic.

A strange song of the self, with its beautiful melody, asks for our attentive ears, yet no single language can capture its meaning. What is said and sung in lyrics is made possible by what is not said and not sung. A playful swing of time and place, with its circular rhythm, asks for our moving visions, yet stasis will prevail without the pull of opposite directions. A dancing is always with the other—even if the dance is solitary—either with the outside other, with the other within, or, more often than not, with both. It is the rhythm flowing simultaneously from both directions of exterior and interior that makes an extraordinary performance. Double orientations stretch the potential, and conflicting doubles give birth to the third space, of multiple possibilities. Decentering, the dual movement of the conflicting double multiplies the potential of the singular in its webbed (dis)connections.

## Identity and Nonidentity at the Crossroads

Our contemporary age can perhaps be captured by the touch of crisis, a crisis provoked by encountering both self and other, both within and without, both East and West, both past and future. "Identity" as both a concept and a reality becomes an enigma in the middle of uncertainty. *Identity* is an alien term, yet to be born in the Confucian world. Foucault prefers the word *nonidentity*, because *identity* is too confining for his rebellion. In Kristeva's psychic picture, *identity* is already always split, a word subverted by the semiotic movement. What does identity mean? Does it mark the boundary of the self? Does it bestow on the subject a transcendental sameness? Does it indicate an implicit sense of belonging, a link "with"? At the crossroads of East and West, woman and man, philosophical subject and psychic self, is there any gesture that will lead us to arrive at the "truth" of identity?

In the borderlands of culture, gender, philosophy, and psyche, ambiguous directions and multiplied opposites are abundant, or, to use the words of Michel Serres's (1997), all reference points are lost in such a third space. Such an unsettled fluidity of identity at the crossroads is troubling: Where can we locate father and mother? How can maternal and paternal functions stay stable if the angle of meeting eyes keeps shifting? What happens when intellectual/spiritual father is transformed into mother in a foreign culture? What happens when a foreign land becomes a mother figure due to the alien's increasing attachment to the nurturance of a new home? Is the appeal of the paternal (of paternal love), after all, not merely symbolic, but also embodied? The moment the contour of identity is sketched, nonidentity sneaks in.

Modern identity in the West, as Charles Taylor (1989) points out, emerges and evolves with inner complexity and contradictions. The Cartesian disengaged rational subject in search of universal human nature and the Montaignian engaged expressive subject in search of the unique essential self take different or even opposite turns. However, both are aimed toward the internalization of identity. "The search for identity can be seen as the search for what I essentially am" (Taylor, 1989, p. 184). Descartes's dream is of the universal, while Montaigne's (self-)knowledge is about the particular, yet both look for the essence of the self. Along with some other contemporary philosophers, Foucault rejects this essentialist assumption of modern identity; he remains suspicious of any identity claim. His subject is transgressive of what is constituted, yet does not lead to any metaphysical sense of "beyond." The beyond of the Foucauldian subject is inherent in creative activities which keep fashioning and inventing the self anew.

Contrary to the common-sense perception of Chinese selflessness, we can find various expressions of "self" in ancient Chinese prose and essays, a self which cannot be confined within the Western language of identity "as" or "beyond" or both. Self-cultivation is one of the keys to unfolding Chinese civilization. In poetry, though, the "I" is usually invisible, a locus of experience that cannot be founded explicitly, which makes direct translation impossible. *Identity* as a term, on the other hand, is seldom used, even in the modern age. The strong connotation of an essential entity is not part of Chinese "identity." *Belonging*, instead of *identity*, is the term commonly used. It is a gesture of identity "with" instead of "as" or "beyond." Due to this refusal to formulate an entity with a transcendental appeal, Chinese philosophy does not strive for either the essence of identity or the "beyond" of nonidentity.

As Western tales of identity in its contemporary mutations begin to trace the unspoken link of "with," modern man's ideal of an autonomous hero in his search for essence is disillusioned. One detail in an American movie, *Three Men and a Baby* (1988)—a hilarious remake of a French comedy about three men charged with the task of taking care of a baby girl—is particularly illuminating. When the baby cries, Peter and Michael have absolutely no idea what to do. Peter suggests that she needs some food:

Peter: Just feed it and it'll shut up!
Michael: I don't know what babies eat!
Peter: Soft stuff. I mean, we were babies once, for God's sake! What did we eat?
Michael: I don't know. It couldn't have been very good. I can't remember!

What is interesting here is *what* is not remembered. What is repressed socially, culturally, and psychically? What connection is lost? That "babies like to be held" is a "discovery." When Michael first picks up the crying baby, he lifts her in front of his eyes and stretches his arms out to keep a distance. However, the memory of touch, tone, milk, and rhythm comes back to these men as they try to take care of the baby, as does the memory of the maternal. William F. Pinar (2001) points out how the fabrication of (racialized) masculinity in the American context is intimately related to the repression of the feminine. The autonomy of the modern Western identity collapses when the whisper of the maternal comes back. The transcendence of essence is drawn back into the web when the lost memories of the relational return.

While the West is alluding to "with," Chinese identity begins to shift its focus toward "beyond." The Chinese conception of unity between the self and the universe, and the Chinese holism of knowing, feeling, will, and acting make it impossible to achieve any transcendental ideal outside of the immanent whole. However, this union is disrupted in the painful process of encountering the Western other. The internal unity of immanence is broken down and the different light of the external comes through the hole. In dealing with the alterity of the other, one has to reach beyond the limits of the self in exchange for what is more in life. The illusion of the union is further dismantled when Chinese women's bound feet are set free. At the intersection of culture (with its focus on relations) and gender (with its focus on self-sacrifice), Chinese women are doubly marginalized. Yet precisely at this double margin their strength and creativity are born, historically and contemporarily. Is Chinese mythology about the strength of *yin* only a myth? In the imagination of the Western public, the Chinese female sex is weak and obedient, yet this peculiar feminine position has inherited its power from Chinese foremothers, and is ready to release its energy beyond the illusion of (patriarchal) union.

After all, identity's "with" and nonidentity's "beyond" become much more intertwined after the sealed shores of both East and West are opened, with the influx of the repressed memory of the maternal. The call from the stranger invites movement toward the beyond, but not beyond into absolute, essential, metaphysical truth. This movement toward the beyond is *with* the web of interconnections. The journey of the self searches for passages *between* the old world and the new, and builds tunnels *between* the underworld and the overworld, traveling with both sun *and* moon. Leaving home, beyond the limit, *crossing* the river, the self lands on a new shore carrying home with her. Only through her efforts to reach *out* can the deep connection *within* be touched, felt, and transformed. In a third space.

**Individuality and Relationality**

An individual, a knotting locus of the web, the web of life, exists only in and through relation. As a knot, it is the result of weaving, infinitely connected to other knots and the web. As an intersection, its independence is nurtured by interdependence. At the crossroads, its relationships enable its own pattern. Allowing other threads to be woven into it, the self is expanded. Pulling out its own inner string to spread the music across the web, the self enriches the whole. A knot is also unique, in its own form, its singular pattern, and its colorful presentation.

Individualism is a creation of man. Written by the Swiss Hermann Hesse (1951), the novel *Siddhartha* demonstrates the spirituality of the East and the West through the story of a young Indian, Siddhartha, raised to be a prince among Brahmins. Siddhartha leaves home to search for the soul's ultimate truth. Right after his encounter with Buddha and refusal to stay with Buddha's teachings, he reaches the moment of awakening. No longer needing any teacher, no longer committed to his father, no longer looking backward, he feels like a thinker, all by himself, alone. As he walks quickly and impatiently with this enlightenment of independence and autonomy, unfortunately, he falls into the worldliness of riches, passion, and power. Is this timing an accident? When one finally believes that one can be torn away from all the connections, one falls right back into the connections, but in another way—often in an unwanted way. Why does the seduction of autonomy produce its opposite? Is it possible to be detached before becoming attached? Can wisdom be touched without experiencing the sensuality of the world and life in its infinite interrelationships? Siddhartha's true enlightenment finally comes after he struggles with his own (unexpected) son, after listening to the thousand different voices of the river in one great song.

Confucian relationality also can turn its back upon itself in unintended directions. Without a sharp distinction between self and other, private and public, the Confucian self, although it expands itself into community, society, and cosmos, runs the risk of a limitless extension of the private ego in the name of serving the public. Here lies the paradox of a socialized self which turns out against the common good of the social. A smooth movement without appropriate boundaries is suffocating rather than regenerating. The Confucian as public intellectual claims his independence in two dramatic ways (among others): one is to sacrifice himself, running the risk of being killed or exiled by the government; the other is to claim scholarly autonomy from official discourse while denouncing political responsibility. In other words, Confucian independence can be easily expelled by the whole of the concentric circular self, which then becomes seamless.

The Foucauldian subject is constituted by the relationality of the social and, at the same time, constitutes itself against social constructions. This double focus captures the inherent tension within the self between individuality and relationality. Yet his project of freedom as *against* does not deal with the issue of *with* successfully: relationality as the limit only serves the purpose of promoting individuality. Is it possible for individuals who are simultaneously *with* and *in* the web of relationships and *against* the constraints of the social to cultivate themselves? From this coexistence of opposite directions sing the poetics of personal and social transformation in a third space, where individuality and relationality intertwine, collide, and interact. Separate yet together, parted yet holding hands, alone yet with the other, such is a story of seeking independence *through* and *for* interdependence. This is a gendered story, Kristeva points out. Woman with a profound sense of interconnection seeks her own room where the silence of the relational and the new words of the singular can begin to speak, in a new tongue.

## Commonality and Differences

Commonality is usually regarded as the key to making connections. Yet cannot differences connect too? This book intentionally picks up the point of rupture between East and West, and the discontinuity within the Eastern and Western histories of thought, to argue for the necessity of relating to what is different. Certainly there are convergent points between East and West. For instance, identity *with* within the Western tradition and identity *beyond* within the Chinese tradition are not difficult to identify. However, the failure to acknowledge and respect difference on its own terms has brought disaster throughout human history. Reliance on a common sense of humanity to bring people together is so easily turned into the violence of reducing otherness into sameness, as manifested in our social and psychic lives. If we search and see in the other's eyes only the reflection of ourselves, the world becomes "ours," and other worlds are shut out of our vision. One of the failures of the Confucian self lies in its inability to see the alterity of the other. Yet, difference not only produces tensions; it also brings attraction and the potential for change. For Kristeva, what we share is difference—within and without—which initiates us into a process of creating new possibilities.

Is difference absolute? If difference is absolute, is any communication between and among people possible? Between and beyond the bipolar positions of erasing difference and denying communion, Kelly Oliver (1998) argues, the distance that is assumed to separate us from others is actually "filled with the elements that sustain us and make relationships possible" (p. 159). The dualism of subject and object produced by privileging vision—the function of eye (I)—makes the modern man stop short at where our vision fails. In the movie *Three Men and a Baby*, what Peter does in response to the crying baby is to hold her at arm's length to "see" what is wrong—touch is unbearable at first. Oliver tells us, "What our eyes cannot see are the elements that fill the space between ourselves and our objects and link us in the circulation of light and air that makes vision possible" (p. 155). Here we can hear the echo of the Chinese wisdom about the immanence of self and universe: We are part of the interconnected web, not the controller of the world. Actually we are in communion with the world all the time, but usually do not acknowledge it.

If we argue for commonality, common hu*man*ity is an inadequate language: we have to account for the songs of birds, the whistle of the wind, the quiet dignity of the mountain, and the unyielding will of water. To single out our common humanity as superior conveys the logic of control and dominance. What is implicit behind the rhetoric of the common is presence of normative criteria which serve to exclude. The language of sharing offers more room than the language of commonality to indicate the connection between self and other without reducing them to the same. Relationship does not have to be built solely upon commonality, and difference can be utilized to build an open intersubjectivity supporting a dynamic subjectivity. This requires us to have a different *vision*, a vision alternative to the subject/object split, a vision which also incorporates other senses to bring the semiotic into the subject, an intuitive vision in which both communion and difference are tangible in the space we share.

Oliver argues for "subjectivity without subject" to elude the violence of objectifying the other and the world, which is echoed, albeit from another direction, in some Chinese scholars' efforts to tease out the (inter)subjective thinking of Chinese thought without moving toward Cartesian objectifying ego. Differences need to be respected for their creative potential—Foucault argues for freeing differences—without sacrificing what we share together in an intersubjective and "interbeing" space. The prefix *inter* already implies the necessity of differentiation, without which interdependence becomes static and independence becomes rootless. The world is multiplied because of difference; so is the space in which we live, which in turn provides more room for us to share. This attending to both difference (singular yet generative) and interbeing (relational yet creative) is a new language we need to speak for the mutual transformation of self, other, and the cosmos.

## Boundary Building and Boundary Crossing

The poetics of fractals (Art Matrix, 1990) vividly shows the movement across boundaries and the simultaneous emergence of new ones. Without boundaries, nothing can exist; without boundary crossing, nothing new can be created. As we paint the contour of a new boundary, we also gesture toward another boundary, old or yet to emerge—to remember, to reconnect with, to imagine otherwise. There is always an opening along the border to "the other heading" (Derrida, 1992) and there is always something more underneath the surface. The other and otherness forever erode the borderline of a boundary.

"As a pause, home is marked off by boundaries, depends upon boundaries, which are made by arrivals and leavings, attachments and detachments" (Martusewicz, 2001, p. 32). Without the intimate boundary of a home, we do not have enough strength to stand up and walk. Yet the boundary of the home always lures us to the possibility of leaving. Without detaching, the familiar bonds us to the given. As a pause, the boundary is uncertain, ambiguous, and ever shifting; as a pause, the boundary holds the intimacy of creativity. Boundary needs to be built; boundary needs to be dissipated. Bound yet free.

Being at home while not being at home is a traveler's tale. Being saturated in our homeplace, we do not want to venture out; alienated from the new places in which the traveler moves, we do not take in what an alien place can offer; having been to new places yet refusing to cast off a skin, we lose the potential for rebirth. Taking the risk to attach, we are vulnerable, yet gently we feel the intimate vibration of life; taking the risk to detach, we are fearful, yet courageously we venture out into a larger web of interconnection. Attachment and detachment both need psychic strength. The double or multiple perspectives an open-minded traveler is willing to take decenter the interior of any boundary and opens up the exterior of the border, lovingly.

Remaining detached yet unconsciously locked up by the memory of the (lost) maternal, Camus's (1942) stranger, Meursault, confronts the possibility of rebirth at the end of his life. Facing death, he is thinking of his mother at her life's end and realizes, "with death so near, Mother must have felt like someone on the brink of freedom, ready to start life all over again" (p. 154). He also feels like starting life all over again—does his outburst against the chaplain at the end of his life, in contrast to his indifference to the language of authority in the court, lead to the birth of an intensified yet peaceful sense of life? Does his ability to reclaim the maternal make possible the necessary detachment to claim his own sense of life? The detachment from the world due to repressing the intimate relations one has with the other does not enable one to leave with steady and firm steps, but makes one float without a grounding for one's feet. The nourishment of attachment is necessary for nurturing one's independence.

Detachment is also required to embrace the vitality of life. As an intellectual exile himself, Edward W. Said (1996) elaborates the status of an outsider and its unsettling affect and effect: "You cannot go back to some ear-lier and perhaps more stable condition of being at home; and, alas, you can never fully arrive, be at one with our new home or situation" (p. 53). In this difficult state of instability and movement, one learns to cultivate a certain sense of being *with* one's surroundings while at the same time going *beyond* the boundary, the old and the new. Taking in the new yet not being totally subsumed and carrying the old yet not being locked up by the memory, such is the demand of the third space, whose borders are at the boundless limit of time and place.

With the comings and goings of the stranger above and underneath the surface, the self carves out its own trajectory, refusing to stay either at the margin or in the center, not even in the middle of the in-between space. Homes are spots that the self builds along its movement, and its course of traveling connects these spots, unexpectedly and anticipatedly.

## Fragments and Holism

The demand for psychic separation produces splits. The appeal of a "limit attitude" privileges multiplicity or fragmentation over unity. The cultivation of independent personality brings temporary ruptures, yet holism prevails. Between fragments and holism is a complicated picture of the self which both spins off the whole and weaves intricate patterns.

Accepting the fleeting nature of all existence and the pain caused by the temporality of human life, the Confucian self does not confront the trauma of separation as Western psychoanalysis attempts to do. The maternal is never really objectified, so there is no need to grapple with the lost object. The trinity of heaven, earth, and man, and the unity between humanity and nature, provide an absorbent ability to compensate for the pains of separa-tion. The temporary rupture from the whole, in its independent ethical claim for "principle," can be brought back to the circular rhythm of the self, in its harmony with society and the cosmos. The fragments produced by failure in practicing "kingliness without" in politics can be woven back into the whole by searching for "sageliness within" through nature and aesthetics. Privileg-ing holism, the Confucian self cannot successfully deal with the issues of fragmentation and division.

The Foucauldian fragmented subject and the Kristevian split subject come from a different tradition: the Western tradition of subject/object dual-ity. The philosophical self and the psychic subject intersect at the objectifi-cation of both the self and the world. Foucault's struggle to break away from the constraints of the social and Kristeva's battle to destabilize the paternal law not only lead to the fragmentation of the subject but also already disrupt any notion of unity. Transgression beyond the limit is the basis for the Foucauldian subject, and separation from the maternal and revolt against the paternal is a psychic necessity for the Kristevian subject. Society, culture, and psychic reality all become the objects of subjective elaboration in such paradigms, which centralize the potential of the self to go beyond the other —human or cosmic—and itself. Pains of separation are assumed to be inevitable and must be encountered.

What is between and beyond the bliss of holism and the pain of separation?

Mikhail Bakhtin asserts the necessity of "unity not as an innate one-and-only, but as a dialogic *concordance* of unmerged twos or multiples" (quoted in Morson & Emerson, 1990, p. 1). Here, unity is not conformity, multiplicity is not division, and the dynamics of unity and multiplicity are preserved by *noncoincidence* of differences and by dialogic *interaction*. In an effort to bring differences together in the borderlands, Gloria Anzaldúa (1999) believes "the self has added a third element which is greater than the sum of its severed parts" (pp. 101–102). This third element is generated not only by the collision of fragments, but also by the encounter between the new part and the whole. It is more than duality *and* the synthesis of the duality. It is something new, not existing before.

The opposite pulls of holism and fragmentation converge in an interactive creative process. Creation needs both the tension of pulling out of the whole and the concordance of diversified forces forming a new pattern, a new way of connecting. The splits resulting from this necessary tension may be woven back into the fabric or left as excess for the further dynamics of self-organization (Doll, 1993). The whole no longer stays the same after the stretching of a creative act: new threads come in and the previous structure is destablized. Fragmentation and holism set each other into motion toward the creativeness of subjectivity situated in both a transcendent sense of *against* and an immanent sense of *with*. The simultaneity of *against* and *with* makes it possible for us to take the pain of invention in a harmonious way of being in the world. Pain no longer splits, but, like the stream of a waterfall, laps against our bodies with regenerative force; harmony refuses to support escapism, but, like the slope of a mountain, accelerates our breath with inspiring interconnectedness. In such a third space, the violence of dualism is gently guided back into a larger life force, and the self-contentedness of holism firmly curves out toward new openings. In and out, back and forth, such is the rhythm of the third.

## Love and Freedom

Holding mother's hand, the baby imagines reaching the star. Maternal love is the air the baby breathes, the food the baby eats, the clothes the baby wears, the pillow on which the baby sleeps, and the pillar to which the baby clings when learning how to walk. Without the power of maternal love, no freedom can be born.

In Kristeva's vision, maternal love mediates between dependency and independency to carve out a space for freedom. It is the prototype of all loving relationships. Our relationship with others is built from this love, which not only provides care for the other but also respects the (baby) other as the (potential) subject who has its own realm of subjectivity.

In *Follow Your Heart,* Susanna Tamaro (1996) tells the story of a woman's journey into love and freedom. Trapped by a marriage for which she has no passion, a woman attempts to journey out so that her "inability" to get pregnant and give birth—symptoms of the depression from which she suffers—can be "cured." Her travel outside of the home brings her the gift of love which helps her gain an extraordinary sense of freedom, even welcoming death. As a result of this freedom enabled by love, a baby girl is born. Later, the successive deaths of her lover and her husband leave her in a depression, during which she wanders along the paths of nature and spirituality to search for a deeper sense of the self. Not until she reaches the realization "on the grass be the grass, under the oak be the oak, among people be a person" (p. 149), that, under a big oak tree, does she set herself free. This realization of freedom *with* instead of *against* the world is echoed by Confucius' ideal of creative unity between self and world.

Love and freedom can be pulled in opposite directions if we see love as merely a relation *with* and freedom as only freeing *from.* In its intensified and supreme moment, love may simultaneously embrace death (the illusion of the final union with the universe) and birth (creation out of a loving relationship). Love can suffocate in a simple mode of *with,* but a genuine sense of being with the other requires labor and the inner strength to carve out the sharp edge of freedom. On the other hand, freedom *from* constraints may bring the sluggish letting go of both self and other. "The mask of freedom often conceals a lack of care, a desire not to get involved" (Tamaro, 1996, p. 47). Care opens rather than encloses. Hanging on a tiny opening out of the familiar and responding to nurture, this hopeful break with the old self are acts of love that uphold freedom. This ability to love usually requires a certain sense of self-assurance, a confident affirmation that there is certain truth and beauty in life. The self's ability to give, to intervene, and to engage with the other brings the gift of love for both.

Ewa Ziarek (2001) proposes a feminist ethic of freedom, defined in relational terms as an engagement with the other beyond objectification for social transformation. Such a freedom is in the domain of the public and serves the need for creating space for democracy. Attending to the needs and voices of the margin, freedom is wedded to the political and social responsibility of forming a nonviolent and nonappropriate—loving—relationship with the other to imagine life otherwise. This ethic requires us to redefine maternity and paternity.

Oliver believes that Western philosophy and psychoanalysis provide us an absent, disembodied father and anti-body culture versus an animal-body mother and antisocial nature. Such an opposition between nature/mother and culture/father is a fiction which supports the tyranny of patriarchy but fails to offer the image of love for our children: Not only is paternal love nonexistent, but maternal love is pushed to a corner and excluded from the social. Maternity is both loving and social, Kristeva says, and paternity is also embodied, Oliver would add. What is excluded from the paternal is its body with its indeterminacy and contingency—"the paternal body necessarily leaks" (Oliver, 1998, p. 143)—which is the object that patriarchy intends to control. Father's body is excluded, mother's body is asocial, and what is left is law emptied by its own disembodiment. Love is lost. Freedom is gone. The connection between words and affects is cut. Meaning is in miscarriage. "The contemporary crisis in meaning is a crisis in love" (Oliver, 1998, p. 134).

If the maternal body is a social body from the very moment when a new life is conceived, the social privilege of the paternal in its disembodied freedom and exclusion of love becomes suspect. Freedom is necessarily connected to love. A singular moment of freedom pregnant with new birth is situated in a shared space of communion.

## Polyphony and Unity in the Borderlands

Here we stand at the crossroads of multiplied conflicting doubles. At the boundary of the borderless border, along the rugged curve of the whole which is constantly pushed by its own parts, identity unites with the differences of nonidentity to narrate the tales of love, freedom, and creativity.

The conflicting double I have outlined is a conceptual differentiation which is traditionally dichotomized, but is actually not a dualism. Rather, it shifts in complex interconnection full of tensions (and attractions) through the dynamics of the third space. The dominance of one party over the other in each pair is displaced, and the dichotomy of the double is dissolved. The third space is born from the mutual transmutation of both, which bounce not only *with* but also *against* each other. The polyphony of the conflicting double is resonant in a new voice of unity (of the third), a unity constantly displaced, in the transitional and the indeterminate. The new voice is not unitary, but multiple, like a symphony. The third space multiplies itself, too, constantly giving new birth in the borderlands, creativity unbounded, moving in countless directions. Attending to the lost memory of what is already gone but does not disappear, and the pregnant possibility of what is yet to come, we are no longer walled by the tyranny of the permitted. The border of the forbidden gives way to the fluidity of traveling unity.

Bakhtin's polyphonic unity brings Foucauldian transgression, Kristevian maternal love, and Confucian relationality together. In this dynamic third space, a new sense of nondualistic creativity, based upon "sacred interconnections" (Griffin, 1990) and "the dream of earth" (Berry, 1988), is in the process of meeting the Eastern ideal of co-emergence of self, other, and universe. In this third space, the potential of the Confucian independent personality is pushed to the limit, meeting the singularity of the Western self, which swings back to the psychic and social web of life. In this third space, woman's deep sense of the relational emerges from the background, diffuses the central paternal figure, and draws the foreground of the male hero back into the interconnection.

Drawn simultaneously by conflicting doubles, the self moves into the third space, embracing simultaneously both the singular and the multiple. The double orientations shift toward new directions at the crossroads. Tales of creation are mixed with tales of love—maternal love, paternal love, "eco-erosic love" (Edgerton, 1996), and divine love. Both *with* the world and *beyond* the world, free as a bird, the self searches for a third space, singing, dancing, nesting, and flying, sometimes with companions, sometimes alone, always already attending to the call of the stranger.

## Body, Psyche, and Inter/Subjectivity

Individual identity and desire must be analyzed within a complex psychological and cultural process which is structured by specific political and social relations.
(Rebecca Martusewicz, 2001, p. 89)

The psychoanalytic subject emerges as simultaneously constituted by social processes of signification and an effect of residual and unresolved psychic conflicts.

(Alice Pitt, 2003, p. 49)

Another conflicting double central to the cross-cultural gendered third space I attempt to articulate here is the philosophical self and the psychoanalytic subject. The Foucauldian subject resists psychic structure and the Confucian self lacks psychic depth, while the Kristevian semiotic disrupts Confucian harmony and destabilizes the Foucauldian symbolic. They open up gaps among one another, while linked and self-intersecting, even if not directly. In this section I briefly discuss the "meeting" between psychic transformation and philosophical self, along the lines of body, psyche, and inter/subjectivity.

Foucault's relation to psychoanalysis is ambivalent, to use Derrida's (1998) phrase, like a hinge that successively "rejects and accepts, excludes and includes, disqualifies and legitimates" (p. 78). Throughout his writings, Foucault both credits and discredits psychoanalysis. On one hand, he acknowledges how Freud's psychoanalytic revolution articulated the relation between power and desire in a more complex way. On the other hand, he questions what he calls the "normalizing functions of psychoanalysis" (1998, p. 5), and points out that by grounding sexuality in the law, desire is surrounded by the "old order of power" (p. 150). According to Foucault, psychoanalysis is implicated in the strategies of knowledge and power through transforming sexuality into discourse, a discourse leading to the secret truth within a disciplinary gaze. Foucault's brief personal experience with psychoanalysis ended "in a fit of pique" (Miller, 1993, p. 62).

Affirming that psychoanalysis can be renewed with its own inherent potential for "nonglobalizable" (Derrida, 1998, p. 114) movement, and acknowledging Foucault's contradictory—thus complicated—gestures toward psychoanalysis, Derrida (1998) asks us to think about how Foucault "attempts to objectify psychoanalysis and to reduce it to that *of which* he speaks rather than to that *out of which* he speaks" (p. 76; emphasis added). In other words, psychoanalysis cannot be reduced to the strategies of knowledge and power, patterns of normalization through essential truth, and Foucault's own discourse is not immune from "infection" by this psychoanalytic "other."

Responding to the charge that psychoanalysis has a globalizing tendency, Kristeva argues for the necessity of *both* historical *and* psychic analysis. "It is a matter of pushing the need for the universal and the need for singularity to the limit in each individual, making this simultaneous movement the source of both thought and language," she (Kristeva, 2000a, p. 19) asserts. According to Kristeva, we need not only to delve deeply into the individual psyche, reaching its particularity in its poetics (which cannot be done only through analyzing social conditions), but also to appeal to the universal structure running through and beyond individuality (this generality being the basis for any theoretical investigation). Her own writing about maternal love, "Stabat Mater" in *Tales of Love* (1987a), is an intentional attempt at articulating this embodied contradiction between the academic generalization and the poetic singular. She adopts two kinds of typeface on the same page: on the left is the literary text, on the right is the academic text. This contradiction between the universal and the individual is coupled with the impossibility of a neutral position for psychoanalytic discourse, in which the engaged involvement of the psychoanalyst is inevitable. The struggle between maintaining a certain ob-

jectivity and engaging with the analytic situation is painful—a doubled position, Kristeva believes, that we need to live with to sustain meaning.

Foucault's project focuses on the singularity and particularity of the subject. His embrace of historical contingency eludes the universal appeal to
truth in its violence, but if violence—in a psychical, not physical, sense—is
part of our inner and social life, perhaps we cannot refuse to confront it. And
this living *with* implies neither *within* nor *without*. Theoretically, actually our
very ability to speak is already implicated in the general structure of language. As long as we are interested in understanding, the universal cannot be
pushed out of the picture. Without excluding the universal, however, we still
need to hold a healthy suspicion about any universalized claim. This doubt
may help us confront the alterity of the other, not as something that can be
assimilated within the self, not even by the stranger within the self, because
our stranger within may not coincide with that otherness. Psychoanalytic
compassion, I would argue, needs to be coupled with the acknowledgment
that the other's difference is irreducible and cannot be universalized into the
sameness of the self. This healthy doubt about the universal is supported by a
cross-cultural analysis of the psyche.

The encounter of psychoanalysis (if it could be reduced to a single framework) with the Chinese self can be illuminating. If the Oedipal story is not a
Chinese story, on what is the psychoanalytic interpretation founded in a different culture? If we must confront Chinese language and Chinese culture,
does not the language of the Oedipal have to go through a certain mutation
first? This does not dispute acknowledgment that Chinese culture has its own
psychic story to tell behind all its historical winding paths. But it needs to be
told in another way.

Standing by a stream, Confucius said, "It passes on just like this! Not
ceasing day or night!" (*The Analects*, 9.17). Tu Wei-ming (1979) interprets
this comment to imply an endless process of self-realization. I would also
read it as recognition of the temporary and contingent nature of both the
world and self. Due to this acknowledgment of flow without permanence, the
sadness that accompanies is not something to be overcome or abandoned, but
is part of the circular movement of human life. Confucius also said that good
music "brings one enjoyment without excess, sorrow without wound" (*The
Analects*, 3.20). This state of sorrow without wound poses a quite different
psychic challenge from the psychoanalytic demand that working through the
wound of separation is necessary for cultivating psychic independence. Confucianism assumes that a wound is an excess and that sorrow is what makes
life interesting or even beautiful, while psychoanalysis assumes that a wound
must be acknowledged so that the loss (of the maternal) can be worked
through. This conflicting orientation is directly related to one of the central

differences between Eastern and Western thought: the line of subject/object duality. If the maternal is never an object from whom one separates in order to become a speaking subject, the Chinese psyche does not have to deal with the scar produced by such a cut. For this same reason, the Confucian self is a transformative self which seldom achieves the sense of transgression characteristic of the Foucauldian subject. Even when a certain moment of transgression happens, it usually ends by being drawn back into the whole rather than disrupting the whole to the degree of changing it once and for all.

Historically and anthropologically, as Kristeva (1977a) argues, Chinese culture has an early matrilineal tradition which still influences the gender picture in the contemporary age. She is amazed by Chinese women's inner strength, courage, and brilliance. Although her comments are criticized as romantic, I believe this romance has a certain truth in it. Psychologically, the emphasis on interdependence rather than autonomy allows the power of the maternal to more strongly influence an individual's psyche. If the Oedipal break with the maternal is not demanded, the post-Oedipal "return" (as Kristeva phrases it) of the maternal semiotic is no longer required. The maternal permeates Chinese culture, art, and psyche, consciously and unconsciously. Aesthetically, this endless imprint of the maternal creates a unique form of art through calligraphy, painting, and music, which in turn contributes to the shaping of an individual psyche.

The important impact of the maternal on the Chinese psyche, however, does not make patriarchy any less painful. It may make patriarchy worse, not so much due to what Kristeva calls "the regression to the maternal," but due to the incorporation of the maternal into the paternal tyranny. This reappropriation of the maternal happens through the control of the paternal, which acknowledges the power of the maternal, yet subsumes this power to serve the interests of a patriarchal system. The intergenerational psychic struggle in an extended family makes it a particularly bitter struggle. It is very difficult for women to have any space of their own.

Traditionally, in the Confucian world, whatever influence women have had in the public sphere has been primarily through their relationships with their husbands. Their influence emotionally has been, primarily, through their relationships with their sons. This complicated web of psychic connections makes women's (emotional) equality with men contingent upon women's ability to compete with the power of the maternal in addition to paternal authority. Although motherhood is always elevated in Chinese culture, it can be easily appropriated psychically and socially to reproduce patriarchy, although it also confers a sophisticated social influence through the strong role of the Chinese family. To understand the collective unconscious of Chinese women in its multiple and conflicting layers of strength and vulnerability and its impact on the contemporary landscape is far beyond what I can elaborate here. But it is sufficient to notice that the Chinese psyche may preserve a certain resistance against the demand to create a wound (the Oedipal break) in dialoguing with the West, but a healthy sense of separation through the necessity of differentiation needs to be upheld so that revolt against patriarchy and hierarchy can be initiated and sustained.

The Chinese self has already confronted a break, as the result of encountering the other for over a century, which has also intensified intracultural encounters—including gendered encounters. If this psychic and cultural split can be worked through, can this process invent what the Chinese tradition has aspired to but never been able to reach? Is it possible that the deepest root is pregnant with the newest possibility, as Serres (1997) argues? Yet, giving birth to such a possibility is a great labor, which requires intercultural and intracultural conversation upheld by the psychic transformation of the personal.

To complicate the Western psychic story with the Chinese situation, not only do I question the claim of the universal psychic structure in psychoanalysis, I also point out the problematics of neglecting psychic struggles in the Chinese philosophical self. The issue of subjectivity and intersubjectivity, coupled with the necessity for both psychic interdependence and independence becomes a cross-cultural gendered tale that needs to be invented. In the Confucian world, not only are the collective and individual psychic stories of Chinese women neglected, but what is lacking is an in-depth analysis of the psychic world. What has been credited to earlier Confucian thought as psychological, such as Mencius' theory of four universal sources of "goodness," which are concerned with human feelings of empathy, shame, reverence, and the sense of right and wrong (*Mencius*, 11.6), usually stays at the level of conventional interpretations of Confucian ethics and morality. There is little probing into what lurks inside. Tu (2000) points out that in-depth psychology such as Freudian theory, especially concerning the darkness of human nature, must be studied in order to transform Confucian thought. The passage of expanding from self-cultivation through family and nation into the universe cannot be channeled successfully without dealing with the turbulence of the psychic world.

This is also true of the notion of harmony. The sense of harmony or unity between self and universe cannot be made fully dynamic without exposing and confronting cultural contradictions and human suffering. Accepting pain without taking the necessary step of psychic differentiation tends to flatten the wave against the limit of the boundary. At times, it can become escapist, running away from the need to make sense out of collision, fragmentation, and splitting. Content to be lost in the depths of the mountains, the Chinese psyche may also lose its ability to speak the unspeakable. "Psychical life is this interior space, this place within, that allows one to take attacks from inside and outside, that is, physiological and biological trauma, as well as social and political aggression" (Kristeva, 2002, p. 267). Refusing to deal with violence in the dark, the Chinese (traditional) notion of the self may lose its ability to take "attacks" from both outside and inside and as a result turn violence back onto itself. In the peaceful melody of classical Chinese music, the calm of the heart is already always disturbed, silently, without words.

This lack of psychic understanding in Chinese thought leaves me particularly suspicious about any theory of subjectivity that does not deal with the psyche, although I remain skeptical about the applicability of Western psychic structures to Chinese culture. While Foucault questions the very possibility of the psychoanalytic potential to empower the self, it would be naive to assume that he refuses to see the role of the psyche. As Miller (1993) points out, "Key Freudian ideas stayed with him [Foucault], though, throughout his life" (p. 62). What Foucault asks of us is to be alert to the danger of any grand theory, including psychoanalysis, and how psychoanalytic "incitements to discourse" on sexuality can reinforce sexual norms. On the other hand, Foucault's historical and social analysis cannot be replaced by psychic analysis. I have argued in Chapter 4 that social space is important for establishing psychic space. To sustain the dynamics of the psychic and the social, we need to not only acknowledge their independence, but also perceive where they cross each other's paths, so that trajectories of both convergence and divergence can be discerned.

Both the (Foucauldian) philosophical subject and the (Kristevian) psychoanalytic subject posit the potential of the subject to go beyond itself, but each locates the sources of resistance differently. Foucault seems to assume an element of the outside, so that the limit of subjectivity is continuously folded back to expose new boundaries (Deleuze, 1994). This outside folds and unfolds, like a hinge which closes and opens. Although Ziarek (2001) argues that "the outside of the historical formation does not have a psychic status" (p. 21), she does not deny that what cannot be assimilated can be haunted by "the psychic remainder." If what is folded back upholds the inside which always touches upon the outside, I would imagine that its depth cannot be reduced, but only multiplied through the active psychic life. It is clear that Foucault does not attempt to locate an outside of the symbolic to register the potential for resistance. The Foucauldian subject subverts itself through ruptures or interstices of the symbolic structure. In Kristeva's discourse, however, it is the semiotic which subverts the symbolic. In other words, the symbolic is incapable of self-subversion. Foucault's and Kristeva's notions of the symbolic are not identical, as the Foucauldian symbolic does not exclude the body. However, without the conceptual alterity of the semiotic, in its utter refusal to be assimilated, the capacity of thought to free differences and to find exits from the past might be limited. What can help elude the danger that the symbolic's self-renewal will lead to reproducing itself instead of breaking new ground? If the (under)current of the psyche is constantly breaking on the shore of subjectivity, would not subjectivity be swept away? It seems to me that the role of the psyche is key to formulating any theory of subjectivity about the limit, at the limit, and beyond the limit. To speak about the psyche does not require psychoanalysis, but insights from psychoanalysis can be helpful in understanding in-depth psychological dynamics.

The psyche is intimately related to the body. The aesthetics of the Foucauldian subject are exercised through the body—or in other words, through queer eroticism—while the body itself is implicated in power relations. As Judith Butler (1997) argues, Foucault's subject has double faces, evident through the double functions of the body: one is the subjection of the body by its normative and normalizing soul; the other is the production of a body exceeding the limit of the social, especially through experimentation with bodily pleasures in queer politics. Butler wonders whether "Foucault has invested the body with a psychic meaning that he cannot elaborate within the terms that he uses" (p. 95) and asks us whether "the unconscious of power itself, in its traumatic and productive iterability" (p. 104) can be elaborated. If the body plays the role of the psyche in its subversive function in Foucauldian subjectivity, there is an interesting twist here because Kristeva's semiotic is contingent upon the maternal *body*, yet this maternal continent is in the world of the unconscious. It would be very difficult (if at all possible) for the Foucauldian body to channel its energy toward the re-creation of the symbolic without going through the transformation of the psyche. In Butler's (1997) words, "The possibilities of resignification will rework and unsettle the passionate [psychic] attachment to subjection without which subject formation— and re-formation—cannot succeed" (p. 105). The otherness of the unconscious provides a site on which social processes of signification are complicated and unsettled by psychic conflicts in the reformulation of subjectivity.

The interconnectedness between body and mind, psychic and social, and subjectivity and intersubjectivity depends upon their differences, and the necessity of opening onto the other requires both differentiation from and engagement with the other. The gap between the two in each dichotomy needs to be sustained so that the potential for both psychic transformation and social change can be opened, rather than enclosed, by collapsing the dichotomies onto a smooth surface. It is through "peering through the opaque depths of the unconscious" (Pinar in Pitt, 2003, p. xv) that the surface of subjectivity cannot be smoothed out, and it is through the imprint of the social that the subject necessarily becomes a shared interspace. At the intersections in the border-lands, the border of body, psyche, and subjectivity no longer merely divides like a straight line, but multiplies in a topology in which crossing over is no longer forbidden but a necessity for constantly changing figurations. Forever transitional, such an imaginative space is enabled by transformative interaction through tensions, attractions, and conflicts.

The Kristevian psychoanalytic self tells the story of the individual psyche—its implications for community are also elaborated but are somehow derivative. But the unconscious is not only individual; it is also collective. This collectivity is not necessarily the mirror for eye(s)/I(s) to see or even reflect upon, but vibrates through the invisible and the inarticulate, and asks for a thorough experiencing of life and a willingness to endure empty space instead of trying to occupy what is perceived as a gap or distance. If we recall Yu Qiuyu's encounter with the intellectual unconscious in an ancient court-yard and listen lovingly to the call from the ghosts of no-name Chinese women, what we touch is beyond the totality of all individual egos, yet not so far away from us. The ability to both let go into a shared space and come out to embrace one's own space depends upon elaborating the psychic differen-tiation of the self through the social body and the cultural past.

Kristeva (2002) speaks about the notion of the "timeless" as archaic memory set against the flow of time. What is the relationship between this archaic memory and cultural archaeology, specifically the cultural uncon-scious? And if body, psyche, and subjectivity meet their own other (not only through the individual, but also through history and culture), would the Kris-tevian intimate revolt be also a collective revolt? On the other hand, can the Confucian independent personality in its social relatedness ever be renewed without probing into individual psychology? Can the Foucauldian outside-of-historical-formation emerge without the transformation of the psyche? The re-articulation of the philosophical self meeting the psychic transformation of the personal through both social–historical analysis and psychic analysis pro-vides complementary inspirations for a path yet to be traversed, along the curved, dispersed, and intersecting line of "intercivilizational dialogue" (Smith, 1999a, 2000; Yu & Tu, 2000) and intracultural conversation, an inter-subjective tale, and an intrapsychic story.

The links, as well as divergences, between and among body, psyche, and inter/subjectivity in Foucault's, Confucius', and Kristeva's theories of the self not only underscore an irreducible element of antagonism but also point to a possibility for conversing. Antagonism and conflict through their double movement press the self to step toward the third space at the crossroads of culture, gender, and identity, a process whose outcome cannot be predicted. My aspiration for a cross-cultural gendered self is situated in this third space of im/possible meeting between East and West, between the psychic and the social, between the feminine and the masculine. It is a meeting never meant to be fully realized. It eludes the final fusion of any conflicting double. Yet the elements of the double search for each other, never abandon the efforts to reach out toward each other, so that meetings are always expected. Double-edged, nevertheless, the third space forms its own border—so that it never disperses into disappearance—at the borderless limit. This is a space words are not sufficient to express. Yet the unspeakable must be felt, the outside must be discerned, and the invisible must be touched, at the crossroads.

### Speaking the Unspeakable: Toward a Third Space of Self

I think or I love, therefore I am not; I think or I love, therefore I am not me; I think or I love, therefore I am no longer there, I have cast off from being there.

(Michel Serres, 1997, p. 29)

*Tao* gives birth to one
One gives birth to two
Two gives birth to three
Three gives birth to universe

(Lao Zi)

Wherever they put the light . . . there was always a shadow somewhere.

(Virginia Woolf, 1927, p. 114)

Language loses its power in a third space. At least its defining power. Like the elusive stranger, as soon as words are spoken to describe it, the third space shifts away. It is invisible, beyond the gaze of eyes. It is inarticulate, beyond the shape of uttering. It is inaudible, beyond the mastering of language. Refusing to be arrested, invested in its own absence, the third space keeps renewing itself precisely at the moment when its own location is displaced.

How can I speak about the unspeakable third space,[1] especially in a language not my own? But is not what I speak already a third language, a language no longer singular, a language with double edges? I speak in a third language imbued by Chinese and English—the latter as an adopted tongue, the former with a foreign accent.

Speaking the unspeakable in a foreign language. Perhaps a foreign language can take the edge off the intimate turbulence, so that the difficult can manage to emerge in words before it is lost, and the impossible can be spoken before it is effaced. The unspeakable takes residence in the alien world. Our own ghosts dance toward the surface beside our pillows, whispering unheard stories. Attending to the shadow within, closing our eyes, lovingly, we learn another language, the language of the underground, the invisible foundation of what keeps sinking. Not only in the paternal utterance, but also in the maternal tongue, the bilingual connects. Different languages, different worlds, and different ways of speaking are connected. The foreground of the paternal order fading into the background of the maternal continent, the feminine other speaks, through the opaque veil of the unsayable and the unseen. What is uttered in the shadow is no longer sustained by its own silence, and the bilingual revolts, intimately. Connecting and disrupting, the language of the ineffable shifts to becoming a third.

At dusk, the red, perfectly round, peaceful sun, without dazzling light, is ready to descend, while simultaneously the opaque, aspiring, and full moon quietly rises to be its counterpart. Looking up into the sky from one locus to another, we may have a moment of suspicion: Which one is sun; which one is moon? Can the moon become red while the sun becomes silver? At the moment of transition (a temporal change, perhaps decisively, marking the split of day and night), a third space is born. Being lost in the double of sun and moon, light and dark, a third space weds daylight laughter with nighttime intimacy, bridges words and memories, and connects motion with meditation. At dawn, isn't the descending moon also accompanied by the rising sun? The archaic, distant touch of a forever-retreating past, the recurring voice of a present which does not repeat, and the vision of a future which is open to its own alterity welcome simultaneous differences in a nonlinear movement. The moment also marks the fusion of horizons—the horizon of sun and the horizon of moon, moving toward a topology of shifting lines, mutable borders, and irreplaceable holes. In the topography of sinking in and surfacing beyond, with, and against the flow of time, in the temporality where social geography and psyche meet and struggle (Pinar, 1991), a third space emerges. Dwelling in and stretching out. A conflicting hybrid interplay of positioning and displacement.

A third space is ineffable. It does not belong to the realm of logic or rationality. What cannot be reasoned becomes the other. It is a space of multiple others interacting through different times and places. What is straight becomes curved, what is bright becomes shadowed, and what is filled becomes empty. The third space is produced by the other in me, which keeps eluding the direct route to the destination. The destination becomes unknown when all reference points are lost (Serres, 1997), as we journey into the third space.

This journey is different from any tourist notion of travel, which risks a glancing over landscapes without taking in anything new. One can search for exotic scenery and jump at the very sight of differences, or what is perceived as surprising discoveries. The resilience of the given, however, can quickly enclose what has just been opened, and exclude the exotic by shutting it outside of the self. The psychic attachment to the given allows surprise, but does not allow the permeation of the other through the boundary. To journey in a third space, we must be engaged in a polyphonic conversation to displace the psychic affiliation. Such an engagement—a process of both receiving and giving—makes the transformation of both self and space possible. Engaged and engaging, such a journey does not take over the places it visits. Refusing to occupy and conquer, a third space is "nomadic" (Roy, 2003).

"Questions of travel" (Kaplan, 1996) ask us to be vigilant about the danger of occupying the other's territory as if it were one's own. Resisting colonization, we have to dwell in a new space in order to let go and allow the old self to be transformed. Without such a dwelling, no becoming can emerge. Without cultivating a new attachment to a specific site on which people, history, and location mingle, one's next move is not grounded. Yet arriving in a new place is never quite completed, as full arrival is both anticipated and suspended. *Becoming* and *being* need to accompany each other to transform the self through the paradoxical movement of placement and displacement. Paradoxically, a third space *is* and *becomes* unspeakable—but not mute; it nevertheless speaks through conflicting and hybrid movement.

Traveling on a road full of old obstacles and newly fallen stones, the journey of the feminine crosses many ancient thresholds and new doorways, positioning herself firmly and deeply both within and against a location that cannot be placed. Meeting with what holds her back, she plants the seeds of restlessness along the way. Restless, she nevertheless connects, spreads roots, and cultivates the possibility of rebirth. The strength of the masculine conquers the land, while the power of the feminine dwells in the land as she moves. Transforming the land but not *dominating* the land, she transforms herself. Her own voice gradually emerges, fades, and then surfaces again. Deeply tied to the maternal underworld, she negotiates contradictions as she travels in and through the landscape. The feminine stranger comes and goes, displacing the center and multiplying the margin. The whole landscape shifts with her unique and unexpected steps. Flowing but positioned, located but displaced, loyal to mother but inventing her own language, the feminine other speaks through subverting her own absence and decentering her own struggle for presence. "The second sex" searches for the third. Longing for the freedom of the sky, a lover of the sea, she swims like a flying bird with delicate but powerful wings. Holding baby's hands, she balances her unbalanced rising and finds her own way to reach stars. Dark branches stroking her lightened face, she rises.

A third space is playful. It is the play of the personal "in the transitional space where inner and outer reality can be experienced together" (Pitt, 2003, p. 94). Experienced together, the inner and the outer move toward the limit, the fold, the intersecting line of meeting, while the interior and the exterior move away from each other, leaving a crack, a gap, an in-between space which cannot be filled. It is the play of the cultural which connects social body through time and place. "Enter(tain)ing" (Gazetas, 2003) a third space, the self plays through history and culture, reaching deeply into the psyche and coming out to embrace the universe. Preserving lingering warmth, the ashes of the night turn to dew in the morning to moisten grass and flowers. Dipping into this warmth that lingers, culturally and personally, our fingers connect to the traces of what has not yet been formed into words, our ancestors' wildest dreams, the traces of what is yet to be reborn, and our own newest longings. The flow of milk and music nourishes our imagination in the wildness *with* the land. Sensing the current underneath the surface, we invent —through love—new words.

A third space is about passage and making passages. Between the midnight sun and the midday moon, the passage is contingent upon the moment of seeing both of them in the sky. Half-buried in the sand, footprints connect dreams of the sea and stories of the land. The interstices between rocks embrace the contour of the mountains and the inner bursting of the valley. The third space is knotted by conflicting doubles. Pulling any one single thread only tightens the knot. The knot can change its shape but cannot dissolve an intricate binding which is pulled in opposite directions.

A good weaver discerns unnoticed connections and potential relatedness. Unrealized relation, hidden, is drawn and pulled, until the invisibility of the joint is caught by hands. To join the unseen threads requires border crossing. The very act of crossing the border does not erase the boundary once and for all, but multiplies limits in the borderlands. This multiplication is abundant with new potential relationships.

Simultaneously differentiated and integrated, the creativity of the third space lies in "a process of transforming positions which gives dynamic presence to the absence of otherness" (Budick & Iser, 1989, p. xiv). As we think and live together, compassion and tenderness toward the other is the tunnel in which we position ourselves in relations. Our hands are forever linked— through suffering, through unspeakable pain, through heartfelt joy, and through collective efforts at making sense of our tears and laughter. The passage is created when our eyes meet, a thousand times, as if for the first time. Deep in the connection, both instant and distant, we meet people we have never met, go places we have never been, hear stories we have never heard, dwell in landscapes we have never seen. In the candlelight in the passageway, weaving allows empty space; connecting cherishes silence. Being affirmative through what is absent, the silence can be the loudest; the emptiness can be the fullest. Interstices ask us to open "soft eyes" (Fleener, 2002) for the complexity of interrelatedness and the deeper layers of hidden order. Full of meanings, a third space speaks through the unsayable. Is it possible to allow "the unsayable to speak for itself?" (Budick & Iser, 1989, p. xi)

The unsayable speaking for itself, a third space is one's *own* space, singular through and beyond the multiple. Immersing into the web, it comes out with new, original patterns. In solitude under the night sky, it exchanges profound thoughts with blinking stars. Driving into the darkness without companions, it locates its own positions among all flowing directions. However alluring union is, be it social, cosmic, or personal, it is permanently temporary. The return of aloneness after union, after giving up one's self, after taking in multiplicity and differences, is crucial for the emergence of a third space. Without the demand for the singular, the third is no longer necessary if we can choose to merge with either side of the shore. Between the semiotic and the symbolic, between the psychic and the social, between memory and promise, between East and West, the third space moves toward the one, the ever-changing, double-faced, original one. Though original, the third space nevertheless splits and moves away, yet iterates back to an always already-lost origin. Enriched by one's tours through other landscapes, other texts, other languages, and other selves, one's own space multiplies itself wherever it swirls. The third space is many and one, one and many.

What is a third space? Can it really be defined? It is simultaneously the third, the one, and the multiple—beyond either/or, beyond in-between, and beyond both/and. The third space comes out of the conflicting double—embodying and flying over both/and into the one; of one's *own*, of independence embedded in interdependence. Interdependence gives birth to the multiple, the multiple of regeneration and creation, the multiple of the interaction between the one and the third. Playing with, rather than being trapped by, in-between, a space of one's own both bends itself to let go and spirals up to reach beyond. Either/or is replaced by doubling, in-between is folded by netting, and both/and leads to another unexplored path.

One's third space shifts as one interacts with each person, with each text, in each situation. Transformative, it hosts ambivalence, contradictions, and fragmentation, yet not without attraction. Affirmative, it regenerates through conflicts and passages. Creative, it holds endless love and boundless energy. If the *Tao* which gives birth to one, to two, to three, and then to the universe, cannot be defined, this third space is also impossible to specify. It is a mystery knotted by unsettled and unsettling strings. Constantly moving, yet with motionless rooting, it creates but does not occupy. Not occupying, it positions itself at the intersection between the subterranean lake and the cave on the hill, holding out, and embracing back at the limit. Dwelling, it casts off the hard shell of yesterday lovingly, and lands the shadow of tomorrow onto today's heavy shoulder. Impossible meetings are both bridged and suspend-ded. Before arrival, the departure already begins. The tragedy and fortune of the double, the split and whole of one, are the magic of the third.

Finally I am home, in a third space. Dancing home, through the body, down to the psyche, in the boats traveling along the river, the river of mem-ory, the river across borders, the river flowing to unfamiliar shore. In a third space, I am no longer at home. Endless homecoming lands in the stranger's kingdom, the queendom of homeless singing. The journey continues, at the interminable beginning through a "complicated conversation" (Pinar, Rey-nolds, Slattery, & Taubman, 1995) that is curriculum.

## Note

1.   While I was troubled by how to proceed with this chapter, Donna Trueit's insightful questions helped to bring me to write about the unspeakable. I would like to thank her for helping me go beyond the (seemingly) dead end.

# Chapter 6
# Curriculum in a Third Space

A beautiful autumn day. On the train from Nanjing to Shanghai. We are on a trip back from Nanjing where we once studied American culture in a bilingual educational center, almost ten years ago. My friend Lydia sits in the seat opposite me. I pull out a piece of paper, smiling at her: "Lydia, I've got the framework for the last chapter of my dissertation." She smiles at me in silence and watches me record my thoughts. After finishing my play with words, we resume our conversation.

A sunny winter day. On the flight from Stillwater, Oklahoma, to Long Beach, California. I am on a vacation. Thoughts and ideas racing through my mind as the plane takes off. Suddenly, I "see" the structure of this chapter you are now reading. I don't have a piece of paper at hand, so I wait until receiving a napkin to sketch the outline.

Is it not amazing that I tend to have inspirations, almost out of nowhere, on trips, all kinds of trips, in the process of being in transit? Is not this the very process of curriculum in a third space, a journey of my own education, in a movement simultaneously both outside and inside?

I had a chance to revisit Nanjing with Lydia during my second trip back to China.[1] It had a profound impact on me. During the trip, I was translator for my American Ph.D. advisor, Dr. Doll, as he made an academic tour throughout China. It was a struggle, albeit an inspirational one, for me to attempt to live with the third space as I took up the task of translation in a broad sense—cultural, educational, and personal. Now I have a new home in Stillwater, where I teach curriculum studies to American graduate students. As I intend to practice teaching in a third space here, other sets of stories unfold. When the contexts shift, the challenges I face shift, too.

With a renewed understanding of the human/woman self, I invite you to travel with me back and forth between China and the United States to be engaged in curriculum as a creative journey home, in a third space.

## An Intimate Transcendent Space

Everyone experiences, and continues to have the possibility of experiencing the transcending of present forms of life, of finding that life is more than what is presently known or lived. This is what education is about.

(Dwayne Huebner, 1999, p. 345)

We need to "look within" ourselves to look beyond what we have already seen. Looking within is part of preparing ourselves for engaging in reflective and mindful practice.

(Hwu Wen-song, 1998, p. 29)

### Shanghai, China

I am checking in at the counter of a hotel in Shanghai. I am still in shock about how much Shanghai has changed during the four years since I left. The newly established Pudong International Airport, shaped like a bird on the shore of the sea, was my first impression of a dynamic Shanghai. I cannot recognize many places with which I used to be familiar. As I turn around, my Chinese advisor, Professor Zhong, is already here to welcome us. I can sense his pride in Shanghai's ever-changing mentality and in China's recent curriculum change.

The emergent focus upon the individual person (Chen, 1988; Deng, 2000; Ding, 1989; Hu, 1989; Yun, 1993; Zhong, 1989, 1994, 1997; Zhang, 2000; Zuo, 1992) situated in sociality has become an important educational wave in the last two decades. A new notion of individuality and relationality based upon transformative interaction between individual and interconnections is in curricular formation. Curriculum as a journey in this age of social change and cultural fluidity in China calls for a simultaneous movement toward personal reflection and cultural transformation. This collective effort to go beyond traditions cannot be successful without serious and critical encounters by educators with their own pasts and with the historical landscapes of the nation.

Dr. Doll lectures to doctoral students in Shanghai on his postmodern perspective on curriculum. He always leaves time for me to hold a discussion with students in Chinese. I ask them not to think too much about the label of "postmodernism," but to think more about the challenges that postmodernism brings to Chinese society and education, and the meaning of the deconstruction of Western traditions to us Chinese in terms of questioning our own traditions. With enthusiasm and open-mindedness, we struggle together with multilayered questions; we argue with each other and seek passage through difficult channels. Impressed by the students' critical thinking and articulate openness, I am also surprised by my own ease in difficult translations across languages, education, and cultures. I feel grounded: the change in me, as a result of my cross-cultural encounters, has reoriented my sense of self and home. This coming home from a distance, yet feeling more comfortable with the self, cannot be achieved without an immersed engagement with the other *and* a deep attachment to home. While Rebecca Martusewicz argues that "detachment is at the heart of education" (2001, p. 34) and wonders how "one deals with the tension between home and nomadism" (p. 37), I believe a detached attachment which values both connection and critique makes curriculum a transcendent journey through intimate dwelling.

Historically, Shanghai is a place where East and West collide, often violently, and intersect. Recently emerging as an international city, it is becoming a location where genuine dialogues in multiple languages take place. Facing the West across the ocean, it tells complicated stories about intercivilizational encounters and intracultural reflections. But my own personal experience of this city carries mixed feelings, as I continually have to deal with the difficulties that my nonnative dialect causes in supermarkets and on buses.[2] Open-minded to the West, yet still provincial, Shanghai has to confront its own arrogance before being truly open to differences, the stranger both within and without. This confrontation, psychically, is "intimate," to use Kristeva's term—an intimacy that requires both memory working in the interior world and a singular invention yet to come.

## Stillwater, Oklahoma

Coincident with the September 11, 2001 tragedy, my initial teaching experience in Stillwater is almost another cultural shock. The radical nature of my doctoral studies and the cross-cultural nature of my personal journey have already positioned me with certain assumptions—such as the belief in social justice, the need to interrogate privileges, and the necessity for change and transformation, all of which have become organic parts of me. However, many of my students hold a quite different set of assumptions—that each person is responsible for *him*self; society has progressed well. Why bother with so much change? Racism is something irrelevant to me because I'm never prejudiced against anyone, they tell me.

This gap between us presents a mutual challenge, and sometimes intense mutual resistance, for both teacher and student. This is where, as Alice Pitt (2003) points out, the teacher's own pedagogical assumptions may not meet the expectations of the students, but since "we resist learning precisely where we are most implicated" (p. 6), this gap is an educational site for all of us. As time has passed and I have persistently refused to position myself as an authority figure in relation to my students, I have come to understand more and more that my teaching en*gender*s an unsettling process, in which students' identity formation (and re-formation) is registered, and which in turn asks me to rework my teaching and personal identity. I realize that I must deal with my own emotions as an alien in this post–September 11 era in order to teach. In other words, I must lead myself when I call students out of their own comfort zones. A sense of transcendence is necessarily intimate in a pedagogical effort to cope with suffering. Then teacher and student can journey together.

Now, every time I walk into a multicultural education class, I tell my students: I don't have any purpose for this class and I assure you that we will not walk out of this class at the end of the semester with any overarching consensus; it is the *experiencing* of thoughts and the reexperiencing of life and self that really matter. Students usually do not realize how much "burden" and anxiety (an anxiety different from that of attempting to meet the teacher's expectation) this claim of uncertainty can produce until they study readings and engage in heated debates.

Pedagogical outcomes are ambiguous and uncertain in promoting an open-ended inquiry in the classroom. When I am astonished and excited by students' new awareness, they may the next moment fall into a depressed mood in which they feel helpless to confront social injustice. If I find myself frustrated by the stubborn psychic "attachment to subjection" (Butler, 1997, p. 105) of the self to the social norms, unexpected breakthrough may come after a while. The initial resistance can turn into a change that will last; an initial acceptance can cover the prevailing of hidden psychic resistance. But if pedagogy genuinely engages a process of leading out, it must have the capacity to endure uncertainty and work with contradictions—not in order to achieve final consensus, but to reach another level of understanding and sympathy—and to reach beyond: not in order to finally settle down, but to nurture the original moments of creativity.

## Transcendence in Intimacy

At first hearing, transcendence and intimacy do not sound attuned to each other, but I would argue (Hwu Wen-song [1998] also articulates a sense of transcendence in immanence) that they must be copresent and intertwined in our search for a third space in which to teach. A journey must be simultaneously a journey out and a journey in. The educative process of leading out to reach new forms of life (Huebner, 1999) is coupled with a leading in and a leading back so that meaning making is imbued with the semiotic return, to support the singularity of a creative act and to sustain the communality of loving encounter. Transcendence implies the necessity of leaving home, while intimacy asks for dwelling and dancing in the shadows—yet both are the task of education. Denying a certain sense of returning has an effect similar to staying at home all the time, since the former is lost in a permanent wandering (of masculinity away from the maternal), while the latter is lost in an enclosed domestic boundary. This boundary is not necessarily maternal, as it can be a symbolic structure, erect like a dam against all tides of the semiotic. Intimacy is the dwelling of the semiotic on the shore of the symbolic to transform the process of meaning making into singular events of invention, which makes transcendence possible. Transcendence in intimacy cannot "be" *and* "become" without a community of co-journeyers who support one another's efforts with love, courage, and compassion.

Martusewicz (2001) argues for leaving home as a necessity for one's education. I also want to argue for the importance of revisiting previous homes. Traveling back is the seeking of passages beyond the old home and the new home, pointing to new directions for further journeying. As Sandra Majors (2002) nicely puts it, "I see myself crossing many borders; bringing much back, never being the same, but always coming home. As for my students, I hope to take them on many journeys across borders ... and bring them back" (p. 8). The very act of crossing itself already implies a certain sense of connection, and this connection becomes more explicit and generative if border crossing also brings enrichment back home. The intertextual nature of education itself asks the teacher and students to keep looping, making recursive returns to previous texts, so that a transformative curriculum can be built through a matrix of interconnections, webbed with room for disconnection (Doll, 1993, 1998a).

A simultaneous movement between departure and return is particularly important for women who have been denied the self for so long. Woman's journey attends to the strangeness which has not been historically legitimated. When silenced whispers are heard, when invisible traces are followed, when denied connections are rebuilt, the suppressed female self in the male other will be reconstructed and the implication of the male self in the female other can be rethought. With the deepening of self-understanding, the woman educator will no longer accept the imposed task of serving others. She will create her own womanhood, made possible by building creative bridges between femininity and masculinity, and recursively traveling through texts, new places, and unfamiliar people. The Kristevian semiotic return must follow every departure to nurture her inner self. In this way, the woman teacher can claim a new sense of self as both fully grounded inside and expanded outside.

Teachers cannot engage in students' personal transformations without first reaching beyond the teacher's self—culturally, socially, and personally. Kristeva (1996) believes that the art of teaching is to "read the unknown that students [bring to the teacher]" instead of seeing students as "looking for our own ideas" (p. 50). The invitation to call forth the unknown within students is also a call for teachers to reach their own unknown. Teachers and students need to not only share knowledge but also share their lives in an "engaged pedagogy" (hooks, 1994a). Sharing is a process of simultaneously reaching inside and outside to meet the other. The student is our "other": can we meet our student as we would meet 'the stranger' (Huebner, 1999)? This pedagogical openness to student-as-stranger who has unrecognized potential with irreducible singularity reflects back to the teacher's necessity to confront her own otherness within. Reading what is behind the surface of students' resistance, we may find a new world of possibilities that calls for our pedagogical imagination. By no means does this openness to the students' own worlds mean giving up pedagogical responsibility and offering students only what they want, but it is precisely in not filling in the pedagogical gap that further labor—emotionally and intellectually—on the part of both teacher and student is always required. Not looking for her own expectations to be fulfilled, the teacher also resists students' demands for certainty and guides them by a third-space orientation—beyond both teaching content and students' comfort level—to call potential into existence.

The intimate transcendent space in which curriculum is situated is much more than knowledge. In deeply experiencing life in its various modes, in its contradictions and suffering, in its embodied meanings which are always open to new extensions, a third space is indeed imaginative (Greene, 1995), requiring the difficult task of envisaging alternative landscapes. Pinar (1994) poetically asks us to see knowledge and intelligence as wings "by which we take flight, visit other worlds, returning to this one to call others to futures more life affirmative than the world we inhabit now" (p. 247). The wings of intelligence do not take us anywhere when the unexpected, the unpredictable, and the imaginative are constantly missing in our classrooms. The profound impact of aesthetic experiences in transforming the ordinary into the extraordinary and opening a magical window to surprise, spontaneity, and the unspeakable aspect of life, needs to be introduced into schools. Rather than merely presenting ideas and making rational arguments, I have learned to use novels, autobiographies, movies, and in-class performance to "touch" students, pulling them out of their comfort zones to reexamine their life stories, to reexperience their connections with others and the world, and to speak about difficult topics through feeling the world differently. When smells, sounds, visions, touch, and vivid depictions of life are activated, imagination connects the intimacy of words and the web of creative forces.

My efforts to lead students—Chinese or American—out to an active engagement with both self and other are highly contextualized, requiring different styles of teaching and of questioning and different ways of relating to students. Yet complicated interplays between desire and knowing and between the psychic and the social are articulated in all classrooms. A third space, enabled by both transcendence and intimacy, does not close pedagogical gaps, but rather, opens them up further, leading to self-organization of both curriculum and its lived participants.

## Beyond the Middle: Positioning, Suffering, and "Home"coming

The moment we choose to love we begin to move against domination, against oppression. The moment we choose to love we begin to move towards freedom, to act in ways that liberate ourselves and others. That action is the testimony of love as the practice of freedom.

(bell hooks, 1994b, p. 250)

To save our children. The individuality of the child must be freed so s/he can be engaged in a lively, active, dynamic, and holistic process of development.

(Hu Keying, 1989, p. 19)

### Harbin, China

Ironically, I lose my passport in my hometown, Harbin, before we go to Beijing. I cannot fly anymore. However, the best thing about it is that after my American guests leave, I can steal some time to play with my nephew, Mengmeng. A smart, articulate, and sensitive nine-year-old and teacher's headache or pride (depending on the occasion), he has his own logic and seldom fails to argue his own points until adults use their privilege to overrule his arguments, while secretly amused by his intelligence. We play with cards and then with a balloon. Almost from the very beginning, I find out that he plays only competitively. I call it to his attention: "Hey, Mengmeng, we are playing!" He grimaces and plays the same. I begin to play according to his rules: he cannot beat me any more, but the game becomes short and boring. I ask him: "Mengmeng, which is more enjoyable, playing for fun, or playing to win?" He looks at me and thinks a little bit. He does not say anything, but the game is changed.

Home is supposed to be a loving space in which children grow up, but it can be turned into a place for fighting, too. Traditionally, education has been dear to the hearts of Chinese parents and they expect their children to become honorable persons. Intensified by the current one-child policy, the high expectations of parents and grandparents have increased the burden on the vulnerable shoulders of children in an unprecedented way. Mengmeng is no exception. He began his practice of calligraphy at the age of four. He gave it up after more than two years of practice—as a protest, I suspect—although he was already doing beautifully. He is only nine, but he can read classical

Chinese novels due to his early calligraphy experience. For better or worse, the work he picks up and of which he is particularly fond is *The Romance of Three Kingdoms*, a novel describing the art of war in ancient China. Now, as a schoolboy, he has to fight for time to read novels. School is worse than home, especially considering its institutional impersonalism. The impositional parental mode of education is intensified by the institutionalization of teacher/student authoritative relationships. Mengmeng is not a disciplined child, and teachers try to restrain him as strictly as possible. It pains me to think about what he has to go through.

Suffering is part of personal cultivation in (Confucian) Chinese traditions (Tu, 1993), and it is true that the capacity for bearing pain is essential to a person's coming into maturity. The experiences of pain also can nurture compassion and sympathy toward others. But what bothers me is the unnecessary burden and universal norms we adults impose on young children, always assuming that we know better than they do. Actually it is we adults who do not know how to endure the frustration caused by the child in the newness of his or her unbounded exploration. Refusing to learn from the child, we impose rules, and the child, in turn, learns from us to invent games of impositions. My commitment to the field of education was directly motivated by my sensitivity to the suffering and pain that children endure in school, starting with my own elementary education. As one of the pioneers in initiating an educational movement in China for freeing the child's individuality, Hu Keying (1989) calls for saving our children, which is still an unfulfilled educational and cultural challenge.

## Tulsa/Stillwater, Oklahoma

A perfect spring day. Back in Stillwater. Stepping down from the commuter bus which carries me between Stillwater and Tulsa to teach a multicultural education class at Oklahoma State University–Tulsa, I reach into my handbag absentmindedly, still thinking about the class, but I am immediately startled. I have lost my keys—the key to my office, the key to my apartment, and the key to my car. Walking back and forth trying to locate them, I finally give up—I must have left them in Tulsa.

Near midnight, standing in the darkness, with nowhere to go, I am lost. Suddenly, I am hit by the return of a long-departed memory, the repressed memory of a personal trauma situated in a national trauma, loaded with the hidden yearning of an unspeakable hurt. Tears come to my eyes.

Riding on the bus between Stillwater (my new home) and Tulsa (a place historically renowned for a horrendous race riot in the 1920s), I have unknowingly been approaching my own hidden turbulence, the intimate touching of which has transformed my approach to pedagogy.

The repression of hurt and burial of trauma in general or "the denial of guilt" (Pinar, 1993) in racial contexts in particular is more devastating than the negative feelings themselves. In the class together with my students, as I painstakingly try to articulate and understand the notion of racism as a "communally shared trauma" (Berlak, 1996) in which all of us are implicated, my own memory comes back. Repressed feelings are recognized, although the contexts of the trauma are different. This acknowledgment of the wound is essential to my healing process. One of my dilemmas in teaching multicultural education in an American classroom is my concern about not "hurting" students, trying to protect them from the assault of suffering while challenging them to learn. But the good intention of preventing hurt is blind to the fact that hurt is already there, both socially and personally, as students from different racial, gender, class, and sexual backgrounds, in their various individualities, walk into the classroom. Precisely in order to teach for understanding, sharing, and working together, there is no "middle" position, especially for a multicultural educator. How can we work together without addressing hurt in order to let it go so we can come back together? A truly loving classroom is where "conflicts and anger, tears and pain, [and] unpredictable directions" (Kohli, 1991, p. 45) can be endured and shared, along with ideas. A third space must be beyond the middle in confronting suffering, in order to move on.

It is in the darkness where I get in touch with the returned; it is in turbulence where I find peace with unbearable pain; it is in suffering where I'm most kind, touching others while being touched; it is in crisis when I am open to the most loving aspect of wisdom, wisdom in its youth, vibrant yet sensitive. I have experienced the overwhelming impact of what can be opened up by confronting the wound, which, in turn, cultivates my faith in my students to grapple with their own inner struggles. I begin to let go of my protectiveness, engage students with difficult readings and open discussions, directly ask them to "feel" the articles, not just read them, yet without giving up pedagogical patience; to wait, lovingly, for students' opening to new insights; to guide them without pressure but affirmatively. This patience also allows students to keep their own positions and to prolong the process of resistance while seeking chances for any breakthrough, as tiny as it might be, and hanging onto this opening until new landscapes sneak in. Without this faith in students' own capacity for self-transformation, education loses its power. Without this positioning of turning toward goodness and justice, pedagogy loses its inner beauty.

## Pedagogy of Suffering, Love, and Play

Two different pictures of pedagogy and suffering unfold before us, in contradictory directions—one asking us to relieve the child from suffering imposed by adults, the other inviting us to dwell with suffering in order to take on pedagogical responsibility. It is indeed on this conflicting site that we need to situate ourselves as educators.

Martusewicz (2001) speaks about a "pedagogy of suffering," a pedagogy that intends to transform suffering into meaning-making and social compassion through confronting the pain of human existence and responding to suffering. Acknowledging the pedagogical functions of suffering, she asks teachers, "What kinds of temporary shelter can we provide as our students venture out? What kinds of relational and conceptual security can we provide as they learn to weather the storm brought on by our questions?" (2001, p. 107). Suffering teaches as it is transformed, and the loving guidance of the teacher becomes essential in helping students meander through their discomfort to reach the other side of the world. Along the way, the pain—social, personal, or psychic—is alleviated (although perhaps not totally gotten rid of) through creating new meanings for both self and community.

There is indeed a tension within our notion and practice of love of our children: a tension between leaving them alone to go wherever they want and challenging them to be engaged in personal cultivation. In the words of John Dewey (1902), we need to find an alternative role for the teacher, "between forcing the child from without, or leaving him entirely alone." Dwayne Huebner (1999) asks us to acknowledge the student as the stranger who confronts the teacher with his or her own unrealized newness. The metaphor of the stranger asks teachers to listen more attentively to children, to look more engagingly into their eyes, and to perceive their souls insightfully, so that the novelty of each child can be affirmed and brought forth. If we adults really open our eyes, ears, and hearts, a lively child like my nephew Mengmeng may teach us many lessons, not only about childhood, but also about new ways of understanding and interpreting life. Hardly implying that teachers need to give themselves up to be merged with students, this opening burdens teachers with a Derridian sense of responsibility—of living with aporias to invent new pedagogical gestures in guiding students. The rigorous and sharp edge of compassion and tenderness toward the other is not in letting the other go but in opening the other's capacity for self-renewal, and the teacher's role as the third party between external imposition and anarchical letting go is to play with pedagogical distance, inspiring students to journey upward through touching what is swirling inside.

As a loving encounter with the student, curriculum does not deny the existential human condition of suffering; neither does it ignore the importance of challenging students to surpass their limits. However, such an encounter, to the extent that it is a loving relationship, must encourage students to carve out a space wherein they may move around. More often than not, this freedom to explore new territories means colliding with adults' complicity in enforcing social stability, which in turn challenges teachers and transforms curricula. Love would be suffocating without freedom, and freedom would be lost without love. Sympathy and compassion themselves cannot work magic without being grounded in a "limit attitude," as Foucault phrases it. Therefore a pedagogy of suffering is made possible by a simultaneous refusal and acceptance of pain in order to transcend, to come home for yet another time, to create a more compassionate world together. Such a homecoming becomes a journey, since home is already transformed by one's loving encounter with new realms of knowledge and life. The recursive fluidity of homecoming also defies a neutral, middle position of the teacher. One cannot *educate* without moving oneself.

Suffering can open our sensitivity to the fragility of life and the vulnerability of humanity; however, it may also bind our feet from moving, cripple our wings (of intelligence) from flying. In order to prevent suffering from blocking our ability to create, play enters the picture. Play softens the edge of conflicts and brings the potential-at-the-limit into existence. If we observe closely what young children do on the playground, it is not difficult to see that they are far more willing to risk playing with the limits than we allow, and that they are quite at home with the discomforts caused by their adventures. However, the spirit of being playful with the world diminishes as they grow up and go to school for "education." Their desire to play with the uncomfortable is increasingly frustrated by "the quest for certainty" (Slattery & Morris, 1999; Quinn, 2001). Thus, the game of domination replaces the play of experiment. Students no longer play with contradictions and paradoxes. Triumphant are the rules of control for certainty, and lost are the poetic songs of creation through ambiguity.

This sense of playfulness does not exist in Chinese schools. Our intellectual traditions do not leave much room for children to play. It surprises me, though, that meaningful play is also absent in American schools. In my fantasy, schools are places for American children to play, just as parents dropping off their children at school usually say: "Have fun." The figure of Dewey is so rooted in Chinese educators' imagination that they take for granted that experientially based pedagogy happens in American classrooms. Doll (2002) contests this image by depicting Dewey as a ghost hovering over the American curriculum. Dewey is misunderstood when schooling stays at the level of hands-on experience without reaching the level of intellectual reflection. Reflective thinking is the key to making play meaningful. Meaningful play is hard work, and play without meaningfulness may amuse but does not inspire. The mental activities of play, when both emotionally charged and intellectually engaged, can transform both the child and the curriculum. The purpose of playing with differences and contradictions is not merely to make learning interesting, but also to touch upon new ground, to experiment with new ideas, and to reconstruct the world in a different way.

To be playful with identity politics in a multicultural education classroom requires not only knowledge of social, political, and economic suffering, but also ironic performative display of the impact of social violence, so that hurt can be displaced onto humor—a serious humor which inspires class members to think, feel, and desire social change. However, without first exposing and addressing pain, humor can be insensitive and offensive. This exposure is not necessarily only through verbal communication, but through images, gestures, music, or bodily movements. Even silence can play a powerful role in sharpening one's sense of what is hidden. At certain points, however, letting go of intense feelings and sharp conflicts for the possibilities of further experience and inquiry is also crucial to create communality, working together for social justice. Tears can touch; laughter can incite; play can be a bridge to connect.

A pedagogy of suffering, love, and play is registered in a paradoxical zone in which the teacher's positioning can hardly be geared toward any neutral ground. Gentle with compassion, affirmative with rigor, inspiring with humor, the teacher is the loving third, who connects students' tears with new visions and their smiles with words. She leads them out and leads them back, and travels with them to curve new landscapes of self. Beyond the middle, pedagogical positioning is fluid, shifting with student's movements. Not fixed to any particular point, the teacher nevertheless guides students in "the upward journey" (Quinn, 2001) toward what is good, beautiful, and true in our lives, that which we can never really reach, but always aspire to.

## A Historical and Cultural Space

The path to moral training, the ideal of sagehood, the ideal of nobleman, if it intends to communicate with the contemporary world, must enter into a more thorough experience of living. We need to truly express our puzzlement about life, the shock from life, even the splitting of life deeply hidden in our hearts.

(Yu Qiuyu, in Yu & Tu, 2000, p. 158)

Today is heavy with tomorrow—
the future was planted yesterday.
Hope is a burden all of us shoulder
though we might stumble under the load.

(Shu Ting, 1991, p. 93)

Curriculum understood as *currere* is a form of social psychoanalysis, a complicated conversation with myself and others, the point of which is movement: autobiographic, political, cultural.

(William Pinar, 2001, p. 2)

## Beijing, China

I am sitting in a hotel preparing a talk on contemporary curriculum theories and the Chinese cultural spirit for graduate students. In front of me is a small red box I got from a restaurant. There are two Chinese characters on it, meaning "affection for home." The big character, *home*, in its complicated stroke, looks so dear to me. The small character, *affection*, is beside a teapot with steam coming out. On the table I also have a book on dragon painting. Incidentally, Cixous's *Rootprint* and Foucault's *The Care of the Self* are also there. What a mix! It is precisely due to this mixture and contrast that I am able to see my own culture through a new angle, with more appreciation and a sharper critique. My (loving) encounter with the other (culture) enables my deeper self-understanding and sets my feet in search of a third space in which self and other can interact creatively to promote both personal and cultural transformation.

Contemporary Chinese scholars struggle to critically reflect on the already divided, multiplied, and fragmented Chinese self and culture. A historical break between traditions and modernization in China makes it both complicated and necessary to search for alternatives through both loving critique and creative regeneration. Situated in the broad framework of cultural reflection and my personal cross-cultural journey, I ask myself: what questions can I ask to invite students to participate in intercivilizational dialogues, intracultural reflections, and curriculum conversations?

As I guide my American guests on a tour of the Forbidden City, I notice that the image of double dragons playing with a pearl between them is almost everywhere—on the doors, windows, and the exterior walls of buildings. The image is not only part of ancient Chinese buildings, it is also seen in folk art such as dragon dancing. We had one king—the embodiment of the dragon—but there often are two dragons playing with each other in art and folktales. Starting with what students are familiar with, perhaps I can ask them to look behind the surface in engaging cultural critiques: Which part of tradition would one like to bring to life in the classroom? One lonely, stern king? or two playful companioning dragons? Psychologically speaking, one dragon could be the other (hidden) part of the one manifest through the double, playing with each other (Donna Trueit, personal communication, November 2000). Yet, is not the very transmutation of one into two more fascinating?

What does the myth and the image of a dragon invented from the multiple (see details in the next section) mean for becoming an open-minded educator in contemporary China? Can we follow the winding course and embrace the multiple and the different as descendents of the dragon? Or do we look upon only one authority to constrain ourselves to one path toward one goal? Of what would the spirit of the dragon (of the playful and multiple) advise us regarding the approach to the other, such as Western culture? These are not only historical and cultural questions; they are personal questions. Students will need to grapple with their own identities as teachers and as Chinese.

## Stillwater, Oklahoma

I am overwhelmed by students' storytelling, to the point of not knowing what to say in response. Deeply touched, I am speechless. Honestly, I had no idea what I was getting myself into when I initiated the discussion. Today, in a graduate seminar on curriculum research, we are reading *The Tao of Life Stories* by Li Xin (2002), a book focusing on Chinese women immigrants' cross-cultural experiences situated in both the Chinese Cultural Revolution and current North America, research conducted through a life-history approach. Though beautifully written and emotionally appealing to me, I was worried that students from a dramatically different culture and history might have difficulty relating to the author's stories. At the beginning of the class, I asked students to work in pairs to discuss three questions:

1. Which story in the book reminds you of your own experience? Tell both the story and the experience to your partner.
2. What emotions are provoked by the book's story that you chose?
3. What do you think about the author's narration and analysis?

Then I asked students to share their partner's story, emotion, and thoughts (rather than their own) with the class after finishing their discussion.

When we came back to share our stories related to the book, I unexpectedly heard deep personal resonance from the students. Together as a class, many themes come out—on life and death, divorce and marriage, neglected children at school and adopted children in loving families, oppression and healing, sacrifice and gender injustice, beauty and the handicapped, and parental expectations versus one's own dream, among other essential questions about human life, and echoing themes in the book. I was particularly moved by the unspoken emotions behind students' calm narrations. Struggling to express my appreciation (I often feel regret about not letting silence play its own pedagogical role), I ask students to discuss the experience of listening to another person narrate his or her own story, especially what happens to them as they experientially try to relate to a text that tells dramatically different stories.

Through multiple layers of one's relation with a text, with another person, and with the class, this storytelling event is not only deeply personal but also profoundly cultural. Story is closely related to culture (Doll, 1998b), and cultural aspects of the stories we tell in the class in responding to the author's cross-cultural journey are explicit. Against the tradition of life story "seen as the individual construction of the autonomous self" (Goodson, 1998, p. 5), the life-history approach adopted by the book invites students to situate their personal stories through history and culture, to which students respond in their own storytelling.

In "future-oriented" American culture, where memory is not valued, where history is forgotten (intentionally or unintentionally) by the majority, and where the individual is the center of the universe, I often find it difficult to guide class discussions to in-depth analysis of history and culture. The very mention of culture seems already a conspiracy against individual choice and freedom. Sometimes, however, powerful encounters with historical biographies such as Li's book can bring unexpected breakthroughs and moving pedagogical moments which cannot be stimulated by any lecture or mere presentation of ideas.

## Curriculum as an Intercultural and Historical Journey

Particularly for some radical Western scholars, culture is often regarded as something conservative. The role of intellectuals or artists is to disrupt the given culture and create something new. Although this differs from the assumptions of rugged individualism, which elevates individual autonomy over culture, culture is still a background *against* which new visions of life can be imagined. In my Chinese mind, though, culture is intricately related to the aesthetic, intellectual, and spiritual realms of human life through its history, history which embodies multilayered and contradictory symbols of both transmission and transcendence, continuity and creativity. It can touch me profoundly and inspire me beyond what I can imagine; it can also upset and suffocate me beyond what I can bear to speak about. I do not think culture is inherently conservative. Cultural transformation through history is marked by both break and repetition. Now, teaching in an American university with a predominantly white student body, I find it imperative to understand curriculum as a historical and cultural text, as the myth of individualism is so deeply rooted in these students' minds. Actually, this is a *cultural* myth, which does not exist in many other countries. Without recognizing how one is situated historically and culturally (itself a form of cultural critique), is it ever possible to become an individual capable of critically engaging one's life and making one's own choices, rather than going with the flow of the main-stream?

The "significance of place" (Kincheloe & Pinar, 1991) is simultaneously historical, cultural, and personal. Beijing is a city where modern radical cultural and political movements erupt, although it is still burdened with its long history of being an ancient capital of an ancient kingdom. It was Beijing where I was devoted to studies in the Beijing Library, and where I was overwhelmed by students' pro-democracy movements. For me, traveling through Beijing means both a continuous fascination and a critical reflection. Culture and history as critique (Joseph et al. , 2000) become key. As Grumet (1988) points out, "The place that is familiar can be the place where we are most lost" (p. 65).

Acknowledging this sense of being lost in the familiar opens up the possibility of reaching deeply inside to rememorize what is not recognized. This asks us to travel out and come back with new eyes. In the contemporary age when the world is increasingly interconnected but more fragmented, place is simultaneously local and global. The theme of "inter" becomes crucial to reach the depth of "intra," hence teaching as a cultural journey is usually intercultural, as scenes in both Beijing and Stillwater have shown so vividly. The individual self is permeated by intercultural encounters which are at the same time deeply personal. These encounters, when meaningful, need the crafting of (pedagogical) translation. Working on the border between autobiography and cultural studies, Susan Edgerton (1996) intends to translate curriculum by "gaining insight into *self* and *other*, how I construct who the *other* is, how I am constructed as the *other*, and how a sense of place is itself built on notions of the *other*" (p. 134; emphasis in original). The intersubjective, intertextual (along with literary readings), inter/intracultural nature of understanding curriculum not only mobilizes any notion of the self but also situates the self in a complicated web of interconnections and intraconnections bordering on the edge of openness to the other.

William Ayers (2001) points out how (white) Americans tend to forget the past—not all of the past, but "the bad part," the "other" part of history, which cannot get through the filter of (cultural) remembering. However, African Americans, it seems, cannot afford to forget. Curriculum as *currere*, as a cultural and historical journey, enables us to hear unheard stories. Pinar (2001) traces the birth of the United States as a nation and how the notion of the "self-made man" (specifically, white masculinity) has structured that peculiar (Pinar prefers "queer") institution of "race." At the intersection of race and gender, the memory of that which is historically (and personally) unbearable returns to move the self out of its frozen zone. Such an opening to "difficult knowledge" (Britzman, 1998) requires the hard work of memory—

not the memory of make-believe good things, but of what is suppressed beneath the gate of the forbidden.

Engaging "the ongoing memory work which must be done" (Munro, 1998b, p. 285) to en*gender* curriculum history, Petra Munro (1998a, 1998b) attempts to mess up our neat recollections about founding fathers, rebellious sons, and obedient daughters so that we can remember women teachers' original contributions, which have been erased from the official records. To reiterate, I insist that there is a generative potential within history and culture that can be released if we go beyond the official curriculum and tell different stories. What manages to be forgotten by the public is usually what we are most ambivalent about, what is too painful to remember. But it can be the most vital part of traditions—the inerasable human spirit of not being crushed—that we may rekindle. The regeneration of this vitality is dependent upon our capacity to weave into today's fabric *those* threads of our culture which are often already broken but can still be reconnected through our loving labor. Such a reconnecting helps us participate in creating a new culture.

Working with a difficult and painful memory collectively asks us to infuse emotions into culture. The emotional appeal of stories and life histories, as Li's book has shown, may connect us unexpectedly at the points of departure. However, our teaching is rarely wedded to emotion, especially feelings provoked by memories of traumas. As Deborah Britzman (1998) and Ayers (2001) point out in different ways, in presenting to our children a rosy picture of "everything is going to be all right," we miss the educative function of memory, its psychic richness and capacity for teaching, and we fail to respond to social injustice. The relational notion of the Chinese self, its unity of intellect and emotion, may ignore the necessity of attending to what is buried inside emotions. When feelings are neglected, what is buried is hidden more deeply; it turns into unspeakable pain, silently eroding children's capacity for imagination. In an expressive culture such as that of the United States, expressions of feelings, especially positive feelings, are expected. However, privatization of emotions and the privilege of reason have taken the discourses of suffering and hurt to the security of the psychoanalytic couch. My American students frequently comment that they will take "troubled" students to counselors because they don't know what to do; it is not their job to treat any "abnormal" kid. The norm of excluding strong feelings provoked by social and personal suffering from the public domain serves only to intensify suffering and cover up social traumas. Taking emotions out of the private domain, understanding their social and historical constructions in American culture, or taking them out of the union with intellect to understand their alterity in Chinese culture, is also part of the memory work with which we must be engaged.

The texts and pedagogical approaches I have adopted sometimes provoke strong emotions on the part of students, often at unexpected moments, like those I just described in our curriculum research class. I find that this makes a greater demand on me as a teacher to pass through more difficult channels than I would ever have expected. A balance between encouraging students to be comfortable with their feelings and challenging them to take one step forward (or backward) toward new ways of perceiving is quite difficult to achieve. Still, in the middle of struggle, I believe that we as teachers cannot bypass what is provoked emotionally in students by their lives or by our teaching. We need to learn how to live with emotions in a pedagogy of suffering, love, and play.

Working at the intersections of gender, class, and the exiled immigrant, Carolyn Steedman in *Landscape for a Good Woman* (1997) asks, "Where is the place that you move into the landscape and can see yourself?" She reminds us that the vista seen from "the curtainless windows of a terraced house" (p. 2) is essentially different from that of a central position or the ground floor. A journey of relandscaping the self to retell those impossible stories through time and place requires multiple positionings of the stranger, be it a woman, the poor, a foreigner, or all of them. When what is absent becomes present, and when what is fixed becomes mobilized, the stranger comes and goes, a stranger whose vibrant calling continuously echoes, shaking mountains and reverberating in valleys, to enrich and transform the whole landscape.

Too often, our school curricula stay fixed and tell only one dominant story, effacing the concreteness and particularity of human life. Schoolgirls are, more often than not, positioned as diligent, hardworking, and passive, still achieving less than naughty, playful, and active schoolboys. As Valerie Walkerdine (1990) points out, this is a fiction, a sexualized fantasy, daily played out in schools. This positioning produces an irony in being both a woman and a teacher—a good girl herself at school but somehow hating being good at it—who is quite ambivalent toward her female students (Walkerdine, 1998), and who often fails to encourage schoolgirls' intellectual pursuits. With the burden of gendered baggage, I wonder how women can sustain their confidence throughout their own journeys into the world. Perhaps *into* of the world will not do much good; a journey *with* the world is crucial to re-landscaping gendered realities.

Curriculum as a cultural and historical journey is both collective and personal, meandering through (our memory) banks to pave new ways of becoming; wandering along the edges of the landscape to uncover what is previously invisible; and curving around the window on the border to generate new visions of self and life.

## A Complicated Space: Harmony, Polyphony, and Creativity

It is the task of recognizing unity in what we see as separate, the task of claiming exemption, as well, from the universal law and claiming separateness despite the wish for unity.

(Madeleine Grumet, 1988, p. 191)

It requires of us a love of ambiguity which is at once a love of the generativity of new life as a gift bestowed from the Earth.

(David Jardine, 1998, p. 31)

### Suzhou/Hongzhou, China

Suzhou and Hongzhou are historically known as paradise on earth. Both of them have traditional gardens, with Suzhou being especially famous for them. Revisiting these gardens—with the help of my American guests' unique perspectives—brings me to a new eye to see the familiar: "Every meeting a first encounter" (Bei, 1991, p. 11). One theme particularly striking to me is the sense of harmony in differences in Chinese aesthetics. The discourses about differences in the United States, especially in poststructuralism and postmodernism, do not have any strong sense of harmony; the theme of struggle through contradictions is dominant. As I tour Chinese gardens everywhere, I am surprised by the patterns of architecture, detailed in the designs and shapes of windows and doors, never repetitive but achieving an aesthetically pleasing harmony. Complicated networks of landscape through multiple doors and windows disclose surprising scenes as we tour. Rockeries, water, and buildings are scattered through the spread-out paths, trees, flowers, and grass, an intricate combination of both density and looseness, "so sparse as to let a horse walk, so dense as not to let a breeze in." The design of layer upon layer and space within space brings out a sense of infinity within a finite boundary. A small garden can give one a view so multilayered and dynamic that the spirit of nature and the universe can flow through humanity to embrace difference, diversity, and harmony.

The sense of the many in the one can be traced to the myth of the dragon. As Wang Dong (2000) tries to argue, the dragon does not (merely) symbolize religious worship; it is a cultural creation. Embodied in the ideal of the dragon, the Chinese cultural spirit includes the unity of humanity and the universe, harmonious relationships between self and other and among groups. There is tolerance of cultural diversity, interaction between *yin* and *yang*, and the creative integration of antithesis and contradictions. In other words, the dragon is the symbol of harmony in differences.

The shape of the dragon itself is already fascinating: a dragon is composed of—according to one common saying (Song, 1999)—the head of an ox, the mouth of a lion, the moustache of a sheep, the feelers of a shrimp, the horn of a deer, the mane of a horse, the body of a snake, and the tail of a fish. The image of the dragon has been shown in almost all realms of Chinese art in its various forms of movement, twisting, curves, and playfulness. We also have a folktale of the dragon giving birth to nine sons (the number nine in ancient Chinese refers to multiple), none of whom is in the shape of the dragon; each has his own image and symbolic meaning. These sons' images can be seen on stone monuments, on the ridges of roofs and heads of bridges in architecture, on the knobs of bells (a common musical instrument in ancient China), on the handles of swords, and on door knockers. Dragon myths are outside my speculations here, yet the refreshing and creative potential in this ancient prototype fascinates me as my second homecoming continually inspires me to rethink culture, self, and curriculum.

The notion of harmony in Chinese aesthetics, I believe, is grounded not in conformity, but in dynamics set in motion by difference and multiplicity shifting in a network of creative imagination. Under the brush of artists and craftsmen, what makes the landscape harmonious is what sets it into movement, not what makes it uniform or common. More often than not, an aesthetically pleasing form is not an individual object; rather, it is situated in a complex, artistically arranged network, comprising space, place, objects, paths, nature, and humanity. The inner harmony within gardens is also expanded by borrowing shadows of pagodas, shapes of mountains, or mirrors of water outside of the gardens, matching what is inside. Such arrangements of gardens outside of gardens (and also gardens within gardens) directly challenge any rigid distinction between inside and outside, inner and outer, and boundary and fluidity. Such a blending between inner and outer also echoes a Confucian sense of the self which cultivates itself within while expanding outward. The multiplicity of space arrangements, the movement of the layout, and the intricate relationships among every part of a garden all mark the dynamics of harmony which make a poetic creation possible through shifting interconnections.

## Tulsa, Oklahoma

Confrontations between ideas are not much of a problem for many, if not most, Americans. Watching debates on TV can be an ordeal for me; sometimes I can barely hear any voice clearly because several persons are trying to speak at the same time. When this happens in the class, I usually ask students to speak one by one. But not always. Polyphonic voices sometimes need to be encountered in an intensified way so that deeper understanding can be sparked. In this Tulsa class, half of the students are from nonmainstream backgrounds, and debates are abundant. After I let go of my desire to "protect" students, I hold myself back even when I want to jump right into the debate, to disperse the tangled focus and divert the heat of discussion. Today, halfway through the semester, we are engaged in a discussion about whether or not culture counts—a theme already getting worn out, since we have been discussing it throughout the class. One middle-aged white male student has traveled to other parts of the world and intends to settle down in a foreign country. He is the one who is most resistant to the notion that understanding students' cultural backgrounds is important for effective teaching. While he argues again, forcefully, for respecting individuals as individuals and nothing more than that, other class members, of African-American heritage, attempt to explain why race does matter. Their arguments have become more and more emotionally charged, but I hold back and listen, listening to them talk back and forth, until the white student blurts out: "It's absurd to say that culture doesn't count—that's not what I am saying! But why would you see your student not as a person but as a person with a color?"

He had never before said in class that culture matters! It was a moment of clarification and repositioning for many of us. I take up the space of silence to ask for further explanation. Here he touches upon the tricky zone of achieving a balance between understanding one's situatedness in culture and one's singularity as a person. The discussion goes on, but it reaches a point where opposition may not be so opposite as we assume.

In students' weekly responses after this class, one of them exclaimed that she had not understood his position until that moment. Although this does not lead to any consensus, complex layers of identity and education are nevertheless articulated, and understanding (even if not mutual) is deepened.

Polyphony also exists within the individual person. Students from racial minority backgrounds often find it very difficult to hear their white classmates speak about not knowing the history of racial hatred and how their lives have not been touched by racism. The emotional underpinnings of this difficulty are often too painful to discuss, so these students choose to either withdraw from the class discussion or turn anger into words that are too powerful for their white classmates to bear. However, in their individual writings, the majority express their desire to see others as persons and not label them according to their race. They also refuse to be positioned as victims and firmly believe that they have been in charge of their own lives while being committed to social change.

This aspect of the self is sometimes lost in the heated class discussions. The burden of pointing out their classmates' privilege is usually met by resistance, sometimes from their white peers who have suffered their own marginalized positions. For those students, it is difficult to acknowledge they are the beneficiaries of racism while they have to suffer at the margin. A gay man, for instance, may not be happy that black students are outspoken about racial inequality but do not recognize the dignity of the homosexual identity. A white student who does not feel that he belongs to mainstream white culture may resist being seen in the "normal" category as a "white man." Although these students do appreciate the role of power relationships in an individual's life, this appreciation cannot be articulated adequately in class debates as they hold onto their "innocence" from the racial construction of reality.

To recognize the potential other in each student and to understand his or her multiple identities, positions me ambiguously. More often than not, mutual understanding in the class is a luxurious hope. If mutuality cannot be reached, I gear the discussion to the very site of dispute and let polyphony, both within and without, play out its own drama. What usually happens is that discussion leads to the point at which students depart from each other, yet remain connected by the other within the self, which is usually unspoken or implicit. In confronting differences, what is unspoken begins to speak, either publicly or privately, and powerful emotions are not only released but also validated, enriching one another's understanding and bringing curriculum to another level of complexity.

## Teaching through Harmony and Polyphony

Harmony in differences in Chinese aesthetics is a creative act with rich implications for reinventing "curriculum dynamics" (Fleener, 2002). I am suspicious, however, about the role of difference in harmony. To what degree can multiplicity and dissonance be allowed when they do not fit into the overall pattern? To what degree can unmerged breaks and discontinuity be encouraged in order to move the unity of the whole in unexpected directions? To what degree, as multiple and shifting as it is, can harmony resist the closure of the boundary? As creative and dynamic as it can be, the theme of harmony indicates a certain merging toward an overall form of beauty. Mikhail Bakhtin also talks about unity, understood not as a totalizing converged force, "but as a dialogic *concordance* of unmerged twos or multiples" (quoted in Morson & Emerson, 1990, p. 1). This unity is not incompatible with the Chinese tradition of harmony in tensions, but Mikhail Bakhtin's notion of polyphony as a new form of art, a new way of understanding, emphasizes more the role of heterogeneity, uncertainty, and openness to alterity in promoting nonconsensual dialogues across differences. A polyphonic dialogue between self and other in a relationship of "simultaneity in difference" (Bakhtin, 1993) allows disagreement and emphasizes the unfinalizability of becoming. Here conflicts, disharmony, and dissonant voices become generative, not merely elements to be harmonized. Harmony in differences focuses on harmony, while polyphony in unity focuses on polyphony, although each is open to its conflicting double. A creative curriculum tunes in with harmony and dances with polyphony.

In a polyphonic curriculum, dissonant voices are welcomed and disharmony can be woven *with* unity, not merely *within* unity. However, as Maxine Greene (1995) reminds us, we cannot abandon the search for common ground to create a democratic classroom in which dialogue enriches members of the community, instead of dividing or separating them. In other words, harmony in differences is also needed to promote a communal inquiry with the trust that, however different we might be, we still can connect with one another. In such an inquiry, students are more willing to journey into new territories, unafraid of mistakes or dead ends. And so are teachers. Creative harmony flows with (not against) contradictions; it both respects and transforms differences. It is important to notice that harmony does not advocate the "neutrality of the curriculum" for making everything understandable, as Denise Egéa-Kuehne (1996) points out. Instead, students are led through multiple layers of connections, as in an ancient Chinese garden, to face complexity in its movements. The newness of the world brought forth by these curriculum dynamics invites students into the realm of the mysterious and the unknown with the promise that they are not alone but with companions. Rethinking "curriculum as polyphonic coauthoring of selfhood" (Wang, 1997), I suggest that curriculum also needs to be infused by the spirit of dynamic harmony.

In a curriculum which values both harmony and polyphony, teaching becomes a creative process situated in a space of ambiguity which calls for teachers' "dialogic intuition" (Bakhtin, 1984, p.61) and "practical wisdom" (Garrison, 1997) to perceive students' inner conflicts and lead students out of themselves. When "shut-down moments" (Morris, 1996) happen, nurturing this silence might be more productive than confronting students with what they are currently resisting. In silence, one can experience and harmonize conflicting voices simultaneously without facing the demand to choose one path. Immersing oneself in contradictory directions, in fact, one may come out anew after traversing the quiet turbulence of the semiotic. In silence, one also can close one's eyes to see what polyphonically stirs inside. When one begins to speak, a new voice may emerge with a different tongue. While "shut-down" moments can be cherished, "polyphonic eruption" moments also need to be respected, as my class episode in Tulsa shows.

Unexpected harmony can be brought about by the intensification of eruptions or interruptions. The clash of rugged edges may eventually erode the sharpness of conflicts and bring students closer to each other. Intellectual and emotional sparks emanating from harmony or polyphony require pedagogical attentiveness as an act of love listening to the other voice in the students. Between a pedagogical smile of hearing new words from students and an educative patience for "an emergent order out of chaos" (Doll, 1993) are the delicate and daring strokes of a teacher who paints on the canvas of the classroom with her compassionate intelligence.

In a Kristevian paradoxical community where the stranger is welcome to sing, polyphony brought by the stranger's songs does not intend to radicalize differences. Rather, it aims to connect us back to the maternal continent. Creativity flows from this reconnection at the border between feminine and masculine. Wendy Atwell-Vasey (1998a, 1998b) addresses the need to bring nourishing words back to schools from their exile in standards, formulas, and (masculine) structures. When the central position of masculinity in language is displaced and bodily experiences, passions, desires, and maternal relationships come "home," words no longer play an exclusive role of separation. Instead, they nurture the student's venturing out toward the third space, where both masculinity and femininity can be expressed and transformed creatively and compassionately. As a negotiator between and among polyphonic realms, leading the student into his/her own negotiation, the teacher needs to reposition herself. Keeping nourishing relationships alive, but not merging with mother, refusing the tyranny of the symbolic, but participating in its transformation, women teachers can situate themselves in a third space where they can build bridges and seek passages.

Winding through harmony in difference and polyphony in unity, curriculum multiplies itself through movements both within and across differences. Teaching inspires an aesthetic way of experiencing life, and community becomes a verb. Exclusive attention to procedures and methods, either through slack, hands-on activities or worksheet ways of teaching, can no longer sustain the eventfulness and the spontaneity of pedagogy. In its efforts to stage curriculum through the performance of life, teaching becomes alive.

## Journeying in a Third Space:
## The Dancing of Curriculum with the Stranger

[The Third Space] may allow for the reconstituting of new pedagogies in the interstices between different cultural worlds in the manner Trinh has developed in her own ethnographies. It also may provide possibilities for links to and connections with alternative ways of negotiating differences.

(Aristides Gazetas, 2003, pp. 113–14)

A transformative curriculum, then, is one that allows for, encourages, and develops this natural capacity for complex organization; and through the process of transfor-

mation the curriculum continually regenerates itself and those involved with it.
(William Doll, 1993, p. 87)

Reading Tuan Yi-fu's (1999) book *Who Am I? An Autobiography of Emotion, Mind, and Spirit* is a pedagogical event for me. A Chinese-American humanistic geographer, Tuan Yi-fu is a highly accomplished scholar, whose achievement in geography, which is dominated by American "self-assured maleness" (p. 120), is quite remarkable. A gay man who was conscious of his own "sexual bent" at the age of fifteen but never really came out, devoting his life to space, place, aesthetics, and the spirituality of geography, Tuan confesses only after his retirement that "except for a brief period in childhood, I have been afraid of life" (p. 119), a life vitalized through intimate human relationships.

Running away from the stranger within himself, Tuan chooses to be immersed with nature-as-stranger. His solitary dancing with nature is imbued with both intoxications with the lunar sky in the desert and meditations about the relationships between humanity, landscape, and cosmos—meanings of life and existence. As a result of profound engagement with nature, his writings can no longer be confined by the traditional boundary of geography, and his contribution is original. While his confession about his failure to confront his own ghost is particularly touching for me, my own reading of this remarkable life "that is seamed in ambivalence" takes a turn that the author may not have intended. A sense of being alone is an existential condition that may not speak the same language for all but has a certain universal tone. The difference is in how people deal with it. In Tuan's case, it was pushed to the extreme of shying away from intimate personal (sexual) relationships, and also to an extreme of originality cultivated in aloneness, as well as an extreme of departure from the norm. An intimate consciousness of this aloneness, however, can be the springboard for social sympathy and cosmic unity. Without acknowledging and accepting the self's aloneness, how can one realize, feel, and respect the other's separate aloneness? Without a solitary experience of land and the universe, how can one become aware of the self as part of the landscape?

I have argued throughout this book that the self is situated in a shifting web of interpersonal and cosmic relationships. However fluid and relational the self can be, the singular experiencing of life—*not* at the expense of intimacy—in traveling through and with multiple worlds is essential for cultivating a sense of the self. Being alone without making efforts to relate to others (as Tuan regrets about his life) leaves a residue of sadness in the creativity he has achieved through immersing his emotion, mind, and spirit with landscape. Reading Tuan's book, however, inspires me to imagine a third space as one's *own*, created by the co-journeying and co-experiencing of self and the world. The return of aloneness after touring multiple texts and multiple landscapes *and* passionately engaging oneself with others, makes possible the movement toward the originality of a third space. Only when tensions between self and other are felt and addressed does a new sense of self-affirmation become imperative in order to find one's own path. In such a journey, one feels at home but with one foot always stepping out of the gate; one accompanies others but remains truthful to the self; and one both gives up and claims oneself. The conflicting gesture in its double directions requires the birth of the third space in its constant renewal to generate one's own space. In the meantime, one's own space is also a *multiple* space, in which independence can be claimed only through interdependence.

Curriculum in a third space is a dancing curriculum in which unique steps of the self are enabled by its interaction with the stranger—as other, as text, as being within the self. Hosting a chaotic creativity, a curriculum with rich initial beginnings, multiple perspectives, open-ended inquiries, and recursive looping structures (Doll, 1993) encourages students to make connections out of ambiguity, to play with boundaries, and to move toward the third space. Within, between, and among teacher, student, and text, multiple layers of conflicting doubling complicate the tales of curriculum along the borders in its movement with the stranger.

Ambivalence in the third space is a generative site on which contradictory directions may move toward each other, without the demand that they meet in the middle, or move away from each other, without splitting. It is the *tension* of the movement that issues new ways of connecting and constructing. It is the process of trying to reach out for the other that stretches the boundary. Swinging in both directions simultaneously, one neither fully submits to the pull of any one pole, nor does one hold onto only one's own posture. One has to move with the swing but maintain balance. This is the teacher's position. The teacher's love for her students mixes with the teacher's wisdom in guiding students through their own personal journeys. Such process-oriented guidance requires of the teacher both self-affirmation and an unyielding pedagogical faith in the students' potential for change. A pedagogy open to ambiguity welcomes the unpredictable and the undecidable. Such an embracing of unsettling provocation without a certain sense of play, tolerance, and humor can be unbearably painful if the quest for certainty is the standard. The magic of the third space is unfolded in the classroom by playing with the in-between dimension, enduring the coexistence of doubling opposites, and detouring through passages of both/and.

Curriculum in a third space upholds the moments of silence and the openness of empty spaces. "Understanding curriculum as silence and solitude" (Slattery, 1999) has become a key theme in curriculum studies. Moments of silence and solitude can enable one to remember, to make sense of random thoughts, and to be fully immersed with oneself and simultaneously fully aware of the world. A pedagogical nourishment of silence in the class—bringing moments of discomfort and interruption—encourages students to examine themselves and stimulates their independent thinking. How to polyphonically orchestrate the noises of a communal space with the quietude of a solitary space to reach the richness and fullness of experiences and thoughts is a pedagogical wisdom that we need to cultivate. In the same vein, empty space can also bring us surprises. Not only is it full of potential for new possibilities, but it also plays the role of connector in an unexpected way. Playing with these empty spaces with "soft eyes" (Fleener, 2002), we may find more rooms for imagination and creativity if we are willing to walk with students along what is absent and what is hidden in our schooling. Such a play is not an issue of occupying that which is empty, but precisely through not filling up the interstices, curriculum swirls around the "hole" for a constant regeneration. Curriculum in a third space is open to silent time in empty space, not only in the present, but also historically and psychically.

Revisiting her book *Teacher as Stranger* (1973), Maxine Greene (2000) not only acknowledges that she did not take feminist points of view, but also suggests that the stranger must become an active participant in the "community-in-the-making" to be engaged in transforming society and culture at large. The stranger as a participant brings to the community a fluidity which is crucial for creating a democratic classroom. However, I also insist that the stranger cannot risk becoming an insider completely; otherwise, the metaphorical and radical lure of the stranger for something *different*, for something *other* than we already have, or for something we can never anticipate or fully grasp but which we will continue longing for, will be lost. When the danger of the stranger is excluded, the possibility of the stranger opening up new horizons is also closed. The dance of the third space is impossible without the call from the stranger.

Curriculum in a third space can hardly be achieved by any individual teacher alone. No teacher, however wonderful and insightful, can reach every student in the classroom, as the teacher's teaching style cannot match all students' needs. It becomes important that a loving and critical community of teachers and students be built, which differences help to construct. I believe differences are *necessary* in order for teachers to respond to students' different struggles. Every student's own space is different and can be crafted only by different approaches. When one student's fragile voice fails to reach one teacher, another teacher's ears might be open. When one student's silent tears fail to be seen by one teacher, another teacher's insightful eyes might be comforting. When one student's eager desire for expression fails to be noticed by one teacher, another teacher's hands might be stretching and supportive. The goal of teacher collaboration is to expand the communal space and to reach as many students as possible in the third space. Working together, we as teachers are moving toward a shifting space which remains open to different callings, different fears, and different dreams, our own and those of our students.

The teacher's third space shifts and emerges through interaction with students' own spaces to communally open new possibilities. Dialogue and conversation with texts are also situated in a third space, inviting students to reach out, to experience, to understand, to experiment, and to reconstruct their own sense of self. Students who are engaged in an educational journey through the dynamics of the third, the one, and the multiple also can enlarge a communal space in which they can respond to one another's callings and dreams. We also need to respect students' refusal to come into the third space and allow them to stay where they are. Pedagogical compassion for students requires a patience for delayed responses and delayed understanding (in a psychoanalytic sense, understanding is always delayed [Pitt, 2003])— but we as teachers must hold students persistently with the faith that openings will happen eventually, however postponed they might be, even after our formal teacher/student relationships are ended.

These curriculum dynamics of (conflicting) double and third, one and multiple, dance in the magic of life, the mysterious interconnections we consciously or unconsciously experience. There is always an element of the unspeakable which leads us down and pushes us up, pushing us across thresholds, allowing us to imagine and experience a life different from what we currently have. This dance with the stranger cannot be taught; it must be lived, felt, and touched, in its movement, rhythm, and attunement to the music of the heart. David Jardine (1998) poetically asks us to renew "our love of language and our sense for its aromas, our ears for its harmonies" (p. 143), love lost in our schools. Children's passions for words can be sustained only if the sensuality of language can be playfully present. Creating a rich pedagogical environment through bodily experiences of texts, the mystery of the third space lures students beyond the given toward the surprise of openings enabled by the comings and goings of the stranger. Journeying in the third space, students form and reform their own sense of self.

The most creative dynamics of conflicting doubles (such as transcendence and intimacy, cultural and personal, harmony and polyphony, etc.) bring curriculum into a third space in which the positioning of the teacher moves with the students' callings, and complicated pedagogical interactions nurture one's authoring of selfhood. Attentive to the sound and the touch of the memory, aspiring to the blink and the light of the star, we respond to the call from the stranger in a creative journey home that invites a unique expression of both femininity and masculinity, invents new images/imaginings of intersubjectivity, and transforms us by casting off the old skins of the self. This journey hosts a dynamics of singularity, relationality, and difference, engages polyphonic intercultural and intracultural conversation, and enchants with lyrics of love, freedom, and creativity.

As a final note, this cross-cultural, intercultural, gendered space I have attempted to articulate is not a model; it is not universally applicable. It cannot be confined within any model. As an invitation, it intends only to inform and inspire those who desire to move with the third space. Cross-cultural experiences may not lead to fragmentation or ambivalence for a particular person. I have no intention to write this book particularly for "foreigners" who have traveled out of their native countries. The profound conflicts I have experienced have led me to the stranger, and to move toward the third space with the purpose of composing my own singular melody. This personal journey is also echoed by many who confront the issue of multiple identities in this complicated contemporary age in which the personal, the collective, the national, or the international constantly reach their own limits and risk the uncertain. As a call, this book invites all those who are in search of new spaces to join in this journey, a journey essentially educational.

Is it now time for conclusion? How am I going to conclude a journey which is always ongoing and has an unpredictable trajectory? How can I skillfully reiterate the already spoken in order to open up instead of close down? Even saying "no conclusion" as a conclusion does not seem to serve me well. This simple and yet complicated life I have is infinitely enriched and expanded by histories, herstories, cultures, places, and people I have met and loved. From these ruminations about education and curriculum, embedded in my life which stretches back to the past and forward to the future, burdening my present, I may still have much to share. Yet, oddly at the moment of conclusion, I feel I have little to say. I had hoped to stand upon the shoulders of Confucius, Foucault, and Kristeva to fly, yet I am still on the ground of my own labor. Finally I feel grounded, not only by them but also by myself, an ordinary, timid, yet persistent soul longing and searching for her own space. I am still going down the path; even if I might lose ground again, somehow, somewhere, I will manage to stand again. Jim Garrison says, "If we allow ourselves to grow, we will lose our 'selves,' our personal identity, many times along the way" (1997, p. 38).

Considering the nature of my project, what I really want my conclusion to be is not a neat summary of my struggles with issues regarding the human/woman self and curriculum, but to point to alternative directions after this initial beginning of a gendered East/West inquiry. Conclusion can be departure instead of summary. Still on the path, though, I have yet to know. I resist weaving my analysis back into a seamless whole—you have heard my conflicting voices, sensed my struggles, and seen my shifting positions—in the hope that I may permit myself to plant some seeds which will grow later. But before I can start all over again, may I ask you to listen to the call of Bei Dao (1991), a contemporary Chinese poet, for departure:

> Let's go,
> dry leaves blowing down the valley,
> homeless, singing.
>
> Let's go,
> moonlight on river ice,
> overflowing.
>
> Let's go,
> watching the same patch of sky,
> hearts drumming in the dusk.
>
> Let's go,
> we know by heart
> the way to the fountainhead.
>
> Let's go
> down the road, strolling through drifts
> of scarlet poppies.

Let us restart our journey with our children, to the embrace of the valley, the mysterious yet intimate whisper, singing the voiceless song of the stranger. Let us travel to the crystal source of fountain, touching upon the gentle wave of water to flow into creative melodies of life. Let us return to the call of the sky, the stern yet loving voice, flying beyond the edge of the familiar and what is at hand, in the music, dancing into the unknown. Let us renew our journey to swing, yet again, to the wilderness, this time under moonlight, to reexperience our deep connection with our land, earth, and sky, flowing with both the feminine and the masculine, to be carried away by the homeless tide back home. One's own home in a shifting third space. Please listen, listen carefully, listen to yourself, listen to the other, listen to the distant, strange, yet intimate calling from other worlds.

Co-journeying into a world or many worlds different from what we have, returning to our own world to rebuild homes, we and our children are forever on the road in a third space to create new realms of life with tears, laughter, screams, love, pain, and prayer. Are we ready—side by side, connected yet apart—to go?

## Notes

1. My second trip back to China was not a quiet one. I was with William E. Doll, Jr. and Donna Trueit as their translator and assistant. We toured seven cities together and Dr. Doll gave speeches at four universities. As I struggled with the impossible task of translation, I began my efforts to articulate a third space.
2. Yu Qiuyu (1992) has an amusing article about "Shanghai-ese" in his book *Bitter Travel in Culture*.

# References

Ames, Roger T. (1984). The meaning of body in classical Chinese thought. *International Philosophical Quarterly, 24*, 39–54.

*The Analects.* In *The four books* (bilingual) (1992) (James Legge Trans.). Changsha: Hunan Publisher.

Anzaldúa, Gloria (1999). *Borderlands / La Frontera.* San Francisco: Aunt Lute Books.

Art Matrix (1990). *Mandelbrot and Julia sets: Mathematics for lovers* [Video]. Ithaca, NY.

Atwell-Vasey, Wendy (1998a). *Nourishing words: Bridging private reading and public teaching.* Albany: State University of New York Press.

———. (1998b). Psychoanalytic feminism and the powerful teacher. In William F. Pinar (Ed.), *Curriculum: Toward new identities* (pp. 143–156). New York: Garland.

Ayers, William (2001). *Fugitive days: A memoir.* Boston: Beacon Press.

Bakhtin, Mikhail M. (1984). *Problems of Dostoevsky's poetics.* Trans. from Russian by Caryl Emerson. Minneapolis: University of Minnesota Press.

———. (1993). *Toward a philosophy of the act.* Trans. from Russian by M. Holquist & V. Liapunov. Austin: University of Texas Press.

Bei Dao (1991). Let's go. In *A splintered mirror: Chinese poetry from the democracy movement* (p. 5). Trans. Donald Finkel and Carolyn Kizer. San Francisco: North Point Press.

Berlak, Ann C. (1996). Teaching stories: Viewing a cultural diversity course through the lens of narrative. *Theory into practice, 35*, 93–101.

Bernstein, Richard J. (1991). *The new constellation: The ethical-political horizons of modernity/postmodernity.* Cambridge, MA: MIT Press.

Berry, Thomas (1988). *Creative energy: Bearing witness for the earth.* San Francisco: Sierra Club Books.

———. (1990). *The dream of the Earth.* San Francisco: Sierra Club Books.

Berthrong, John H. (1998). *Concerning creativity: A comparison of Chu Hsi, Whitehead, and Neville.* Albany: State University of New York Press.

Bhabha, Homi K. (1990). The third space: Interview with Homi Bhabha. In Jonathan Rutherford (Ed.), *Identity: Community, culture, difference* (pp. 207–221). London: Lawrence & Wishart.

Birge, Bettine (1989). Chu Hsi and women's education. In Wm. Theodore de Bary & John W. Chaffee (Eds.), Neo-Confucian education: The formative stage (pp. 325–367). Berkeley, CA: University of California Press.

Bond, Michael H. (1996). *The handbook of Chinese psychology.* Oxford: Oxford University Press.

Bordo, Susan (1993). *Unbearable weight: Feminism, Western culture, and the body.* Berkeley and Los Angeles: University of California Press.

Britzman, Deborah (1998). *Lost subjects, contested objects: Toward a psychoanalytic inquiry of learning*. Albany: State University of New York Press.

Brooks, E. Bruce, & Brooks, A. Taeko (1998). *The original Analects*. New York: Columbia University Press.

Budick, Sanford, & Iser, Wolfgang (Eds.) (1989). *Languages of the unsayable*. New York: Columbia University Press.

Butler, Judith (1989). The body politics of Julia Kristeva. *Hypatia, 3*, 104–119.

———. (1990). *Gender trouble: Feminism and the subversion of identity*. New York: Routledge.

———. (1997). *The psychic life of power*. Palo Alto, CA: Stanford University Press.

Camus, Albert (1942). *Stranger*. Trans. from French by Stuart Gilbert. New York: Alfred A. Knopf, 1978.

Cao Wenxuan (2001). 《二十世纪末中国文学作品选》 [An anthology of Chinese literature at the end of the 20th century]. Beijing: Beijing University Press.

Chen Hsuan-chih (1996). Chinese reading and comprehension: A cognitive psychology perspective. In Michael Harris Bond (Ed.), *The handbook of Chinese psychology* (pp. 43–62). Hong Kong and New York: Oxford University Press.

Chang Kang-i Sun, & Saussy, Haun (1999). *Women writers of traditional China*. Palo Alto, CA: Stanford University Press.

Chaves, Jonathan (1975). *Heaven my blanket, Earth my pillow: Poems from Sung-Dynasty China by Yang Wan-li*. New York: Weatherhill.

Chen Jianxiang (1988). 《人的个性发展与教育改革》 [The development of individuality and educational reform]. 《教育研究》, 7, 7–16.

Chernin, Kim (1994). *In my mother's house*. New York: HarperPerennial.

Chiao Chien (1992). *Involution and revolution in gender equality: The Chinese experience*. Hong Kong: Hong Kong Institute of Asia-Pacific Studies.

Ching, Julia (1986). Zhu Xi on personal cultivation. In Wing-tsit Chan (Ed.), *Zhu Xi and Neo-Confucianism* (pp. 273–291). Honolulu: University of Hawaii Press.

Chodorow, Nancy (1978). *The reproduction of mothering: Psychoanalysis and the sociology of gender*. Berkeley and Los Angeles: University of California Press.

Cixous, Hélène (1994). *The Hélène Cixous Reader*. New York: Routledge.

Dawson, Raymond (1993). *Confucius: The analects*. Oxford and New York: Oxford University Press.

de Bary, William T. (1991). *Learning for one's self: Essays on the individual in neo-Confucian thought*. New York: Columbia University Press.

———. (1998). *Asian values and human rights*. Cambridge, MA: Harvard University Press.

de Beauvoir, Simone (1952). *The second sex* [1949]. Trans. from French by H. M. Parshley. New York: Bantam.

Deleuze, Gilles (1994). Foldings, or the inside of thought (subjectivation). In Michael Kelly (Ed.), *Critique and power: Recasting the Foucault/Habermas debate* (pp. 315–346). Cambridge, MA: MIT Press.

Deng Zhiwei (2000). 《个性化教学论》 [Individualized pedagogy]. Shanghai: Shanghai Educational Press.

Derrida, Jacques (1991). *Derrida reader: Between the blinds*. Edited and Trans. From French by Peggy Kamuf. New York: Columbia University Press.

———. (1992). *The other heading*. Trans. from French by P. Brault & M. B. Naas. Bloomington: Indiana University Press.

————. (1993). *Aporias*. Trans. from French by Thomas Dutoit. Palo Alto, CA: Stanford University Press.

————. (1995). *The gift of death*. Trans. from French by David Wills. Chicago: University of Chicago Press.

————. (1998). *Resistances of psychoanalysis*. Trans. from French by Peggy Kamuf et al. Palo Alto, CA: Stanford University Press.

Dewey, John (1902). *The school and society / The child and the curriculum*. Chicago: University of Chicago Press, 1990.

Ding Gang (1989). 《先秦教育思想简论》 [An introduction to educational research in the Qin dynasty]. 《教育研究》, *1*, 52–56.

Doane, Janice, & Hodges, Devon (1992). *From Klein to Kristeva: Psychoanalytic feminism and the search for the "good enough" mother*. Ann Arbor: University of Michigan Press.

*The doctrine of the mean*. In *The four books* (bilingual) (1992) (James Legge Trans.). Changsha: Hunan Publisher.

Doll, Mary A. (1995). *To the lighthouse and back: Writings on teaching and living*. New York: Peter Lang.

————. (2000). *Like letters in running water: A mythopoetics of curriculum*. Mahwah, NJ: Lawrence Erlbaum.

Doll, Jr., William E. (1993). *A post-modern perspective on curriculum*. New York: Teachers College Press.

————. (1998a). Curriculum and concepts of control. In William F. Pinar (Ed.), *Curriculum: Toward new identities* (pp. 295–323). New York: Garland.

————. (1998b). The spirit of education. *Early Childhood Education, 31*, 3–7.

————. (2001). Struggles with spirituality. In Thomas Oldenski & Dennis Carlson (Eds.), *Educational yearning: The journey of the spirit and democratic education condition*. New York: Garland.

————. (2002). Ghosts and the curriculum. In William E. Doll Jr. & Noel Gough (Eds.), *Curriculum visions* (pp. 23–70). New York: Peter Lang.

Doll, Jr., W. E., & Gough, N. (Eds.) (2002). *Curriculum visions*. New York: Peter Lang.

Ebrey, Patricia B. (1993). *The inner quarters: Marriage and the lives of Chinese women in the Sung period*. Berkeley and Los Angeles: University of California Press.

Edgerton, Susan H. (1996). *Translating the curriculum: Multiculturalism into cultural studies*. New York: Routledge.

Egéa-Kuehne, Denise (1995). Deconstruction revisited and Derrida's call for academic responsibility. *Educational Theory, 45*, 293–310.

————. (1996). Neutrality in education and Derrida's call for "double duty." In Frank Margonis (Ed.), *Philosophy of Education* (pp. 154–163). Urbana, IL: Philosophy of Education Society.

Eppert, Claudia (2000). Relearning questions: Responding to the ethical address of past and present others. In Roger I. Simon, Sharon Rosenberg, & Claudia Eppert (Eds.), *Between hope and despair: Pedagogy and the remembrance of historical trauma* (pp. 213–230). Lanham, MD: Rowman & Littlefield.

Fleener, Jayne M. (2002). *Curriculum dynamics: Recreating heart*. New York: Peter Lang.

Foucault, Michel (1970). *The order of things: An archaeology of the human sciences* [1966]. New York: Pantheon Books.

————. (1973). *Madness and civilization: A history of insanity in the age of reason* [1961]. Trans. from French by Richard Howard. New York: Vintage Books.

————. (Ed.) (1975). *I, Pierre Riviere, having slaughtered my mother, my sister, and my brother . . .* New York: Pantheon Books.

————. (1977). *Discipline and punish.* Trans. from French by Alan Sheridan. New York: Pantheon Books.

————. (1978). *The history of sexuality* (Vol. 1). Trans. from French by Robert Hurley. New York: Vintage Books.

————. (1981). Sexuality and solitude. In Paul Rabinow (Ed.) (1997), *Ethics: Subjectivity and truth* (pp. 175–184). New York: The New Press.

————. (1982a). Sex, power, and the politics of identity. In Paul Rabinow (Ed.) (1997), *Ethics: Subjectivity and truth* (pp. 163–173). New York: The New Press.

————. (1982b). Technologies of the self. In Paul Rabinow (Ed.) (1997), *Ethics: Subjectivity and truth* (pp. 223–251). New York: The New Press.

————. (1982c). An interview by Stephen Riggins. In Paul Rabinow (Ed.) (1997), *Ethics: Subjectivity and truth* (pp. 121–133). New York: The New Press.

————. (1982d). Sexual choice, sexual act. In Paul Rabinow (Ed.) (1997), *Ethics: Subjectivity and truth* (pp. 141–156). New York: The New Press.

————. (1982e). The subject and power. In Hubert L. Dreyfus & Paul Rabinow, *Michel Foucault: Beyond structuralism and hermeneutics* (pp. 208–226). Chicago: University of Chicago Press.

————. (1983a). Structuralism and post-structuralism. In James D. Fubion (Ed.) (1998), *Aesthetics, method, and epistemology* (pp. 432–459). New York: The New Press.

————. (1983b). On the genealogy of ethics: An overview of work in progress. In Paul Rabinow (Ed.) (1997), *Ethics: Subjectivity and truth* (pp. 253–280). New York: The New Press.

————. (1984a), What is enlightenment? In Paul Rabinow (Ed.) (1997), *Ethics: Subjectivity and truth* (pp. 303–319). New York: The New Press.

————. (1984b). The ethics of the concern for self as a practice of freedom. In Paul Rabinow (Ed.) (1997), *Ethics: Subjectivity and truth* (pp. 281–301). New York: The New Press.

————. (1984c). What is an author? [1969] In Paul Rabinow (Ed.), *The Foucault Reader* (pp. 101–120). New York: Pantheon.

————. (1985). *The use of pleasure.* Trans. from French by Robert Hurley. New York: Vintage Books.

————. (1986). *The care of the self.* Trans. from French by Robert Hurley. New York: Vintage Books.

————. (1988). Truth, power, self: An interview. In Luther H. Martin, Huck Gutman, & Patrick H. Hutton (Eds.), *Technologies of the self* (pp. 9–15). Amherst: University of Massachusetts Press.

————. (1997). *Ethics: Subjectivity and truth.* Ed. Paul Rabinow; trans. From French by Robert Hurley et al. New York: The New Press.

————. (1998). *Aesthetics, method, and epistemology.* Trans. from French by Robert Hurley et al. New York: The New Press.

————. (2000). *Power.* Ed. James D. Faubion; trans. From French by Robert Hurley et al. New York: The New Press.

*The four books* (bilingual) (1992). Trans. from Chinese by James Legge. Changsha: Hunan Publisher.

Fraser, Nancy (1994). Michel Foucault: A "young conservative"? In Michael Kelly (Ed.), *Critique and power: Recasting the Foucault/Habermas debate* (pp. 185–210). Cambridge, MA: MIT Press.

Fung Yu-lan (1983). *A history of Chinese philosophy* (Vol. 2, p. 535). Princeton, NJ: Princeton University Press.

Garrison, Jim (1997). *Dewey and eros: Wisdom and desire in the art of teaching*. New York: Teachers College Press.

———. (1998). Dewey, Foucault, and self-creation. *Educational Philosophy and Theory, 30,* 111–134.

Gazetas, Aristides (2003). Re-constituting pedagogies: The (im)possibilities for Inter/nationalizing curriculum studies. In Donna Trueit, William E. Doll, Jr., Hongyu Wang, & William F. Pinar (Eds.), *The internationalization of curriculum studies* (pp. 103–115). New York: Peter Lang.

Goldin, Paul R. (2000). The view of women in early Confucianism. In Li Chengyang (Ed.), *The sage and the second sex: Confucianism, ethics, and gender* (pp. 133–162). Chicago: Open Court.

Goodson, Ivor (1998). Storying the self: Life politics and the study of the teacher's life and work. In William F. Pinar (Ed.), *Curriculum: Toward new identities* (pp. 21–40). New York: Garland.

*The great learning*. In *The four books* (bilingual) (1992) (James Legge Trans.). Changsha: Hunan Publisher.

Greene, Maxine (1973). *Teacher as stranger*. Belmont, CA: Wadsworth.

———. (1995). *Releasing the imagination: Essays on education, the arts, and social change*. San Francisco: Jossey-Bass.

———. (2000). Reflections on *Teacher as Stranger*. *Journal of Curriculum Theorizing, 16,* 85–88.

Griffin, David R. (Ed.) (1990). *Sacred interconnections: Postmodern spirituality, political economy, and art* (pp. 1–14). Albany: State University of New York Press.

Grumet, Madeleine R. (1988). *Bitter milk: Women and teaching*. Amherst: University of Massachusetts Press.

Hall, David L., & Ames, Roger T. (1987). *Thinking through Confucius*. Albany: State University of New York Press.

———. (2000). Sexism, with Chinese characteristics. In Li Chengyang (Ed.), *The sage and the second sex: Confucianism, ethics and gender* (pp. 75–96). Chicago: Open Court.

Hekman, Susan J. (Ed.) (1996). *Feminist interpretations of Michel Foucault*. University Park: Pennsylvania State University Press.

Hesse, Hermann (1951). *Siddhartha*. Trans. from German by Hilda Rosner. New York: New Directions.

hooks, bell (1994a). *Teaching to transgress: Education as the practice of freedom*. New York: Routledge.

———. (1994b). *Outlaw culture: Resisting representations*. New York: Routledge.

Hoy, David Couzens (1986). *Foucault: A critical reader*. Oxford: Basil Blackwell.

Hu Keying (1989). 《 "人"在呼唤》 [The call from "human"]. 《教育研究》, 17–19.

Hu Shi (1931). Women's place in Chinese history. In Li Yu-ning (Ed.), *Chinese women through Chinese eyes* (pp. 3–15). New York: East Gate, 1992.

Huebner, Dwayne (1999). *The lure of the transcendent: Collected essays by Dwayne E. Huebner*. Ed. Vikki Hillis. Mahwah, NJ: Lawrence Erlbaum.

Hwu Wen-song (1998). Curriculum, transcendence, and Zen/Taoism. In William F. Pinar (Ed.), *Curriculum: Toward new identities* (pp. 21–40). New York: Garland.

Infinito, Justen (2003). Ethical self-formation: A look at the later Foucault. *Educational Theory, 53,* 155–171.

Irigaray, Luce (1985). *This sex which is not one*. Trans. from French by Catherine Porter and Carolyn Burke. Ithaca, NY: Cornell University Press.

jagodzinski, jan (2002). The ethics of the "real" in Levinas, Lacan, and Buddhism: Pedagogical implications. *Educational Theory, 52*, 81–96.

Jardine, David (1998). *To dwell with a boundless heart: Essays in curriculum theory, hermeneutics, and the ecological imagination*. New York: Peter Lang.

Jin Guantao & Liu Qinfeng (1984). 《兴盛与危机》 [Prosperity and crisis]. Changsha: Hunan People's Press.

Joseph, Pamela B., et al. (Eds.) (2000). *Cultures of curriculum*. Mahwah, NJ: Lawrence Erlbaum Associates.

Kaplan, Caren (1996). *Questions of travel*. Durham, NC: Duke University Press.

Kelly, Michael (Ed.) (1995). *Critique and power: Recasting the Foucault/Habermas debate*. Cambridge, MA: MIT Press.

Kincheloe, Joe L., & Pinar, William F. (1991). *Curriculum as social psychoanalysis: The significance of place*. Albany: State University of New York Press.

Kingston, Maxine Hong (1989). *The woman warrior*. New York: Vintage Books.

Ko, Dorothy (1994). *Teachers of the inner chamber: Women and culture in seventeenth-century China*. Palo Alto, CA: Stanford University Press.

Kohli, Wendy (1991). Postmodernism, critical theory and the "new" pedagogies: What's at stake in the discourse? *Education and Society, 9*, 39–46.

Kristeva, Julia   (1974). *Revolution in poetic language*. Trans. from French by Margaret Waller. New York: Columbia University Press, 1984.

———. (1977a). *About Chinese women*. Trans. from French by Anita Barrows. New York: Urizen Books.

———. (1977b). Women's time. In Kelly Oliver (Ed.), *The portable Kristeva* (pp. 249–269). New York: Columbia University Press, 1997.

———. (1980). *Desire in language: A semiotic approach to literature and art*. Ed. Leon S. Roudiez; trans. from French by Thomas Gora et al. New York: Columbia University Press.

———. (1981). *Language the unknown: An initiation into linguistics* [1981]. Trans. from French by Anne M. Menke. New York: Columbia University Press, 1989.

———. (1984b). Julia Kristeva in conversation with Rosalind Coward. In Kelly Oliver (Ed.), *The portable Kristeva* (pp. 331–343). New York: Columbia University Press, 1997.

———. (1986). A new type of intellectual: The dissident. In Toril Moi (Ed.), *Kristeva reader* (pp. 292–300). New York: Columbia University Press.

———. (1987a). *Tales of love*. Trans. from French by Leon S. Roudiez. New York: Columbia University Press.

———. (1989). *Black sun: Depression and melancholia*. Trans. from French by Leon S. Roudiez. New York: Columbia University Press.

———. (1991). *Strangers to ourselves*. Trans. from French by Leon S. Roudiez. New York: Columbia University Press.

———. (1993a). *Nation without nationalism*. Trans. Leon S. Roudiez. New York: Columbia University Press.

———. (1993b). Foreign body: A conversation with Julia Kristeva and Scott L. Malcomson. *Transition*, 172–183.

———. (1995). *New maladies of the soul*. Trans. from French by Ross Guberman. New York: Columbia University Press.

————. (1996). *Julia Kristeva: Interviews.* Ed. Ross Mitchell Guberman. New York: Columbia University Press.

————. (1999). Famale genius: General introduction. In Kelly Oliver (Ed.), *The portable Kristeva: Updated edition* (pp. 399–408). New York: Columbia University Press, 2002.

————. (2000a). *The sense and non-sense of revolt.* Trans. from French by Jeanine Herman. New York: Columbia University Press.

————. (2000b). *Crisis of the European subject.* Trans. from French by Susan Fairfield. New York: Columbia University Press.

————. (2001). *Melanie Klein.* Trans. from French by Ross Guberman. New York: Columbia University Press.

————. (2002). *Intimate revolt: The powers and limits of psychoanalysis.* Trans. from French by Jeanine Herman. New York: Columbia University Press.

《老子》 [Lao Zi] (1992). Changsha: Hunan University Press.

Lee, Jung H. (1999). Neither totality nor infinity: Suffering the other. *The Journal of Religion, 79*, 250–275.

Lerner, Gerda (1993). *Creation of feminist consciousness.* New York: Oxford University Press.

Levy, Howard S. (1966). *Chinese footbinding.* New York: Walton Rawl.

Li Chengyang (2000). *The sage and the second sex: Confucianism, ethics, and gender.* Chicago: Open Court.

Li Leyi (1993). 《汉字演变五百例》 [Tracing the roots of Chinese characters: 500 cases]. Beijing: Beijing Language and Cultural University Press.

————. (1996). 《简化字源》 [The origins of simplified Chinese characters]. Beijing: Sinolingua.

Li Yu-ning (Ed.) (1992). *Chinese women through Chinese eyes.* New York: East Gate Book.

Li Xin (2002). *The Tao of life stories: Chinese language, culture, and poetry in education.* New York: Peter Lang.

Liang Xiaobin (1980). China, I lost my key. In Cao Wenxuan (Ed.) (2001), 《二十世纪末中国文学作品选》 [An anthology of Chinese literature at the end of the 20th century] (pp. 7–8). Beijing: Beijing University Press.

Lin Yusheng. (1983). 《思想与人物》 [Thoughts and people]. Taibei: Lianjing Press.

————. (1986). 《中国意识的危机：五四时期激烈的反传统主义》 [Crisis of Chinese consciousness: The radical anti-tradition movement in the May Fourth Period]. Guiyan: Guizhou People's Press.

Lin Yutang (1936). Feminist thought in ancient China. In Li Yu-ning (Ed.), *Chinese women through Chinese eyes* (1992; pp. 34–58). New York: East Gate.

————. (1959). *From pagan to Christian.* Cleveland: The World Publishing Company.

Liu, Shuxian (1989). 《大陆与海外：传统的反省与转化》 [Mainland and oversea: Reflection and transformation of traditions]. Taibei: Yunchen Cultural Corporation.

Lo Ping-cheng (1993). Zhu Xi and Confucian sexual ethics. *Journal of Chinese Philosophy, 20* (4), 465-479.

Lu Tonglin (Ed.) (1993). *Gender and sexuality in twentieth-century Chinese literature and society.* Albany: State University of New York Press.

Lu Xun (1918). *Diary of a madman.* Trans. From Chinese by William A. Lyell (1990). Honolulu: University of Hawaii Press.

Majors, Sandra (2002). *Multicultural pedagogies: Crossing borders, illuminating hidden rules of class, and contextualizing cultures.* Unpublished manuscript.

Marshall, James D. (1996). *Michel Foucault: Personal autonomy and education*. Dordrecht, The Netherlands: Kluwer Academic Publishers.

Martusewicz, Rebecca A. (2001). *Seeking passage: Post-structuralism, pedagogy, ethics*. New York: Teachers College Press.

McNay, Lois (1992). *Foucault and feminism*. Boston: Northeastern University Press.

———. (1994). *Foucault: A critical introduction*. Cambridge: Polity Press.

*Mencius*. In *The four books* (bilingual) (1992) (James Legge Trans.). Changsha: Hunan Publisher.

Meng Peiyuan (1997). 《中国哲学主体思维》 [Subjective thinking in Chinese philosophy]. Beijing: People's Press.

Miller, James (1993). *The passion of Michel Foucault*. New York: Simon & Schuster.

Miller, Janet. (1990). *Creating spaces, finding voices*. Albany: State University of New York Press.

Morris, Marla (1996). Toward a ludic pedagogy: An uncertain occasion. *JCT: Journal of Curriculum Studies, 12* (1), 29–33.

———. (2001). *Curriculum and the Holocaust: Competing sites of memory and representation*. Mahwah, NJ: Lawrence Erlbaum.

Morson, Gary S., & Emerson, Caryl (1990). *Mikhail Bakhtin: Creation of a prosaic*. Palo Alto, CA: Stanford University Press.

Munro, Donald J. (Ed.) (1985). *Individualism and holism: Studies in Confucian and Taoist values*. Ann Arbor: University of Michigan Press.

Munro, Petra (1998a). Engendering the curriculum. In William F. Pinar (Ed.), *Curriculum: Toward new identities* (pp. 263–294). New York: Garland.

———. (1998b). *Subject to fiction: Women teacher's life history narratives and the cultural politics of resistance*. Philadelphia: Open University Press.

Muo Fei (1997). Garden without time. In Cao Wenxuan (Ed.) (2001), 《二十世纪末中国文学作品选》 [An anthology of Chinese literature at the end of the 20th century] (pp. 357–375). Beijing: Beijing University Press.

Nikolchina, Miglena (1991). The lost territory: Parables of exile in Julia Kristeva. *Semiotica*, 231–246.

Noddings, Nel (1999). Caring. In William F. Pinar (Ed.), *Contemporary curriculum discourses: Twenty years of JCT* (pp. 42–55). New York: Peter Lang.

O'Farrell, Clare (1989). *Foucault: Historian or philosopher?* New York: St. Martin's Press.

Oliver, Kelly (1993). *Reading Kristeva: Unraveling the double-bind*. Bloomington: Indiana University Press.

———. (Ed.) (1997). *The portable Kristeva*. New York: Columbia University Press.

———. (1998). *Subjectivity without subjects*. Lanham, MD: Rowman & Littlefield.

———. (2002a). Psychic space and social melancholy. In K. Oliver & S. Edwin (Eds.), *Between the psyche and the social: Psychoanalytic social theory* (pp. 49–65). Lanham, MD: Rowman & Littlefield.

———. (Ed.) (2002b). The portable Kristeva: Updated edition. New York: Columbia University Press.

Oliver, Kelly, & Edwin, Steve (Eds.) (2002). *Between the psyche and the social: Psychoanalytic social theory* (pp. 49–65). Lanham, MD: Rowman & Littlefield.

Pagano, Jo A. (1990). *Exiles and communities: Teaching in the patriarchal wilderness*. Albany: State University of New York Press.

Peterson, Barbara B., et al. (Eds.) (2000). *Notable women of China: Shang dynasty to the early twentieth century*. Armonk, NY: M. E. Sharpe.

Pinar, William F. (1991). Curriculum as social psychoanalysis: On the significance of place. In Joe L. Kincheloe & William F. Pinar (Eds.), *Curriculum as social psychoanalysis: The significance of place* (pp. 167–186). Albany: State University of New York Press.

———. (1993). Notes on understanding curriculum as a racial text. In Cameron McCarthy & Warren Crichlow (Eds.), *Race, identity, and representation in education* (pp. 60–70). New York & London: Routledge.

———. (1994). *Autobiography, politics and sexuality: Essays in curriculum theory 1972–1992.* New York: Peter Lang.

———. (Ed.) (1998). *Curriculum: Toward new identities.* New York: Garland.

———. (1999). Caring: Gender considerations: A response to Nel Noddings' "Caring." In William F. Pinar (Ed.), *Contemporary curriculum discourses: Twenty years of JCT* (pp. 56–60). New York: Peter Lang.

———. (2001). *The gender of racial politics and violence in America: Lynching, prison rape, and the crisis of masculinity.* New York: Peter Lang.

———. (2003). *International handbook of curriculum research.* Mahwah, NJ: Lawrence Erlbaum.

Pinar, William F., & Grumet, Madeleine R. (1976). *Toward a poor curriculum.* Dubuque, IA: Kendall/Hunt Publishing Company.

Pinar, William F., Reynolds, William M., Slattery, Patrick, & Taubman, Peter M. (1995). *Understanding curriculum: An introduction to the study of historical and contemporary curriculum discourses.* New York: Peter Lang.

Pitt, Alice (2003). *The play of the personal: Psychoanalytic narratives of feminist education.* New York: Peter Lang.

Porche-Frilot, Donna (2002). A perspective on "the call from the stranger: Dwayne Huebner's vision of curriculum as a spiritual journey." In William E. Doll, Jr. & Noel Gough (Eds.), *Curriculum Visions* (pp. 300–303). New York: Peter Lang.

Poster, Mark (1986). Foucault and the tyranny of Greece. In David Couzens Hoy (Ed.), *Foucault: A critical reader* (pp. 205–220). Oxford: Basil Blackwell.

Quinn, Molly (2001). *Going out, not knowing whither: Education, the upward Journey, and the faith of reason.* New York: Peter Lang.

Reid, Tom R. (1999). *Confucius lives next door: What living in the East teaches us about living in the West.* New York: Random House.

Ren Hongxuan (1988). I only want to walk into a Chinese character. In Cao Wenxuan (Ed.) (2001), 《二十世纪末中国文学作品选》 [An anthology of Chinese literature at the end of the 20th century] (pp. 199–200). Beijing: Beijing University Press.

Rich, Adrienne (1984). Compulsory heterosexuality and lesbian existence. In Ann B. Snitow, Christine Stansell, & Sharon Thompson (Eds.), *Desire: The politics of sexuality* (pp. 212–241). London: Virago.

Rorty, Richard (1999). *Philosophy and social hope.* New York: Penguin.

Roy, Kaustuv (2003). *Teachers in nomadic spaces: Deleuze and curriculum.* New York: Peter Lang.

Said, Edward W. (1996). *Representations of the intellectual: The 1993 Reith lectures.* New York: Vintage Books.

Sawicki, Jana (1991). *Disciplining Foucault: Feminism, power and the body.* New York: Routledge.

———. (1994). Foucault, feminism and questions of identity. In Gary Gutting (Ed.), *The Cambridge companion to Foucault* (pp. 286–313). Cambridge: Cambridge University Press.

194                    *The Call from the Stranger on a Journey Home*

Schrag, Calvin O. (1997). *The self after postmodernity*. New Haven, CT: Yale University Press.
Serres, Michel (1997). *The troubadour of knowledge*. Trans. from French by Sheila Faria Glaser & William Paulson. Ann Arbor: University of Michigan Press.
Shu, Ting (1991). Also all. In *A splintered mirror: Chinese poetry from the democracy movement* (p. 93). Trans. from Chinese by Donald Finkel and Carolyn Kizer. San Francisco: North Point Press.
Slattery, Patrick (1999). Understanding curriculum as silence and solitude. *Journal of Curriculum Theorizing, 15*, 5–9.
Slattery, Patrick, & Morris, Marla (1999). Simone de Beauvoir's ethics and postmodern ambiguity: The assertion of freedom in the face of the absurd. *Educational Theory, 49* (1), 21–36
Smith, Anna (1996). *Julia Kristeva: Readings of exile and estrangement*. New York: St. Martin's Press.
———. (1998). *Julia Kristeva: Speaking the unspeakable*. London: Pluto Press.
Smith, David Geoffrey (1996). Identity, self and other in the conduct of pedagogical action: An East/West inquiry. *JCT: An Interdisciplinary Journal of Curriculum Theorizing, 12*, 6–11.
———. (1999a). Globalization and education: Prospects for postcolonial pedagogy in a hermeneutic mode. *Interchange, 30*, 1–10.
———. (1999b). *Pedagon: Interdisciplinary essays in the human sciences, pedagogy, and culture*. New York: Peter Lang.
———. (2000). The specific challenges of globalization for teaching and vice versa. *Alberta Journal of Educational Research, 66*, 7–26.
Song Haolin (1999). 《宋浩霖画龙》 [Song Haolin paints dragons]. Hefei: Anhui Arts Press.
Steedman, Carolyn K. (1987). *Landscape for a good woman*. New Brunswick, NJ: Rutgers University Press.
Tagore, Rabindranath (1916). *Fruit gathering*. New York: Macmillan.
Tamaro, Susanna (1996). *Follow your heart*. Trans. from Italian by Avril Bardoni. London: Minerva.
Tamney, Joseph B., & Chiang, Linda H. (2002). *Modernization, globalization, and Confucianism in Chinese societies*. Westport, CT: Praeger.
Taylor, Charles (1989). *Sources of the self: The making of the modern identity*. Cambridge, MA: Harvard University Press.
Thich Nhat Hanh (1993). *Love in action: Writings on nonviolent social change*. Berkeley, CA: Parallax Press.
Trueit, Donna, Doll, Jr., William, Wang, Hongyu, & Pinar, William F. (2003). *The internationalization of curriculum studies*. New York: Peter Lang.
Tu, Wei-ming (1979). *Humanity and self-cultivation: Essays in Confucian thought*. Berkeley, CA: Asian Humanities Press.
———. (1985a). *Confucian thought: Selfhood as creative transformation*. Albany: State University of New York Press.
———. (1985b). The continuity of being: Chinese visions of nature. In Tu Wei-ming, *Confucian thought: Selfhood as creative transformation*. Albany: State University of New York Press.
———. (1993). *Way, learning, and politics: Essays on the Confucian intellectual*. Albany: State University of New York Press.
———. (1998). Join East and West. *Harvard International Review 20*, 44–49.

Tyler, Sally M. (2001). *Catharine Maria Sedgwick's* Hope Leslie: *Clues to a woman's journey.* Unpublished doctoral dissertation, Louisiana State Univerity, Baton Rouge, Louisiana.

Walkerdine, Valerie (1990). *Schoolgirl fictions.* London: Verso.

———. (1998). *Counting girls out: Girls and mathematics.* London: Falmer Press.

Wang Dong (2000). 《中国龙的新发现》 [New discoveries of Chinese dragon]. Beijing: Beijing University Press.

Wang Hongyu (1997). Curriculum as polyphonic authoring: A pedagogy through the "loophole." *Journal of Curriculum Theorizing, 13,* 20–24.

Wang Jiaxin (1993). Words. In CaoWenxuan (Ed.) (2001), 《二十世纪末中国文学作品选》 [An anthology of Chinese literature at the end of the 20th century] (pp. 276–283). Beijing: Beijing University Press.

Wolin, Richard (1986). Foucault's aesthetic decisionism. *Telos, 67,* 71–86.

Woolf, Virginia (1929). *A room of one's own.* New York: Harcourt Brace.

———. (1927). *To the lighthouse.* San Diego: Harvest/Harcourt, 1981.

Wu Jei-tun, & Liu In-mao (1996). Chinese lexical access. In Michael Harris Bond (Ed.), *The handbook of Chinese psychology* (pp. 30–42). Hong Kong and New York: Oxford University Press.

Xu Yuanhe (1994). 《儒学与东方文化》 [Confucianism and Eastern culture]. Beijing: People's Press.

Yao Xinzhong (1996). Self-construction and identity: The Confucian self in relation to some Western perceptions. *Asian Philosophy, 6,* 179–195.

Tuan Yi-fu (1999). *Who am I? An autobiography of emotion, mind, and spirit.* Madison: University of Wisconsin Press.

Young, Russell L. (1998). Becoming American: Coping strategies of Asian Pacific American children. In V. O. Pang & L. L. Cheng (Eds.), *Struggling to be heard: The unmet needs of Asian Pacific American children* (pp. 61–73). Albany: State University of New York.

Yu Qiuyu (1992). 《文化苦旅》 [Bitter travel in culture]. Shanghai: East Publishing Center.

———. (1999). 《山居笔记》 [Mountain dwelling essays]. Shanghai: WenHui Publishing House.

Yu Qiuyu & Tu Wei-ming (2000). 《寻找文化的尊严》 [In search of the dignity of culture]. Changsha: Hunan University Press.

Yun Zhaoshi (Ed.) (1993). 《走向未来的学校》 [Schools towards the future]. Beijing: People's Educational Press.

Zhang Hua (2000). 《经验课程论》 [Studies on experiential curriculum]. Shanghai: Shanghai Educational Press.

Zhang Shiying (1995). 《天人之际》 [Between heaven and man]. Beijing: People's Press.

Zhao Liming (1995).《女书与汉字》 [*Nushu* and the Chinese language]. In L. Zhao, B. Bai, & J. Shi (Eds.), 《全国女书学术考察研讨会文集》 [The mystery of *Nushu*—the women's script] (pp. 87–93). Beijing: Beijing Language College Press.

Zhong Qiquan (1989). 《现代课程论》 [Modern curriculum theory]. Shanghai: Shanghai Educational Press.

———. (1994). 《选修制度与个性发展》 [Elective system and the development of individuality]. 《比较教育研究》, *3,* 19–23.

———. (1997). 《个性差异与质量教育》 [Individual differences and quality education]. 《教育理论与实践》, *4,* 12–19.

Zhu Xi [Chu Hsi] (1990). *Learning to be a sage: Selections from the conversations of master*

*Chu, arranged topically*. Trans. from Chinese by Daniel K. Gardner. Berkeley and Los Angeles: University of California Press.

Zhuang Zukun (1997). 《契合与转化: 基督教与中国文化革新之路》 [Juncture and transformation: The path to Christianity and the transformation of Chinese culture]. Ontario: Canadian Gospel Association.

Ziarek, Ewa P. (2001). *An ethics of dissensus: Postmodernity, feminism, and the politics of radical democracy*. Palo Alto, CA: Stanford University Press.

Zuo Qipei (1992). 《个性的发展与教育》 [The development of individuality and education], 《教育理论与实践》, 4, 8–9.

# INDEX

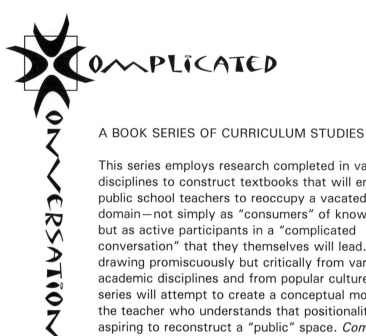

# OMPLICATED

## CONVERSATION

A BOOK SERIES OF CURRICULUM STUDIES

This series employs research completed in various disciplines to construct textbooks that will enable public school teachers to reoccupy a vacated public domain—not simply as "consumers" of knowledge, but as active participants in a "complicated conversation" that they themselves will lead. In drawing promiscuously but critically from various academic disciplines and from popular culture, this series will attempt to create a conceptual montage for the teacher who understands that positionality as aspiring to reconstruct a "public" space. *Complicated Conversation* works to resuscitate the progressive project—an educational project in which self-realization and democratization are inevitably intertwined; its task as the new century begins is nothing less than the intellectual formation of a public sphere in education.

The series editor is:

Dr. William F. Pinar
Department of Curriculum and Instruction
223 Peabody Hall
Louisiana State University
Baton Rouge, LA 70803-4728

To order other books in this series, please contact our Customer Service Department:

(800) 770-LANG (within the U.S.)
(212) 647-7706 (outside the U.S.)
(212) 647-7707 FAX

Or browse online by series:

www.peterlangusa.com